The Poetical Works Of John Keats. With A Memoir

Keats, John, 1795-1821, Lowell, James Russell, 1819-1891

ib

vol

olor

abr

JOHN KEATS.

THE

POETICAL WORKS

OF

JOHN KEATS.

WITH A MEMOIR,

BY JAMES RUSSELL LOWELL.

WITH ILLUSTRATIONS.

NEW YORK

HURST & COMPANY

PUBLISHERS

CONTENTS.

CONTENTS.

iv

CONTENTS.

THE LIFE OF KEATS.

THERE are few poets whose works contain slighter hints of their personal history than those of
Keats; yet there are, perhaps, even fewer, whose
real lives, or rather the conditions upon which they
lived, are more clearly traceable in what they have
written. To write the life of a man was formerly
understood to mean the cataloguing and placing of
circumstances, of those things which stood about the
life and were more or less related to it, but were
not the life itself. But Biography from day to day
holds dates cheaper and facts dearer. A man's life
(as far as its outward events are concerned) may
be made for him, as his clothes are by the tailor, of
this cut or that, of finer or coarser material, but the
gait and gesture show through, and give to trap-
pings, in themselves characterless, an individuality
that belongs to the man himself. It is those essen-
tial facts which underlie the life and make the
ind.vidual man, that are of importance, and it is
the cropping out of these upon the surface, that
gives us indications by which to judge of the true
nature hidden below. Every man has his block
given him, and the figure he cuts will depend very
much upon the shape of that — upon the knots and
twists which existed in it from the beginning. We
were designed in the cradle, perhaps earlier, and
it is in finding out this design, and shaping ourselves to it, that our years are spent wisely It

the vain endeavor to make ourselves what we are not that has strewn history with so many broken purposes and lives left in the rough.

Keats hardly lived long enough to develop a well-outlined character, for that results commonly from the resistance made by temperament to the many influences by which the world, as it may happen then to be, endeavors to mould every one in its own image. What his temperament was we can see clearly, and also that it subordinated itself more and more to the discipline of art.

John Keats, the second of four children, like Chaucer, was a Londoner, but, unlike Chaucer, he was certainly not of gentle blood. Mr Monckton Milnes, who seems to have had a kindly wish to create him gentleman by brevet, says that he was "born in the upper ranks of the middle class." This shows a commendable tenderness for the nerves of English society, and reminds one of Northcote's story of the violin-player who, wishing to compliment his pupil, George III, divided all fiddlers into three classes, those who could not play at all, those who played very badly, and those who played very well, assuring his majesty that he had made such commendable progress as to have already reached the second rank. The American public will perhaps not be disturbed by knowing that the father of Keats (as Mr. Milnes had told us in an earlier biography) " was employed in the establishment of Mr. Jennings, the proprietor of large livery-stables on the Pavement in Moorfields, nearly opposite the entrance into Finsbury Circus." So that, after all, it was not so bad; for, *first*, Mr. Jennings was a *proprietor; second*, he was the proprietor of an *establishment, third*, he was the proprietor of a *large* establishment; and, *fourth*, this large establishment was *nearly* opposite Finsbury Circus, — a name which vaguely dilates the imagination with all sorts of conjectured grandeurs It is true, Leigh Hunt asserts that Keats "was a little too sensitive on the score of his origin," * but we can find no trace of such a feeling either in his poetry, or in such of his letters as have been printed. We suspect the fact to have been that he resented with becoming pride the vulgar Blackwood and Quarterly standard which measured genius by genealogies. It is enough that his poetical pedigree is of the best, tracing through Spenser to Chaucer, and that Pegasus does not stand at livery even in the largest establishments in Moorfields.

As well as we can make out, then, the father of Keats was a groom in the service of Mr. Jennings, and married the daughter of his master. Thus, on the mother's side, at least, we find a grandfather; on the father's there is no hint of such an ancestor, and we must charitably take him for granted. It is of more importance that the elder Keats was a man of sense and energy, and that his wife was a lively and intelligent woman, who hastened the birth of the poet by her passionate devotion to amusement, bringing him into the world, a seven months' child, on the 29th October, 1795, instead of the 29th December, as would have been conventionally proper. Mr. Milnes describes her as "tall, with a large oval face, and a somewhat saturnine demeanor." † This last circumstance does not agree very well with what he had just before told us of her liveliness; but he consoles us by adding that "she succeeded, *however*, in inspiring her children with the profoundest affection" This was particularly true of John, who once, when between four and five years old, mounted guard at her

---

* Hunt's *Autobiography*, (American edition,) vol. ii. p 36
† Milnes's *Life of Keats*, (American edition,) p. 15.

chamber-door with an old sword, when she was
ill, and the doctor had ordered her not to be disturbed *

In 1804, Keats being in his ninth year, his father was killed by a fall from his horse.   His
mother seems to have been ambitious for her children, and there was some talk of sending John to
Harrow.   Fortunately this plan was thought too
expensive, and he was sent instead to the School
of Mr. Clarke at Enfield with his brothers.   A
maternal uncle, who had distinguished himself by
his courage under Duncan at Camperdown, was
the hero of his nephews, and they went to school
resolved to maintain the family reputation for courage.   John was always fighting, and was chiefly
noted among his school-fellows as a strange com-
pound of pluck and sensibility.   He attacked an
usher who had boxed his brother's ears, and when
his mother died, in 1810, was moodily inconsolable,
(in spite, it seems, of her " saturnine demeanor,")
hiding himself for several days in a nook under the
master's desk, and refusing all comfort from teacher
or friend

He was popular at school, as boys of spirit always are, and impressed his companions with a
sense of his power.   They thought he would one
day be a famous soldier.   This may have been ow-
ing to the stories he told them of the heroic uncle,
whose deeds, we may be sure, were properly fa-
moused by the boy Homer, and whom they proba-
bly took for an admiral at the least, as it would have
been well for Keats's literary prosperity if he had
been   At any rate, they thought John would be
a great man, which is the main thing, for the public opinion of the playground is truer and more dis-
cerning than that of the world; and if you tell us

---

* Haydon tells the story differently, but we think Mr. Milnes's
version the best.

what the boy was, we will tell you what the man longs to be, however he may be repressed by necessity or fear of the police reports

Mr. Milnes has failed to discover anything else especially worthy of record in the school-life of Keats. He translated the twelve books of the Æneid, read Robinson Crusoe and the Incas of Peru, and looked into Shakspeare. He left school in 1810, with little Latin and no Greek, but he had studied Spence's Polymetis, Tooke's Pantheon, and Lemprière's Dictionary, and knew gods, nymphs, and heroes, which were quite as good company as aorists and aspirates. It is pleasant to fancy the horror of those respectable writers if their pages could suddenly have become alive under their pens with all that the young poet saw in them.*

On leaving school, he was apprenticed for five years to a surgeon at Edmonton. His master was a Mr. Hammond, "of some eminence" in his profession, as Mr. Milnes takes care to assure us. The place was of more importance than the master, for its neighborhood to Enfield enabled him to keep up his intimacy with the family of his former teacher, Mr. Clarke, and to borrow books of them.

---

* There is always some one willing to make himself a sort of accessory after the fact in any success ; always an old woman or two, ready to remember omens of all quantities and qualities in the childhood of persons who have become distinguished Accordingly, a certain "Mrs Grafty of Craven Street, Finsbury," assures Mr George Keats, when he tells her that John is determined to be a poet, "that this was very odd, because when he could just speak, instead of answering questions put to him, he would always make a rhyme to the last word people said, and then laugh" The early histories of heroes, like those of nations, are always more or less mythical, and we give the story for what it is worth   Doubtless there is a gleam of intelligence in it, for the old lady pronounces it odd that any one should *determine* to be a poet, and seems to have wished to hint that the matter was determined earlier and by a higher disposing power   There are few children who do not soon discover the charm of rhyme, and perhaps fewer who can resist making fun of the Mrs Graftys of Craven Street, Finsbury, when they have the chance. See Haydon's *Autobiography*, vol. i. p. 361.

In 1812, when he was in his seventeenth year Mr. Charles Cowden Clarke lent him the Faerie Queene. Nothing that is told of Orpheus or Amphion is more wonderful than this miracle of Spenser's, transforming a surgeon's apprentice into a great poet. Keats learned at once the secret of his birth, and henceforward his indentures ran to Apollo instead of Mr. Hammond. Thus could the Muse defend her son. It is the old story, — the lost heir discovered by his aptitude for what is gentle and knightly.

Before long we find him studying Chaucer, then Shakspeare, and afterward Milton. That he read wisely, his comments on the Paradise Lost are enough to prove. He now also commenced poet himself, but does not appear to have neglected the study of his profession. He was a youth of energy and purpose, and, though he no doubt penned many a stanza when he should have been anatomizing, and walked the hospitals accompanied by the early gods, nevertheless passed a very creditable examination in 1817. In the spring of this year, also, he prepared to take his first degree as poet, and accordingly published a small volume containing a selection of his earlier essays in verse. It attracted little attention, and the rest of this year seems to have been occupied with a journey on foot in Scotland, and the composition of Endymion, which was published in 1818. Milton's *Tetrachordon* was not better abused; but Milton's assailants were unorganized, and were obliged each to print and pay for his own dingy little quarto, trusting to the natural laws of demand and supply to furnish him with readers. Keats was arraigned by the constituted authorities of literary justice. They might be, nay, they were Jeffrieses and Scroggses, but the sentence was published, and the penalty inflicted before all England. The differ-

ence between his fortune and Milton's was that between being pelted by a mob of personal enemies,
and being set in the pillory.   In the first case, the
annoyance brushes off mostly with the mud; in
the last, there is no solace but the consciousness of
suffering in a great cause.   This solace, to a certain
extent, Keats had; for his ambition was noble, and
he hoped not to make a great reputation, but to be
a great poet.   Haydon says that Wordsworth and
Keats were the only men he had ever seen who
looked conscious of a lofty purpose.

It is curious that men should resent more fiercely
what they suspect to be good verses, than what
they know to be bad morals.   Is it because they
feel themselves incapable of the one, and not of the
other?   However it be, the best poetry has been
the most savagely attacked, and men who scrupu-
lously practised the Ten Commandments as if there
were never a *not* in any of them, felt every senti-
ment of their better nature outraged by the *Lyrical
Ballads.*   It is idle to attempt to show that Keats
did not suffer keenly from the vulgarities of Blackwood and the Quarterly.   He suffered in proportion as his ideal was high, and he was conscious of
falling below it.   In England, especially, it is not
pleasant to be ridiculous, even if you are a lord;
but to be ridiculous and an apothecary at the same
time, is almost as bad as it was formerly to be ex-
communicated.   *A priori*, there was something
absurd in poetry written by the son of an assistant
in the livery-stables of Mr. Jennings, even though
they were an establishment, and a large establishment, and nearly opposite Finsbury Circus   Mr.
Gifford, the ex-cobbler, thought so in the Quarterly, and Mr. Terry, the actor,* thought so even
more distinctly in Blackwood, bidding the young

* Haydon (*Autobiography*, vol. 1. p. 379) says that he " strong
ly suspects " Terry to have written the articles in Blackwood.

apothecary "back to his gallipots!" It is not
pleasant to be talked down upon by your inferiors
who happen to have the advantage of position, nor
to be drenched with ditch-water, though you know
it to be thrown by a scullion in a garret

Keats, as his was a temperament in which sensibility was excessive, could not but be galled by
this treatment. He was galled the more that he
was also a man of strong sense, and capable of
understanding clearly how hard it is to make men
acknowledge solid value in a person whom they
have once heartily laughed at. Reputation is in
itself only a farthing-candle, of wavering and uncertain flame, and easily blown out, but it is the
light by which the world looks for and finds merit.
Keats longed for fame, but longed above all to
deserve it. Thrilling with the electric touch of
sacred leaves, he saw in vision, like Dante, that
small procession of the elder poets to which only
elect centuries can add another laurelled head.
Might he, too, deserve from posterity the love and
reverence which he paid to those antique glories?
It was no unworthy ambition, but everything was
against him, — birth, health, even friends, since it
was partly on their account that he was sneered at.
His very name stood in his way, for Fame loves
best such syllables as are sweet and sonorous on the
tongue, like Spenserian, Shakspearian In spite of
Juliet, there is a great deal in names, and when the
fairies come with their gifts to the cradle of the
selected child, let one, wiser than the rest, choose
a name for him from which well-sounding deriva-
tives can be made, and best of all with a termina-
tion in *on.* Men judge the current coin of opinion
by the ring, and are readier to take without question whatever is Platonic, Baconian, Newtonian,
Johnsonian. Washingtonian, Jeffersonian, Napol-
eonic, and all the rest. You cannot make a good

adjective out of Keats, — the more pity, — and to say a thing is *Keatsy* is to contemn it Fate likes fine names.

Haydon tells us that Keats was very much depressed by the fortunes of his book. This was natural enough, but he took it all in a manly way, and determined to revenge himself by writing better poetry. He knew that activity, and not despondency, is the true counterpoise to misfortune. Haydon is sure of the change in his spirits, because he would come to the painting-room and sit silent for hours. But we rather think that the conversation, where Mr. Haydon was, resembled that in a young author's first play, where the other interlocutors are only brought in as convenient points for the hero to hitch the interminable web of his monologue on. Besides, Keats had been continuing his education this year, by a course of Elgin marbles and pictures by the great Italians, and might very naturally have found little to say about Mr. Haydon's extensive works, which he would have cared to hear. Mr Milnes, on the other hand, in his eagerness to prove that Keats was not killed by the article in the Quarterly, is carried too far toward the opposite extreme, and more than hints that he was not even hurt by it. This would have been true of Wordsworth, who, by a constant companionship with mountains, had acquired something of their manners, but was simply impossible to a man of Keats's temperament.

On the whole, perhaps, we need not respect Keats the less for having been gifted with sensibility, and may even say what we believe to be true, that his health was injured by the failure of his book. A man cannot have a sensuous nature and be pachydermatous at the same time; and if he be imaginative as well as sensuous, he suffers just in proportion to the amount of his imagination. It is

perfectly true that what we call the world, in these
affairs, is nothing more than a mere Brocken spec
tre, the projected shadow of ourselves, but as long
as we do not know it, it is a very passable giant.
We are not without experience of natures so purely
intellectual that their bodies had no more concern
in their mental doings and sufferings than a house
has with the good or ill fortune of its occupant
But poets are not built on this plan, and especially
poets like Keats, in whom the moral seems to have
so perfectly interfused the physical man, that you
might almost say he could feel sorrow with his
hands, so truly did his body, like that of Donne's
mistress, think and remember and forebode.   The
healthiest poet of whom our civilization has been
capable says that when he beholds

> ——" desert a beggar born,
> And strength by limping sway disabled,
> And art made tongue-tied by authority,"

(alluding, plainly enough, to the Giffords of his
day,)

> " And simple truth miscalled simplicity,"

(as it was long afterward in Wordsworth's case,)

> " And Captive Good attending Captain Ill,"

that then even he, the poet to whom of all others
life seems to have been dearest, as it was also the
fullest of enjoyment, "tired of all these," had noth
ing for it but to cry for " restful Death "

Keats, as we have said, accepted his ill fortune
courageously.   On the 9th of October, 1818, he
writes to his publisher, Mr. Hessey, " I cannot but
feel indebted to those gentlemen who have taken
my part.   As for the rest, I begin to get acquainted
with my own strength and weakness.   Praise or
blame has but a momentary effect on the man
whose love of beauty in the abstract makes him a

severe critic of **his own** works. My own domestic
criticism has given me pain without comparison beyond what 'Blackwood' or the 'Quarterly' could
inflict · and also, when I feel I am right, no exter-
nal praise can give me such a glow as my own solitary reperception and ratification of what is fine.
J. S. is perfectly right in regard to 'the slipshod
Endymion.' That it is so is no fault of mine.
No! though it may sound a little paradoxical, it is
as good as I had power to make it by myself. Had
I been nervous about its being a perfect piece, and
with that view asked advice and trembled over
every page, it would not have been written; for it
is not in my nature to fumble. I will write independently. I have written independently *without
judgment.* I may write independently and *with
judgment*, hereafter. The Genius of Poetry must
work out its own salvation in a man. It cannot be
matured by law and precept, but by sensation and
watchfulness in itself. That which is creative must
create itself. In 'Endymion' I leaped headlong
into the sea, and thereby have become better acquainted with the soundings, the quicksands, and
the rocks, than if I had stayed upon the green
shore, and piped a silly pipe, and took tea and
comfortable advice. I was never afraid of failure; for I would sooner fail than not be among the
greatest '*

This was undoubtedly true, and it was naturally
the side which a large-minded person would display to a friend. This is what he thought; but
whether it was what he *felt*, we think doubtful.
We look upon it rather as one of the phenomena
of that multanimous nature of the poet, which makes
him for the moment that which he has an intellectual perception of. Elsewhere he says something
which seems to hint at the true state of the case

* Milnes's *Life and Letters of Keats*, pp 145–6
2

"I must think that difficulties nerve the spirit
of a man : *they make our prime objects a refuge as
well as a passion.*"   One cannot help contrasting
Keats with Wordsworth ; the one altogether poet,
the other essentially a Wordsworth with the poetic
faculty added ; the one shifting from form to form,
and from style to style, and pouring his hot throbbing life into every mould ; the other remaining always the individual, producing works, and not so
much living in his poems as memorially recording
his life in them.   When Wordsworth alludes to the
foolish criticisms on his writings, he speaks serenely
and generously of Wordsworth the poet, as if he
were an unbiassed third person, who takes up the
argument merely in the interest of literature.   He
towers into a bald egotism which is quite above and
beyond selfishness.   Poesy was his employment ; it
was Keats's very existence ; and he felt the rough
treatment of his verses as if it had been the wound-
ing of a limb.   To Wordsworth, composing was a
healthy exercise ; his slow pulse and unimpressible
nature gave him assurance of a life so long that he
could wait ; and when we read his poems we should
never suspect the existence in him of any sense but
that of observation, as if Wordsworth the poet were
only a great sleepless eye, accompanied by Mr.
Wordsworth, the distributer of stamps, as a rever-
ential scribe and Baruch.   But every one of Keats's
poems was a sacrifice of vitality ; a virtue went
away from him into every one of them ; even yet,
as we turn the leaves, they seem to warm and thrill
our fingers with the flush of his fine senses, and
the flutter of his electrical nerves, and we do not
wonder he felt that what he did was to be done
swiftly.

In the mean time, his younger brother languished
and died ; his elder seems to have been in some
way unfortunate, and had gone to America, and

Keats himself showed symptoms of the hereditary disease which caused his death at last. It is in October, 1818, that we find the first allusions to a passion, which was, ere long, to consume him. It is plain enough beforehand, that those were not moral or mental graces that should attract a man like Keats. His intellect was satisfied and absorbed by his art, his books, and his friends. He could have companionship and appreciation from men; what he craved of woman was only repose. That luxurious nature, which would have tossed uneasily on a crumpled rose-leaf, must have something softer to rest upon than intellect, something less ethereal than culture. It was his body that needed to have its equilibrium restored, the waste of his nervous energy that must be repaired by deep draughts of the overflowing life and drowsy tropical force of an abundant and healthily-poised womanhood. Writing to his sister-in-law, he says of this nameless person: "She is not a Cleopatra, but is, at least, a Charmian; she has a rich eastern look; she has fine eyes, and fine manners. When she comes into a room, she makes the same impression as the beauty of a leopardess. She is too fine and too conscious of herself to repulse any man who may address her. From habit, she thinks that *nothing particular.* I always find myself at ease with such a woman; the picture before me always gives me a life and animation which I cannot possibly feel with anything inferior. I am at such times too much occupied in admiring, to be awkward, or in a tremble. I forget myself entirely, because I live in her. You will by this time think I am in love with her, so, before I go any farther, I will tell you that I am not. She kept me awake one night, as a tune of Mozart's might do. I speak of the thing as a pastime and an amusement, than which I can feel none deeper than a conversation

with an imperial woman, the very *yes* and *no* of
whose life is to me a banquet. . . . . I like her
and her like, because one has no *sensation*, what
we both are, is taken for granted. .   . She
walks across a room in such a manner that a
man is drawn toward her with magnetic power.
. . . . . I believe, though, she has faults, the
same as a Cleopatra or a Charmian might have
had.   Yet she is a fine thing, speaking in a worldly
way; for there are two distinct tempers of mind
in which we judge of things: the worldly, theat-
rical, and pantomimical; and the unearthly, spiritual, and ethereal.   In the former, Bonaparte, Lord
Byron, and this Charmian hold the first place in
our minds; in the latter, John Howard, Bishop
Hooker, rocking his child's cradle, and you, my
dear sister, are the conquering feelings   As a man
of the world, I love the rich talk of a Charmian,
as an eternal being, I love the thought of you.   I
should like her to ruin me, and I should like you
to save me."

It is pleasant always to see Love hiding his head
with such pains, while his whole body is so clearly
visible, as in this extract.   This lady, it seems, is
not a Cleopatra, only a Charmian; but presently
we find that she is imperial.   He does not love her,
but he would just like to be ruined by her, nothing
more.   This glimpse of her, with her leopardess
beauty, crossing the room and drawing men after
her magnetically, is all we have.   She seems to
have been still living in 1848, and, as Mr. Milnes
tells us, kept the memory of the poet sacred.   "She
is an East Indian," Keats says, "and ought to
be her grandfather's heir."   Her name we do not
know.

Between this time and the spring of 1820, he
seems to have worked assiduously.   Of course
worldly success was of more importance than ever

He began *Hyperion*, but had given it up in September, 1819, because, as he said, "there were too many Miltonic inversions in it." He wrote *Lamia* after an attentive study of Dryden's versification. This period also produced the *Eve of St Agnes*, *Isabella*, and the odes to the *Nightingale*, and to the *Grecian Urn*. He studied Italian, read Ariosto, and wrote part of a humorous poem. *The Cap and Bells*. He tried his hand at tragedy, and Mr. Milnes has published among his " Remains," *Otho the Great*, and all that was ever written of *King Stephen* We think he did unwisely, for a biographer is hardly called upon to show how ill his *biographee* could do anything.

In the winter of 1820, he was chilled in riding on the top of a stage-coach, and came home in a state of feverish excitement. He was persuaded to go to bed, and in getting between the cold sheets, coughed slightly. " That is blood in my mouth," he said. " Bring me the candle, let me see this blood." It was of a brilliant red, and his medical knowledge enabled him to interpret the augury. Those narcotic odors that seem to breathe seaward and steep in repose the senses of the voyager who is drifting toward the shore of the mysterious Other World, appeared to envelop him, and, looking up with sudden calmness, he said, "I know the color of that blood; it is arterial blood; I cannot be deceived in that color. That drop is my death warrant; I must die."

There was a slight rally during the summer of that year, but toward autumn he grew worse again, and it was decided that he should go to Italy. He was accompanied thither by his friend, Mr. Severn, an artist After embarking, he wrote to his friend, Mr Brown We give a part of this letter, which is so deeply tragic that the sentences we take almost seem to break away from the rest with a cry of anguish, like the branches of Dante's lamentable wood.

"I wish to write on subjects that will not agitate me much. There is one I must mention and have done with it. Even if my body would recover of itself, this would prevent it. The very thing which I want to live most for will be a great occasion of my death. I cannot help it. Who can help it? Were I in health it would make me ill, and how can I bear it in my state? I dare say you will be able to guess on what subject I am harping: you know what was my greatest pain during the first part of my illness at your house. I wish for death every day and night to deliver me from these pains, and then I wish death away, for death would destroy even those pains, which are better than nothing. Land and sea, weakness and decline, are great separators, but Death is the great divorcer forever. When the pang of this thought has passed through my mind, I may say the bitterness of death is passed. I often wish for you, that you might flatter me with the best. I think, without my mentioning it, for my sake, you would be a friend to Miss —— when I am dead. You think she has many faults, but for my sake think she has not one. If there is anything you can do for her by word or deed, I know you will do it. I am in a state at present in which woman, merely as woman, can have no more power over me than stocks and stones, and yet the difference of my sensations with respect to Miss —— and my sister is amazing: the one seems to absorb the other to a degree incredible. I seldom think of my brother and sister in America; the thought of leaving Miss —— is beyond everything horrible, — the sense of darkness coming over me, — I eternally see her figure eternally vanishing; some of the phrases she was in the habit of using during my

last nursing at Wentworth Place ring in my ears
Is there another life? Shall I awake and find all
this a dream? There must be, — we cannot be
created for this sort of suffering."

To the same friend he writes again from Naples,
(1st November, 1820):

"The persuasion that I shall see her no more
will kill me. My dear Brown, I should have had
her when I was in health, and I should have re-
mained well. I can bear to die; I cannot bear
to leave her. Oh, God! God! God! Everything
I have in my trunks that reminds me of her
goes through me like a spear. The silk lining she
put in my travelling-cap scalds my head My
imagination is horribly vivid about her; I see her
— I hear her. There is nothing in the world of
sufficient interest to divert me from her a moment.
This was the case when I was in England, I cannot recollect, without shuddering, the time that I
was a prisoner at Hunt's, and used to keep my eyes
fixed on Hampstead all day. Then there was a
good hope of seeing her again — Now! — O that I
could be buried near where she lives! I am afraid
to write to her — to receive a letter from her — to
see her handwriting would break my heart — Even
to hear of her anyhow, to see her name written,
would be more than I can bear. My dear Brown,
what am I to do? Where can I look for consolation or ease? If I had any chance of recovery,
this passion would kill me. Indeed, through the
whole of my illness, both at your house and at
Kentish Town, this fever has never ceased wearing
me out."

The two friends went almost immediately from
Naples to Rome, where Keats was treated with great
kindness by the distinguished physician, Dr. (afterward Sir James) Clark.* But there was no hope

* The lodging of Keats was on the *Piazza di Spagna*, in the

from the first.   His disease was beyond remedy, as
his heart was beyond comfort.   The very fact that
life might be happy deepened his despair.   He
might not have sunk so soon, but the waves in which
he was struggling looked only the blacker that they
were shone upon by the signal-torch that promised
safety, and love, and rest.

It is good to know that one of Keats's last pleasures was in hearing Severn read aloud from a volume of Jeremy Taylor.   On first coming to Rome,
he had bought a copy of Alfieri, but finding on the
second page these lines,

> Misera me! sollievo a me non resta
> Altro che il pianto, ed il pianto è delitto,

he laid down the book and opened it no more.   On
the 14th February, 1821, Severn speaks of a change
that had taken place in him toward greater quietness
and peace.   He talked much, and fell at last into a
sweet sleep, in which he seemed to have happy
dreams.   Perhaps he heard the soft footfall of the
angel of Death, pacing to and fro under his win-
dow, to be his Valentine.   That night he asked to
have this epitaph inscribed upon his gravestone,

"HERE LIES ONE WHOSE NAME WAS WRIT IN WATER"

On the 23d, he died, without pain and as if falling
asleep   His last words were, "I am dying; I shall
die easy; don't be frightened; be firm and thank
God it has come!"   .

He was buried in the Protestant burial-ground at
Rome, in that part of it which is now disused and
secluded from the rest.   A short time before his
death, he told Severn that he thought his intensest
pleasure in life had been to watch the growth of
flowers; and once, after lying peacefully awhile, he

---

first house on the right hand in going up the *Scalinata*   Mr
Severn's Studio is said to have been in the *Cancello* over the gar-
den-gate of the *Villa Negroni*, pleasantly familiar to all Ameri-
cans as the Roman home of their countryman Crawford

said, " I feel the flowers growing over me." His grave is marked by a little head-stone, on which are carved somewhat rudely his name and age, and the epitaph dictated by himself. No tree or shrub has been planted near it; but the daisies, faithful to their buried lover, crowd his small mound with a galaxy of their innocent stars, more prosperous than those under which he lived.

In person, Keats was below the middle height, with a head small in proportion to the breadth of his shoulders. His hair was brown and fine, falling in natural ringlets about a face in which energy and sensibility were remarkably mixed up. Every feature was delicately cut; the chin was bold; and about the mouth something of a pugnacious expression. His eyes were mellow and glowing, large, dark, and sensitive. At the recital of a noble action, or a beautiful thought, they would suffuse with tears, and his mouth trembled.* Haydon says that his eyes had an inward Delphian look that was perfectly divine.

The faults of Keats's poetry are obvious enough , but it should be remembered that he died at twenty-four, and that he offends by superabundance and not poverty. That he was overlanguaged at first there can be no doubt, and in this was implied the possibility of falling back to the perfect mean of diction. It is only by the rich that the costly plainness, which at once satisfies the taste and the imagination, is attainable.

Whether Keats was original or not we do not think it useful to discuss until it has been settled what originality is. Mr. Milnes tells us that this merit (whatever it is) has been denied to Keats, because his poems take the color of the authors he happened to be reading at the time he wrote them

* Leigh Hunt's *Autobiography*, ii. 48

But men have their intellectual ancestry, and the likeness of some one of them is forever unexpectedly flashing out in the features of a descendant, it may be after a gap of several generations. In the parliament of the present, every man represents a constituency of the past. It is true that Keats has the accent of the men from whom he learned to speak, but this is to make originality a mere question of externals, and in this sense the author of a dictionary might bring an action of trover against every author who used his words. It is the man behind the words that gives them value; and if Shakspeare help himself to a verse or a phrase, it is with ears that have learned of him to listen that we feel the harmony of the one, and it is the mass of his intellect that makes the other weighty with meaning. Enough that we recognize in Keats that undefinable newness and unexpectedness that we call genius. The sunset is original every evening, though for thousands of years it has built out of the same light and vapor its visionary cities with domes and pinnacles, and its delectable mountains which night shall utterly abase and destroy.

Three men, almost contemporaneous with each other, Wordsworth, Keats, and Byron, were the great means of bringing back English poetry from the sandy deserts of rhetoric, and recovering for her her triple inheritance of simplicity, sensuousness, and passion. Of these, Wordsworth was the only conscious reformer; and his hostility to the existing formalism injured his earlier poems by tingeing them with something of iconoclastic extravagance. He was the deepest thinker, Keats the most essentially a poet, and Byron the most keenly intellectual of the three. Keats had the broadest mind, or at least his mind was open in more sides, and he was able to understand Wordsworth and judge Byron, equally conscious, through his artistic sense, of the greatnesses of the one. and the many littlenesses of the other, while Wordsworth was isolated in a feeling of his prophetic character, and Byron had only an uneasy and jealous instinct of contemporary merit. The poems of Wordsworth, as he was the most individual, accordingly reflect the moods of his own nature ; those of Keats, from sensitiveness of organization, the moods of his own taste and feeling ; and those of Byron, who was impressible chiefly through the understanding, the intellectual and moral wants of the times in which he lived. Wordsworth has influenced most the ideas of succeeding poets ; Keats their forms : and Byron, interesting to men of imagination less for his writings than for what his writings indicate, reappears no more in poetry, but presents an ideal to youth made restless with vague desires not yet regulated by experience nor supplied with motives by the duties of life.

As every young person goes through all the world-old experiences, fancying them something peculiar and personal to himself, so it is with every new generation, whose youth always finds its representatives in its poets. Keats rediscovered the delight and wonder that lay enchanted in the dictionary Wordsworth revolted at the poetic diction which he found in vogue, but his own language rarely rises above it except when it is upborne by the thought Keats had an instinct for fine words, which are in themselves pictures and ideas, and had more of the power of poetic expression than any modern English poet. And by poetic expression we do not mean merely a vividness in particulars, but the right feeling which heightens or subdues a passage or a whole poem to the proper tone, and gives entireness to the effect. There is a great deal more than is commonly supposed in this choice of words. Men's thoughts and opinions are in a great degree vassals of him who invents a new **phrase** or reapplies an old epithet. The thought or feeling a thousand times repeated, becomes his at last who utters it best. This power of language is veiled in the old legends which make the invisible powers the servants of some word. As soon as we have discovered the word for our joy or sorrow, we are no longer its serfs, but its lords. We reward the discoverer of an anæsthetic for the body and make him member of all the societies, but him who finds a nepenthe for the soul we elect into the small academy of the immortals

The poems of Keats mark an epoch in English poetry; for, however often we may find traces of it in others, in them found its strongest expression that reaction against the barrel-organ style which had been reigning by a kind of sleepy divine right for half a century. The lowest point was indicated when there was such an utter confounding of the common and the uncommon sense that Dr Johnson wrote verse and Burke prose The most profound gospel of criticism was, that nothing was good poetry that could not be translated into good prose, as if one should say that the test of sufficient moonlight was that tallow-candles could be made of it. We find Keats at first going to the other extreme, and endeavoring to extract green cucumbers from the rays of tallow; but we see also incontestable proof of the 'greatness and purity of his poetic gift in the constant return toward equilibrium and repose in his latter poems And it is a repose always lofty and clear-aired, like that of the eagle balanced in incommunicable sunshine. In him a vigorous understanding developed itself in equal measure with the divine faculty, thought emancipated itself from expression without becoming its tyrant; and music and meaning floated together, accordant as swan and shadow, on the smooth element of his verse. Without losing its sensuousness, his poetry refined itself and grew more inward, and the sensational was elevated into the typical by the control of that finer sense which underlies the senses and is the spirit of them.

T. R. L.

ENDYMION:

A POETIC ROMANCE.

INSCRIBED TO THE MEMORY OF

THOMAS CHATTERTON.

———————

THE STRETCHED METRE OF AN ANTIQUE SONG

PREFACE.

KNOWING within myself the manner in which this Poem has been produced, it is not without a feeling of regret that I make it public.

What manner I mean, will be quite clear to the reader, who must soon perceive great inexperience, immaturity, and every error denoting a feverish attempt, rather than a deed accomplished. The two first books, and indeed the two last, I feel sensible are not of such completion as to warrant their passing the press; nor should they if I thought a year's castigation would do them any good;—it will not; the foundations are too sandy. It is just that this youngster should die away: a sad thought for me, if I had not some hope that while it is dwindling I may be plotting, and fitting myself for verses fit to live.

This may be speaking too presumptuously, and may deserve a punishment; but no feeling man will be forward to inflict it; he will leave me alone, with the conviction that there is not a fiercer hell than the failure in a great object. This is not written with the least atom of purpose to forestall criticisms of course, but from the desire I have to conciliate men who are competent to look, and who do look with a zealous eye, to the honor of English literature.

The imagination of a boy is healthy, and the mature imagination of a man is healthy; but there is a space of life between, in which the soul is in a

ferment, the character undecided, the way of life
uncertain, the ambition thick-sighted ; thence pro-
ceeds mawkishness, and all the thousand bitters
which those men I speak of must necessarily taste
in going over the following pages.

I hope I have not in too late a day touched the
beautiful mythology of Greece, and dulled its
brightness ; for I wish to try once more before I
bid it farewell.

TEIGNMOUTH, *April* 10, 1818.

ENDYMION.

◆

BOOK I.

A THING of beauty is a joy for ever:
Its loveliness increases; it will never
Pass into nothingness; but still will keep
A bower quiet for us, and a sleep
Full of sweet dreams, and health, and quiet breath
    ing.
Therefore, on every morrow, are we wreathing
A flowery band to bind us to the earth,
Spite of despondence, of the inhuman dearth
Of noble natures, of the gloomy days,
Of all the unhealthy and o'er-darken'd ways
Made for our searching : yes, in spite of all,
Some shape of beauty moves away the pall
From our dark spirits.   Such the sun, the moon,
Trees old and young, sprouting a shady boon
For simple sheep; and such are daffodils
With the green world they live in ; and clear rills
That for themselves a cooling covert make
'Gainst the hot season; the mid-forest brake,
Rich with a sprinkling of fair musk-rose blooms
And such too is the grandeur of the dooms
We have imagined for the mighty dead;
All lovely tales that we have heard or read:
An endless fountain of immortal drink,
Pouring unto us from the heaven's brink.

Nor do we merely feel these essences
For one short hour; no, even as the trees
That whisper round a temple become soon
Dear as the temple's self, so does the moon,

The passion poesy, glories infinite,
Haunt us till they become a cheering light
Unto our souls, and bound to us so fast,
That, whether there be shine, or gloom o'ercast,
They alway must be with us, or we die.

Therefore, 'tis with full happiness that I
Will trace the story of Endymion.
The very music of the name has gone
Into my being, and each pleasant scene
Is growing fresh before me as the green
Of our own valleys: so I will begin
Now while I cannot hear the city's din;
Now while the early budders are just new,
And run in mazes of the youngest hue
About old forests; while the willow trails
Its delicate amber; and the dairy pails
Bring home increase of milk.   And, as the year
Grows lush in juicy stalks, I'll smoothly steer
My little boat, for many quiet hours,
With streams that deepen freshly into bowers.
Many and many a verse I hope to write,
Before the daisies, vermeil rimm'd and white,
Hide in deep herbage; and ere yet the bees
Hum about globes of clover and sweet peas,
I must be near the middle of my story.
O may no wintry season, bare and hoary,
See it half-finish'd: but let Autumn bold,
With universal tinge of sober gold,
Be all about me when I make an end.
And now at once, adventuresome, I send
My herald thought into a wilderness:
There let its trumpet blow, and quickly dress
My uncertain path with green, that I may speed
Easily onward, thorough flowers and weed.

Upon the sides of Latmos was outspread
A mighty forest; for the moist earth fed

So plenteously all weed-hidden roots
Into o'erchanging boughs, and precious, fruits.
And it had gloomy shades, sequester'd deep,
Where no man went, and if from shepherd's keep
A lamb stray'd far a-down those inmost glens,
Never again saw he the happy pens
Whither his brethren, bleating with content,
Over the hills at every nightfall went.
Among the shepherds 'twas believed ever,
That not one fleecy lamb which thus did sever
From the white flock, but pass'd unworried
By any wolf, or pard with prying head,
Until it came to some unfooted plains
Where fed the herds of Pan : ay, great his gains
Who thus one lamb did lose   Paths there were
        many,
Winding through palmy fern, and rushes fenny,
And ivy banks ; all leading pleasantly
To a wide lawn, whence one could only see
Stems thronging all around between the swell
Of tuft and slanting branches   who could tell
The freshness of the space of heaven above,
Edged round with dark tree-tops? through which
        a dove
Would often beat its wings, and often too
A little cloud would move across the blue.

Full in the middle of this pleasantness
There stood a marble altar, with a tress
Of flowers budded newly ; and the dew
Had taken fairy phantasies to strew
Daisies upon the sacred sward last eve,
And so the dawned light in pomp receive.
For 'twas the morn : Apollo's upward fire
Made every eastern cloud a silvery pyre
Of brightness so unsullied, that therein
A melancholy spirit well might win
Oblivion, and melt out his essence fine

Into the winds: rain-scented eglantine
Gave temperate sweets to that well-wooing sun;
The lark was lost in him; cold springs had run
To warm their chilliest bubbles in the grass;
Man's voice was on the mountains; and the mass
Of nature's lives and wonders pulsed tenfold.
To feel this sun-rise and its glories old.

Now while the silent workings of the dawn
Were busiest, into that self-same lawn
All suddenly, with joyful cries, there sped
A troop of little children garlanded;
Who gathering round the altar, seem'd to pry
Earnestly round as wishing to espy
Some folk of holiday: nor had they waited
For many moments, ere their ears were sated
With a faint breath of music, which even then
Fill'd out its voice, and died away again.
Within a little space again it gave
Its airy swellings, with a gentle wave,
To light-hung leaves, in smoothest echoes breaking
Through copse-clad valleys,—ere their death,
     o'ertaking
The surgy murmurs of the lonely sea.

And now, as deep into the wood as we
Might mark a lynx's eye, there glimmer'd light
Fair faces and a rush of garments white,
Plainer and plainer showing, till at last
Into the widest alley they all past,
Making directly for the woodland altar.
O kindly muse! let not my weak tongue falter
In telling of this goodly company,
Of their old piety, and of their glee:
But let a portion of ethereal dew
Fall on my head, and presently unmew
My soul; that I may dare, in wayfaring,
To stammer where old Chaucer used to sing.

Leading the way, young damsels danced along,
Bearing the burden of a shepherd's song;
Each having a white wicker, overbrimm'd
With April's tender younglings : next, well trimm'd
A crowd of shepherds with as sunburnt looks
As may be read of in Arcadian books;
Such as sat listening round Apollo's pipe.
When the great deity, for earth too ripe,
Let his divinity o'erflowing die
In music, through the vales of Thessaly :
Some idly trail'd their sheep-hooks on the ground,
And some kept up a shrilly mellow sound
With ebon-tipped flutes : close after these,
Now coming from beneath the forest trees,
A venerable priest full soberly,
Begirt with ministering looks : alway his eye
Steadfast upon the matted turf he kept,
And after him his sacred vestments swept.
From his right hand there swung a vase, milk-
　　white,
Of mingled wine, out-sparkling generous light;
And in his left he held a basket full
Of all sweet herbs that searching eye could cull :
Wild thyme, and valley-lilies whiter still
Than Leda's love, and cresses from the rill.
His aged head, crowned with beechen wreath,
Seem'd like a poll of ivy in the teeth
Of winter hoar. Then came another crowd
Of shepherds, lifting in due time aloud
Their share of the ditty. After them appear'd,
Up-follow'd by a multitude that rear'd
Their voices to the clouds, a fair-wrought car
Easily rolling so as scarce to mar
The freedom of three steeds of dapple brown :
Who stood therein did seem of great renown
Among the throng. His youth was fully blown,
Showing like Ganymede to manhood grown;
And, for those simple times, his garments were

A chieftain king's, beneath his breast, half bare,
Was hung a silver bugle, and between
His nervy knees there lay a boar-spear keen.
A smile was on his countenance; he seem'd
To common lookers-on like one who dream'd
Of idleness in groves Elysian ·
But there were some who feelingly could scan
A lurking trouble in his nether lip,
And see that oftentimes the reins would slip
Through his forgotten hands · then would they sigh
And think of yellow leaves, of owlets' cry,
Of logs piled solemnly — Ah, well-a-day,
Why should our young Endymion pine away!

Soon the assembly, in a circle ranged,
Stood silent round the shrine: each look was
    changed
To sudden veneration · women meek
Beckon'd their sons to silence; while each cheek
Of virgin bloom paled gently for slight fear.
Endymion too, without a forest peer,
Stood, wan, and pale, and with an awed face,
Among his brothers of the mountain chase.
In midst of all, the venerable priest
Eyed them with joy from greatest to the least,
And, after lifting up his aged hands,
Thus spake he " Men of Latmos! shepherd
    bands!
Whose care it is to guard a thousand flocks:
Whether descended from beneath the rocks
That overtop your mountains; whether come
From valleys where the pipe is never dumb;
Or from your swelling downs, where sweet air stirs
Blue harebells lightly, and where prickly furze
Buds lavish gold; or ye, whose precious charge
Nibble their fill at ocean's very marge,
Whose mellow reeds are touch'd with sounds forlorn
By the dim echoes of old Triton's horn:

Mothers and wives! who day by day prepare
The scrip, with needments, for the mountain **air**;
And all ye gentle girls who foster up
Udderless lambs, and in a little cup
Will put choice honey for a favour'd youth:
Yea, every one attend! for in good truth
Our vows are wanting to our great god Pan.
Are not our lowing heifers sleeker than
Night-swollen mushrooms?   Are not our **wide**
    plains
Speckled with countless fleeces?   Have not rains
Green'd over April's lap?   No howling sad
Sickens our fearful ewes; and we have had
Great bounty from Endymion our lord.
The earth is glad: the merry lark has pour'd
His early song against yon breezy sky,
That spreads so clear o'er our solemnity."

Thus ending, on the shrine he heap'd a spire
Of teeming sweets, enkindling sacred fire;
Anon he stain'd the thick and spongy sod
With wine, in honour of the shepherd-god.
Now while the earth was drinking it, and while
Bay leaves were crackling in the fragrant pile,
And gummy frankincense was sparkling bright
Neath smothering parsley, and a hazy light
Spread grayly eastward, thus a chorus sang:

" O thou, whose mighty palace roof doth **hang**
From jagged trunks, and overshadoweth
Eternal whispers, glooms, the birth, life, death
Of unseen flowers in heavy peacefulness;
Who lovest to see the hamadryads dress
Their ruffled locks where meeting hazels **darken**
And through whole solemn hours dost sit, **and**
    hearken
The dreary melody of bedded reeds —
In desolate places, where dank moisture **breeds**

The pipy hemlock to strange overgrowth,
Bethinking thee, how melancholy loth
Thou wast to lose fair Syrinx — do thou now,
By thy love's milky brow!
By all the trembling mazes that she ran,
Hear us, great Pan!

" O thou, for whose soul-soothing quiet, turtles
Passion their voices cooingly 'mong myrtles,
What time thou wanderest at eventide
Through sunny meadows, that outskirt the side
Of thine enmossed realms : O thou, to whom
Broad-leaved fig-trees even now foredoom
Their ripen'd fruitage ; yellow-girted bees
Their golden honeycombs ; our village leas
Their fairest blossom'd beans and poppied corn ;
The chuckling linnet its five young unborn,
To sing for thee ; low-creeping strawberries
Their summer coolness ; pent-up butterflies
Their freckled wings ; yea, the fresh-budding year
All its completions — be quickly near,
By every wind that nods the mountain pine,
O forester divine !

" Thou, to whom every faun and satyr flies
For willing service ; whether to surprise
The squatted hare while in half-sleeping fit ;
Or upward ragged precipices flit
To save poor lambkins from the eagle's maw ;
Or by mysterious enticement draw
Bewilder'd shepherds to their path again ;
Or to tread breathless round the frothy main,
And gather up all fancifullest shells
For thee to tumble into Naiads' cells,
And, being hidden, laugh at their out-peeping ;
Or to delight thee with fantastic leaping,
The while they pelt each other on the crown
With silvery oak-apples, and fir-cones brown —

By all the echoes that about thee ring,
Hear us, O satyr king!

" O Hearkener to the loud-clapping shears,
While ever and anon to his shorn peers
A ram goes bleating: Winder of the horn,
When snouted wild-boars routing tender corn
Anger our huntsman: Breather round our farms,
To keep off mildews, and all weather harms:
Strange ministrant of undescribed sounds,
That come a-swooning over hollow grounds,
And wither drearily on barren moors:
Dread opener of the mysterious doors
Leading to universal knowledge — see,
Great son of Dryope,
The many that are come to pay their vows
With leaves about their brows!

" Be still the unimaginable lodge
For solitary thinkings; such as dodge
Conception to the very bourne of heaven,
Then leave the naked brain: be still the leaven,
That spreading in this dull and clodded earth,
Gives it a touch ethereal — a new birth:
Be still a symbol of immensity:
A firmament reflected in a sea;
An element filling the space between;
An unknown — but no more: we humbly screen
With uplift hands our foreheads, lowly bending,
And giving out a shout most heaven-rending,
Conjure thee to receive our humble Pæan,
Upon thy Mount Lycean!"

Even while they brought the burden to a close,
A shout from the whole multitude arose,
That linger'd in the air like dying rolls
Of abrupt thunder, when Ionian shoals
Of dolphins bob their noses through the brine.

Meantime, on shady levels, mossy fine,
Young companies nimbly began dancing
To the swift treble pipe, and humming string.
Ay, those fair living forms swam heavenly
To tunes forgotten — out of memory :
Fair creatures! whose young children's children bred
Thermopylæ its heroes — not yet dead,
But in old marbles ever beautiful.
High genitors, unconscious did they cull
Time's sweet first-fruits — they danced to weariness,
And then in quiet circles did they press
The hillock turf, and caught the latter end
Of some strange history, potent to send
A young mind from its bodily tenement.
Or they might watch the quoit-pitchers, intent
On either side, pitying the sad death
Of Hyacinthus, when the cruel breath
Of Zephyr slew him, — Zephyr penitent,
Who now, ere Phœbus mounts the firmament,
Fondles the flower amid the sobbing rain.
The archers too, upon a wider plain,
Beside the feathery whizzing of the shaft
And the dull twanging bowstring, and the raft,
Branch down sweeping from a tall ash top,
Call'd up a thousand thoughts to envelope
Those who would watch.   Perhaps, the trembling
    knee
And frantic gape of lonely Niobe,
Poor, lonely Niobe! when her lovely young
Were dead and gone, and her caressing tongue
Lay a lost thing upon her paly lip,
And very, very deadliness did nip
Her motherly cheeks.   Aroused from this sad mood
By one, who at a distance loud halloo'd,
Uplifting his strong bow into the air,
Many might after brighter visions stare :
After the Argonauts, in blind amaze
Tossing about on Neptune's restless ways.

Until, from the horizon's vaulted side,
There shot a golden splendour far and wide,
Spangling those million poutings of the brine
With quivering ore : 'twas even an awful shine
From the exaltation of Apollo's bow;
A heavenly beacon in their dreary woe.
Who thus were ripe for high contemplating,
Might turn their steps towards the sober ring
Where sat Endymion and the aged priest
'Mong shepherds gone in eld, whose looks increased
The silvery setting of their mortal star.
There they discoursed upon the fragile bar
That keeps us from our homes ethereal;
And what our duties there : to nightly call
Vesper, the beauty-crest of summer weather;
To summon all the downiest clouds together
For the sun's purple couch; to emulate
In ministering the potent rule of fate
With speed of fire-tail'd exhalations;
To tint her pallid cheek with bloom, who cons
Sweet poesy by moonlight : besides these,
A world of other unguess'd offices.
Anon they wander'd, by divine converse,
Into Elysium; vying to rehearse
Each one his own anticipated bliss.
One felt heart-certain that he could not miss
His quick-gone love, among fair blossom'd boughs,
Where every zephyr-sigh pouts, and endows
Her lips with music for the welcoming.
Another wish'd, 'mid that eternal spring,
To meet his rosy child, with feathery sails,
Sweeping, eye-earnestly, through almond vales :
Who, suddenly, should stoop through the smooth
    wind,
And with the balmiest leaves his temples bind;
And, ever after, through those regions be
His messenger, his little Mercury.
Some were athirst in soul to see again

Their fellow-huntsmen o'er the wide champaign
In times long past; to sit with them, and talk
Of all the chances in their earthly walk;
Comparing, joyfully, their plenteous stores
Of happiness, to when upon the moors,
Benighted, close they huddled from the cold,
And shared their famish'd scrips.   Thus all outtold
Their fond imaginations, — saving him
Whose eyelids curtain'd up their jewels dim,
Endymion : yet hourly had he striven
To hide the cankering venom, that had riven
His fainting recollections.   Now indeed
His senses had swoon'd off: he did not heed
The sudden silence, or the whispers low,
Or the old eyes dissolving at his woe,
Or anxious calls, or close of trembling palms,
Or maiden's sigh, that grief itself embalms :
But in the self-same fixed trance he kept,
Like one who on the earth had never stept.
Ay, even as dead-still as a marble man,
Frozen in that old tale Arabian.

     Who whispers him so pantingly and close ?
Peona, his sweet sister : of all those,
His friends, the dearest.   Hushing signs she made,
And breathed a sister's sorrow to persuade
A yielding up, a cradling on her care.
Her eloquence did breathe away the curse :
She led him, like some midnight spirit nurse
Of happy changes in emphatic dreams,
Along a path between two little streams, —
Guarding his forehead, with her round elbow,
From low-grown branches, and his footsteps slow
From stumbling over stumps and hillocks small ;
Until they came to where these streamlets fall,
With mingled bubblings and a gentle rush,
Into a river, clear, brimful, and flush
With crystal mocking of the trees and sky.

A little shallop, floating there hard by,
Pointed its beak over the fringed bank;
And soon it lightly dipt, and rose, and sank,
And dipt again, with the young couple's weight, —
Peona guiding, through the water straight,
Towards a bowery island opposite;
Which gaining presently, she steered light
Into a shady, fresh, and ripply cove,
Where nested was an arbour, overwove
By many a summer's silent fingering;
To whose cool bosom she was used to bring
Her playmates, with their needle broidery,
And minstrel memories of times gone by.

So she was gently glad to see him laid
Under her favourite bower's quiet shade,
On her own couch, new made of flower leaves,
Dried carefully on the cooler side of sheaves
When last the sun his autumn tresses shook,
And the tann'd harvesters rich armfuls took
Soon was he quieted to slumbrous rest:
But, ere it crept upon him, he had prest
Peona's busy hand against his lips,
And still, a-sleeping, held her finger-tips
In tender pressure. And as a willow keeps
A patient watch over the stream that creeps
Windingly by it, so the quiet maid
Held her in peace: so that a whispering blade
Of grass, a wailful gnat, a bee bustling
Down in the bluebells, or a wren light rustling
Among sere leaves and twigs, might all be heard.

O magic sleep! O comfortable bird,
That broodest o'er the troubled sea of the mind
Till it is hush'd and smooth! O unconfined
Restraint! imprison'd liberty! great key
To golden palaces, strange minstrelsy,
Fountains grotesque, new trees, bespangled caves,

Echoing grottoes, full of tumbling waves
And moonlight; ay, to all the mazy world
Of silvery enchantment! — who, upturl'd
Beneath thy drowsy wing a triple hour,
But renovates and lives? — Thus, in the **bower,**
Endymion was calm'd to life again.
Opening his eyelids with a healthier brain,
He said: " I feel this thine endearing love
All through my bosom: thou art as a dove
Trembling its closed eyes and sleeked wings
About me; and the pearliest dew not brings
Such morning incense from the fields of May,
As do those brighter drops that twinkling stray
From those kind eyes. — the very home and haunt
Of sisterly affection. Can I want
Aught else, aught nearer heaven, than such **tears!**
Yet dry them up, in bidding hence all fears
That, any longer, I will pass my days
Alone and sad. No, I will once more raise
My voice upon the mountain-heights; once **more**
Make my horn parley from their foreheads hoar:
Again my trooping hounds their tongues shall loll
Around the breathed boar: again I'll poll
The fair grown yew-tree, for a chosen bow:
And, when the pleasant sun is getting low,
Again I'll linger in a sloping mead
To hear the speckled thrushes, and see **feed**
Our idle sheep. So be thou cheered, **sweet!**
And, if thy lute is here, softly entreat
My soul to keep in its resolved course."

    Hereat Peona, in their silver source,
Shut her pure sorrow-drops with glad **exclaim,**
And took a lute, from which there pulsing **came**
A lively prelude, fashioning the way
In which her voice should wander. 'Twas a **lay**
More subtle-cadenced, more forest wild
Than Dryope's one lulling of her child

And nothing since has floated in the a_
So mournful strange.   Surely some influence rare
Went, spiritual, through the damsel's hand,
For still, with Delphic emphasis, she spann'd
The quick invisible strings, even though she saw
Endymion's spirit melt away and thaw
Before the deep intoxication.
But soon she came, with sudden burst, upon
Her self-possession — swung the lute aside,
And earnestly said: " Brother, 'tis vain to hide
That thou dost k ow of things mysterious,
Immortal, starry ; such alone could thus
Weigh down thy nature.   Hast thou sinn'd in
    aught
Offensive to the heavenly powers ?   Caught
A Paphian dove upon a message sent ?
Thy deathful bow against some deer-herd bent,
Sacred to Dian ?   Haply, thou hast seen
Her naked limbs among the alders green ;
And that, alas ' is death   No, I can trace
Something more high perplexing in thy face !"

   Endymion look'd at her, and press'd her hand,
And said, " Art thou so pale, who wast so bland
And merry in our meadows ?   How is this ?
Tell me thine ailment. tell me all amiss !
Ah! thou hast been unhappy at the change
Wrought suddenly in me.   What indeed more
    strange ?
Or more complete to overwhelm surmise ?
Ambition is no sluggard · 'tis no prize,
That toiling years would put within my grasp,
That I have sigh'd for . with so deadly gasp
No man e'er panted for a mortal love.
So all have set my heavier grief above
These things which happen.   Rightly have they
    done ·
I. who still saw the horizontal sun

4

Heave his broad shoulder o'er the edge of the
    world,
Out-facing Lucifer, and then had hurl'd
My spear aloft, as signal for the chase —
I, who, for very sport of heart, would race
With my own steed from Araby; pluck down
A vulture from his towery perching; frown
A lion into growling, loth retire —
To lose, at once, all my toil-breeding fire,
And sink thus low! but I will ease my breast
Of secret grief, here in this bowery nest.

    " This river does not see the naked sky,
Till it begins to progress silverly
Around the western border of the wood,
Whence, from a certain spot, its winding flood
Seems at the distance like a crescent moon:
And in that nook, the very pride of June,
Had I been used to pass my weary eves;
The rather for the sun unwilling leaves
So dear a picture of his sovereign power,
And I could witness his most kingly hour,
When he doth tighten up the golden reins,
And paces leisurely down amber plains
His snorting four.   Now when his chariot last
Its beams against the zodiac-lion cast,
There blossom'd suddenly a magic bed
Of sacred dittany, and poppies red:
At which I wonder'd greatly, knowing well
That but one night had wrought this flowery spell
And, sitting down close by, began to muse
What it might mean.   Perhaps, thought I, Mor-
    pheus,
In passing here, his owlet pinions shook;
Or, it may be, ere matron Night uptook
Her ebon urn, young Mercury, by stealth,
Had dipp'd his rod in it: such garland wealth
Came not by common growth.   Thus on I thought,

Until my head was dizzy and distraught.
Moreover, through the dancing poppies stole
A breeze most softly lulling to my soul;
And shaping visions all about my sight
Of colors, wings, and bursts of spangly light;
The which became more strange, and strange, and
    dim,
And then were gulf'd in a tumultuous swim:
And then I fell asleep.   Ah, can I tell
The enchantment that afterwards befell?
Yet it was but a dream: yet such a dream
That never tongue, although it overteem
With mellow utterance, like a cavern spring,
Could figure out and to conception bring
All I beheld and felt.   Methought I lay
Watching the zenith, where the milky way
Among the stars in virgin splendour pours;
And travelling my eye, until the doors
Of heaven appear'd to open for my flight,
I became loth and fearful to alight
From such high soaring by a downward glance·
So kept me steadfast in that airy trance,
Spreading imaginary pinions wide.
When, presently, the stars began to glide,
And faint away, before my eager view:
At which I sigh'd that I could not pursue,
And dropp'd my vision to the horizon's verge;
And lo! from opening clouds, I saw emerge
The loveliest moon, that ever silver'd o'er
A shell for Neptune's goblet; she did soar
So passionately bright, my dazzled soul
Commingling with her argent spheres did roll
Through clear and cloudy, even when she went
At last into a dark and vapoury tent —
Whereat, methought, the lidless-eyed train
Of planets all were in the blue again.
To commune with those orbs, once more I raised
My sight right upward: but it was quite dazed

By a bright something, sailing down apace,
Making me quickly veil my eyes and face:
Again I look'd, and, O ye deities,
Who from Olympus watch our destinies
Whence that completed form of all completeness?
Whence came that high perfection of all sweet-
    ness?
Speak, stubborn earth, and tell me where, O
    where
Hast thou a symbol of her golden hair?
Not oat-sheaves drooping in the western sun;
Not — thy soft hand, fair sister! let me shun
Such follying before thee — yet she had,
Indeed, locks bright enough to make me mad;
And they were simply gordian'd up and braided,
Leaving, in naked comeliness, unshaded,
Her pearl round ears, white neck, and orbed brow;
The which were blended in, I know not how,
With such a paradise of lips and eyes,
Blush-tinted cheeks, half smiles, and faintest sighs,
That, when I think thereon, my spirit clings
And plays about its fancy, till the stings
Of human neighbourhood envenom all.
Unto what awful power shall I call?
To what high fane, — Ah! see her hovering feet,
More bluely vein'd, more soft, more whitely sweet,
Than those of sea-born Venus, when she rose
From out her cradle shell.   The wind out-blows
Her scarf into a fluttering pavilion;
'Tis blue, and over-spangled with a million
Of little eyes, as though thou wert to shed,
Over the darkest, lushest bluebell bed,
Handfuls of daisies." — " Endymion, how strange!
Dream within dream!" — " She took an airy
    range,
And then, towards me, like a very maid,
Came blushing, waning, willing, and afraid,
And press'd me by the hand: Ah! 'twas too much

Methought I fainted at the charmed touch,
Yet held my recollection, even as one
Who dives three fathoms where the waters run
Gurgling in beds of coral: for anon,
I felt upmounted in that region
Where falling stars dart their artillery forth,
And eagles struggle with the buffeting north
That balances the heavy meteor-stone;—
Felt too, I was not fearful, nor alone,
But lapp'd and lull'd along the dangerous sky.
Soon, as it seem'd, we left our journeying high,
And straightway into frightful eddies swoop'd;
Such as aye muster where gray time has scoop'd
Huge dens and caverns in a mountain's side:
There hollow sounds aroused me, and I sigh'd
To faint once more by looking on my bliss—
I was distracted; madly did I kiss
The wooing arms which held me, and did give
My eyes at once to death: but 'twas to live,
To take in draughts of life from the gold fount
Of kind and passionate looks; to count, and count
The moments, by some greedy help that seem'd
A second self, that each might be redeem'd
And plunder'd of its load of blessedness
Ah, desperate mortal! I even dared to press
Her very cheek against my crowned lip,
And, at that moment, felt my body dip
Into a warmer air: a moment more,
Our feet were soft in flowers.   There was store
Of newest joys upon that alp.   Sometimes
A scent of violets, and blossoming limes,
Loiter'd around us; then of honey cells,
Made delicate from all white-flower bells;
And once, above the edges of our nest,
An arch face peep'd,—an Oread as I guess'd.

  " Why did I dream that sleep o'erpower'd me
In midst of all this heaven ?   Why not see,

Far off, the shadows of his pinions dark,
And stare them from me?   But no, like a spark
That needs must die, although its little beam
Reflects upon a diamond, my sweet dream
Fell into nothing — into stupid sleep.
And so it was, until a gentle creep,
A careful moving caught my waking ears,
And up I started: Ah! my sighs, my tears,
My clenched hands; — for lo! the poppies hung
Dew-dabbled on their stalks, the ouzel sung
A heavy ditty, and the sullen day
Had chidden herald Hesperus away,
With leaden looks: the solitary breeze
Bluster'd, and slept, and its wild self did tease
With wayward melancholy; and I thought,
Mark me, Peona! that sometimes it brought
Faint fare-thee-wells, and sigh-shrilled adieus! —
Away I wander'd — all the pleasant hues
Of heaven and earth had faded: deepest shades
Were deepest dungeons; heaths and sunny glades
Were full of pestilent light; our taintless rills
Seem'd sooty, and o'erspread with upturn'd gills
Of dying fish; the vermeil rose had blown
In frightful scarlet, and its thorns outgrown
Like spiked aloe.   If an innocent bird
Before my heedless footsteps stirr'd, and stirr'd
In little journeys, I beheld in it
A disguised demon, missioned to knit
My soul with under darkness; to entice
My stumblings down some monstrous precipice:
Therefore I eager follow'd, and did curse
The disappointment.   Time, that aged nurse,
Rock'd me to patience.   Now, thank gentle heaven
These things, with all their comfortings, are given
To my down-sunken hours, and with thee,
Sweet sister, help to stem the ebbing sea
Of weary life."

Thus ended he, and both
Sat silent : for the maid was very loth
To answer ; feeling well that breathed words
Would all be lost, unheard, and vain as swords
Against the encha~ed crocodile, or leaps
Of grasshoppers against the sun.   She weeps,
And wonders ; struggles to devise some blame ;
To put on such a look as would say, *Shame
On this poor weakness !* but, for all her strife,
She could as soon have crush'd away the life
From a sick dove.   At length, to break the pause,
She said with trembling chance · " Is this the cause ?
This all ?   Yet it is strange, and sad, alas !
That one who through this middle earth should **pass**
Most like a sojourning demi-god, and leave
His name upon the harp-string, should achieve
No higher bard than simple maidenhood,
Singing alone, and fearfully, — how the blood
Left his young cheek ; and how he used to stray
He knew not where : and how he would say, ***nay***
If any said 'twas love . and yet 'twas love ;
What could it be but love ?   How a ring-dove
Let fall a sprig of yew-tree in his path
And how he died : and then, that love doth scathe
The gentle heart, as northern blasts do roses ;
And then the ballad of his sad life closes
With sighs, and an alas ! — Endymion !
Be rather in the trumpet's mouth, — anon
Among the winds at large — that all may **hearken**
Although, before the crystal heavens darken,
I watch and dote upon the silver lakes
Pictured in western cloudiness, that takes
The semblance of gold rocks and bright gold **sands**
Islands, and creeks, and amber-fretted strands
With horses prancing o'er them, palaces
And towers of amethyst, — would I so tease
My pleasant days, because I could not mount
Into those regions ?   The Morphean fount

Of that fine element that visions, dreams,
And fitful whims of sleep are made of, streams
Into its airy channels with so subtle,
So thin a breathing, not the spider's shuttle,
Circled a million times within the space
Of a swallow's nest-door, could delay a trace,
A tinting of its quality   how light
Must dreams themselves be ; seeing they're more
    slight
Than the mere nothing that engenders them l
Then wherefore sully the entrusted gem
Of high and noble life with thoughts so sick ?
Why pierce high-fronted honour to the quick
For nothing but a dream ?"   Hereat the youth
Look'd up   a conflicting of shame and ruth
Was in his plaited brow : yet his eyelids
Widen'd a little, as when Zephyr bids
A little breeze to creep between the fans
Of careless butterflies. amid his pains
He seem'd to taste a drop of manna-dew,
Full palatable ; and a colour grew
Upon his cheek, while thus he lifeful spake.

    " Peona ! ever have I long'd to slake
My thirst for the world's praises : nothing base,
No merely slumberous phantasm, could unlace
The stubborn canvas for my voyage prepared —
Though now 'tis tatter'd ; leaving my bark bared
And sullenly drifting : yet my higher hope
Is of too wide, too rainbow-large a scope,
To fret at myriads of earthly wrecks.
Wherein lies happiness ?   In that which becks
Our ready minds to fellowship divine,
A fellowship with essence ; till we shine,
Full alchemized, and free of space.   Behold
The clear religion of heaven l   Fold
A rose-leaf round thy finger's taper   so,
And soothe thy lips : hist l when the airy stress

Of music's kiss impregnates the free winds,
And with a sympathetic touch unbinds
Æolian magic from their lucid wombs:
Then old songs waken from enclouded tombs:
Old ditties sigh above their father's grave;
Ghosts of melodious prophesyings rave
Round every spot where trod Apollo's foot;
Bronze clarions awake, and faintly bruit,
Where long ago a giant battle was;
And, from the turf, a lullaby doth pass
In every place where infant Orpheus slept.
Feel we these things!—that moment have we
        stept
Into a sort of oneness, and our state
Is like a floating spirit's.   But there are
Richer entanglements, enthralments far
More self-destroying, leading, by degrees,
To the chief intensity: the crown of these
Is made of love and friendship, and sits high
Upon the forehead of humanity.
All its more ponderous and bulky worth
Is friendship, whence there ever issues forth
A steady splendour; but at the tip-top,
There hangs by unseen film, an orbed drop
Of light, and that is love: its influence
Thrown in our eyes genders a novel sense,
At which we start and fret: till in the end,
Melting into its radiance, we blend,
Mingle, and so become a part of it,—
Nor with aught else can our souls interknit
So wingedly: when we combine therewith,
Life's self is nourish'd by its proper pith,
And we are nurtured like a pelican brood.
Ay, so delicious is the unsating food,
That men, who might have tower'd in the van
Of all the congregated world, to fan
And winnow from the coming step of time
All chaff of custom, wipe away all slime

Left by men-slugs and human serpentry,
Have been content to let occasion die,
Whilst they did sleep in love's Elysium.
And, truly, I would rather be struck dumb,
Than speak against this ardent listlessness :
For I have ever thought that it might bless
The world with benefits unknowingly ;
As does the nightingale, up-perched high,
And cloister'd among cool and bunched leaves
She sings but to her love, nor e'er conceives
How tiptoe Night holds back her dark-gray hood
Just so may love, although 'tis understood
The mere commingling of passionate breath,
Produce more than our searching witnesseth :
What I know not : but who, of men, can tell
That flowers would bloom, or that green fruit would
          swell
To melting pulp, that fish would have bright mail,
The earth its dower of river, wood, and vale,
The meadows runnels, runnels pebble-stones,
The seed its harvest, or the lute its tones,
Tones ravishment, or ravishment its sweet,
If human souls did never kiss and greet ?

    " Now, if this earthly love has power to make
Men's being mortal, immortal ; to shake
Ambition from their memories, and brim
Their measure of content ; what merest whim,
Seems all this poor endeavour after fame,
To one, who keeps within his steadfast aim
A love immortal, an immortal too.
Look not so wilder'd ; for these things are true.
And never can be born of atomies
That buzz about our slumbers, like brain-flies,
Leaving us fancy-sick.   No, no, I'm sure,
My restless spirit never could endure
To brood so long upon one luxury,
Unless it did, though fearfully, espy

A hope beyond the shadow of a dream.
My sayings will the less obscured seem
When I have told thee how my waking sight
Has made me scruple whether that same night
Was pass'd in dreaming.   Hearken, sweet Peona!
Beyond the matron-temple of Latona,
Which we should see but for these darkening
     boughs,
Lies a deep hollow, from whose ragged brows
Bushes and trees do lean all round athwart,
And meet so nearly, that with wings outraught,
And spreaded tail, a vulture could not glide
Past them, but he must brush on every side.
Some moulder'd steps lead into this cool cell,
Far as the slabbed margin of a well,
Whose patient level peeps its crystal eye
Right upward, through the bushes, to the sky.
Oft have I brought thee flowers, on their stalks set
Like vestal primroses, but dark velvet
Edges them round, and they have golden pits:
'Twas there I got them, from the gaps and slits
In a mossy stone, that sometimes was my seat,
When all above was faint with mid-day heat.
And there in strife no burning thoughts to heed,
I'd bubble up the water through a reed;
So reaching back to boyhood: make me ships
Of moulted feathers, touchwood, alder chips,
With leaves stuck in them; and the Neptune be
Of their petty ocean.   Oftener, heavily,
When lovelorn hours had left me less a child,
I sat contemplating the figures wild
Of o'er-head clouds melting the mirror through.
Upon a day, while thus I watch'd, by flew
A cloudy Cupid, with his bow and quiver;
So plainly character'd, no breeze would shiver
The happy chance: so happy, I was fain
To follow it upon the open plain,
And, therefore, was just going; when, behold!

A wonder, fair as any I have told —
The same bright face I tasted in my sleep,
Smiling in the clear well. My heart did leap
Through the cool depth. — It moved as if to flee —
I started up, when lo! refreshfully,
There came upon my face, in plenteous showers,
Dew-drops, and dewy buds, and leaves, and flowers
Wrapping all objects from my smother'd sight,
Bathing my spirit in a new delight.
Ay, such a breathless honey-feel of bliss
Alone preserved me from the drear abyss
Of death, for the fair form had gone again.
Pleasure is oft a visitant ; but pain
Clings cruelly to us, like the gnawing sloth
On the deer's tender haunches : late, and loth,
'Tis scared away by slow returning pleasure.
How sickening, how dark the dreadful leisure
Of weary days, made deeper exquisite,
By a foreknowledge of unslumbrous night !
Like sorrow came upon me, heavier still,
Than when I wander'd from the poppy hill :
And a whole age of lingering moments crept
Sluggishly by, ere more contentment swept
Away at once the deadly yellow spleen.
Yes, thrice have I this fair enchantment seen,
Once more been tortured with renewed life.
When last the wintry gusts gave over strife
With the conquering sun of spring, and left the
     skies
Warm and serene, but yet with moisten'd eyes
In pity of the shatter'd infant buds, —
That time thou didst adorn, with amber studs,
My hunting-cap, because I laugh'd and smiled,
Chatted with thee, and many days exiled
All torment from my breast ; — 'twas even then,
Straying about, yet coop'd up in the den
Of helpless discontent, — hurling my lance
From place to place, and following at chance,

At last, by hap, through some young trees it struck,
And, plashing among bedded pebbles, stuck
In the middle of a brook, — whose silver ramble
Down twenty little falls through reeds and bramble
Tracing along, it brought me to a cave,
Whence it ran brightly forth, and white did lave
The nether sides of mossy stones and rock, —
'Mong which it gurgled blithe adieus, to mock
Its own sweet grief at parting.   Overhead,
Hung a lush screen of drooping weeds, and spread
Thick, as to curtain up some wood-nymph's home.
  Ah! impious mortal, whither do I roam!'
Said I, low-voiced : ' Ah, whither! 'Tis the grot
Of Proserpine, when Hell, obscure and hot,
Doth her resign : and where her tender hands
She dabbles on the cool and sluicy sands:
Or 'tis the cell of Echo, where she sits,
And babbles thorough silence, till her wits
Are gone in tender madness, and anon,
Faints into sleep, with many a dying tone
Of sadness.   O that she would take my vows,
And breathe them sighingly among the boughs,
To sue her gentle ears for whose fair head,
Daily, I pluck sweet flowerets from their bed,
And weave them dyingly — send honey-whispers
Round every leaf, that all those gentle lispers
May sigh my love unto her pitying!
O charitable Echo! hear, and sing
This ditty to her! — tell her' — So I stay'd
My foolish tongue, and listening, half afraid,
Stood stupefied with my own empty folly,
And blushing for the freaks of melancholy.
Salt tears were coming, when I heard my name
Most fondly lipp'd, and then these accents came:
  Endymion! the cave is secreter
Than the isle of Delos.   Echo hence shall stir
No sighs but sigh-warm kisses, or light noise
Of thy combing hand, the while it travelling cloys

And trembles through my labyrinthine hair.'
At that oppress'd, I hurried in — Ah! where
Are those swift moments! Whither are they fled
I'll smile no more, Peona, nor will wed
Sorrow, the way to death; but patiently
Bear up against it: so farewell, sad sigh;
And come instead demurest meditation,
To occupy me wholly, and to fashion
My pilgrimage for the world's dusky brink.
No more will I count over, link by link,
My chain of grief: no longer strive to find
A half-forgetfulness in mountain wind
Blustering about my ears: ay, thou shalt see,
Dearest of sisters, what my life shall be;
What a calm round of hours shall make my days
There is a paly flame of hope that plays
Where'er I look: but yet, I'll say 'tis nought —
And here I bid it die. Have not I caught,
Already, a more healthy countenance?
By this the sun is setting; we may chance
Meet some of our near-dwellers with my car."

This said, he rose, faint-smiling, like a star
Through autumn mists, and took Peona's hand!
They stept into the boat, and launch'd from land

———————◆———————

BOOK II.

O sovereign power of love! O grief! O balm!
All records, saving thine, come cool, and calm,
And shadowy, through the mist of passed years:
For others, good or bad, hatred and tears
Have become indolent; but touching thine,
One sigh doth echo, one poor sob doth pine,
One kiss brings honey-dew from buried days.

The woes of Troy, towers smothering o'er their
    blaze,
Stiff-holden shields, far-piercing spears, keen blades,
Struggling, and blood, and shrieks — all dimly fades
Into some backward corner of the brain ;
Yet, in our very souls, we feel amain
The close of Troilus and Cressid sweet.
Hence, pageant history ! hence, gilded cheat
Swart planet in the universe of deeds !
Wide sea, that one continuous murmur breeds
Along the pebbled shore of memory !
Many old rotten-timber'd boats there be
Upon thy vaporous bosom, magnified
To goodly vessels ; many a sail of pride,
And golden-keel'd, is left unlaunch'd and dry.
But wherefore this ? What care, though owl did fly
About the great Athenian admiral's mast ?
What care, though striding Alexander past
The Indus with his Macedonian numbers ?
Though old Ulysses tortured from his slumbers
The glutted Cyclops, what care ? — Juliet leaning
Amid her window-flowers, — sighing, — weaning
Tenderly her fancy from its maiden snow,
Doth more avail than these : the silver flow
Of Hero's tears, the swoon of Imogen,
Fair Pastorella in the bandit's den,
Are things to brood on with more ardency
Than the death-day of empires. Fearfully
Must such conviction come upon his head,
Who, thus far, discontent, has dared to tread,
Without one muse's smile, or kind behest,
The path of love and poesy. But rest,
In chafing restlessness, is yet more drear
Than to be crush'd, in striving to uprear
Love's standard on the battlements of song.
So once more days and nights aid me along,
Like legion'd soldiers.

Brain-sick shepherd-prince
What promise hast thou faithful guarded since
The day of sacrifice ?   Or, have new sorrows
Come with the constant dawn upon thy morrows
Alas! 'tis his old grief.   For many days,
Has he been wandering in uncertain ways :
Through wilderness, and woods of mossed oaks ;
Counting his woe-worn minutes, by the strokes
Of the lone wood-cutter ; and listening still,
Hour after hour, to each lush-leaved rill.
Now he is sitting by a shady spring,
And elbow-deep with feverous fingering
Stems the upbursting cold : a wild rose-tree
Pavilions him in bloom, and he doth see
A bud which snares his fancy : lo ! but now
He plucks it, dips its stalk in the water : how
It swells, it buds, it flowers beneath his sight
And, in the middle, there is softly pight
A golden butterfly ; upon whose wings
There must be surely character'd strange things,
For with wide eye he wonders, and smiles oft.

Lightly this little herald flew aloft,
Follow'd by glad Endymion's clasped hands :
Onward it flies   From languor's sullen bands
His limbs are loosed, and eager, on he hies
Dazzled to trace it in the sunny skies.
It seem'd he flew, the way so easy was ;
And like a new-born spirit did he pass
Through the green evening quiet in the sun,
O'er many a heath, through many a woodland dun
Through buried paths, where sleepy twilight dreams
The summer time away   One track unseams
A wooded cleft, and, far away, the blue
Of ocean fades upon him ; then, anew,
He sinks adown a solitary glen,
Where there was never sound of mortal men,
Saving, perhaps, some snow-light cadence

Melting to silence, when upon the breeze
Some holy bark let forth an anthem sweet,
To cheer itself to Delphi Still his feet
Went swift beneath the merry-winged guide,
Until it reach'd a splashing fountain's side
That, near a cavern's mouth, for ever pour'd
Unto the temperate air; then high it soar'd,
And, downward, suddenly began to dip,
As if, athirst with so much toil, 'twould sip
The crystal spout-head: so it did, with touch
Most delicate, as though afraid to smutch,
Even with mealy gold, the waters clear.
But, at that very touch, to disappear
So fairy-quick, was strange! Bewildered,
Endymion sought around, and shook each bed
Of covert flowers in vain; and then he flung
Himself along the grass. What gentle tongue,
What whisperer, disturb'd his gloomy rest?
It was a nymph uprisen to the breast
In the fountain's pebbly margin, and she stood
'Mong lilies, like the youngest of the brood.
To him her dripping hand she softly kist,
And anxiously began to plait and twist
Her ringlets round her fingers, saying: " Youth
Too long, alas, hast thou starved on the ruth,
The bitterness of love: too long indeed,
Seeing thou art so gentle. Could I weed
Thy soul of care, by heavens, I would offer
All the bright riches of my crystal coffer
To Amphitrite; all my clear-eyed fish,
Golden, or rainbow-sided, or purplish,
Vermilion-tail'd, or finn'd with silvery gauze;
Yea, or my veined pebble-floor that draws
A virgin-light to the deep; my grotto-sands,
Tawny and gold, oozed slowly from far lands
By my diligent springs; my level lilies, shells,
My charming-rod, my potent river spells;
Yes, every thing, even to the pearly cup
5

Meander gave me, — for I bubbled up
To fainting creatures in a desert wild.
But woe is me, I am but as a child
To gladden thee ; and all I dare to say,
Is, that I pity thee ; that on this day
I've been thy guide ; that thou must wander far
In other regions, past the scanty bar
To mortal steps, before thou canst be ta'en
From every wasting sigh, from every pain,
Into the gentle bosom of thy love.
Why it is thus, one knows in heaven above :
But, a poor Naiad, I guess not.   Farewell !
I have a ditty for my hollow cell."

   Hereat she vanish'd from Endymion's gaze,
Who brooded o'er the water in amaze :
The dashing fount pour'd on, and where its pool
Lay, half asleep, in grass and rushes cool,
Quick waterflies and gnats were sporting still,
And fish were dimpling, as if good nor ill
Had fallen out that hour.   The wanderer,
Holding his forehead, to keep off the burr
Of smothering fancies, patiently sat down ;
And, while beneath the evening's sleepy frown
Glowworms began to trim their starry lamps,
Thus breathed he to himself : " Whoso encamp
To take a fancied city of delight,
O what a wretch is he ! and when 'tis his,
After long toil and travelling, to miss
The kernel of his hopes, how more than vile !
Yet, for him there's refreshment even in toil
Another city doth he set about,
Free from the smallest pebble-bead of doubt
That he will seize on trickling honey-combs :
Alas ! he finds them dry ; and then he foams
And onward to another city speeds.
But this is human life : the war, the deeds,
The disappointment, the anxiety,

Imagination's struggles, far and nigh,
All human ; bearing in themselves this **good,**
That they are still the air, the subtle food,
To make us feel existence, and to show
How quiet death is. . Where soil is, men **grow,**
Whether to weeds or flowers ; but for me,
There is no depth to strike in : I can see
Nought earthly worth my compassing ; so **stand**
Upon a misty, jutting head of land —
Alone ?   No, no ; and by the Orphean lute,
When mad Eurydice is listening to 't,
I'd rather stand upon this misty peak,
With not a thing to sigh for, or to seek,
But the soft shadow of my thrice-seen love,
Than be — I care not what.   O meekest dove
Of heaven ! O Cynthia, ten-times bright and **fair** !
From thy blue throne, now filling all the air,
Glance but one little beam of temper'd **light**
Into my bosom, that the dreadful might
And tyranny of love be somewhat scared !
Yet do not so, sweet queen ; one torment **spared,**
Would give a pang to jealous misery,
Worse than the torment's self: but rather **tie**
Large wings upon my shoulders, and point **out**
My love's far dwelling.   Though the playful **rout**
Of Cupids shun thee, too divine art thou,
Too keen in beauty, for thy silver prow
Not to have dipp'd in love's most gentle **stream.**
O be propitious, nor severely deem
My madness impious ; for, by all the **stars**
That tend thy bidding, I do think the **bars**
That kept my spirit in are burst — that I
Am sailing with thee through the dizzy sky !
How beautiful thou art !   The world how **deep** !
How tremulous-dazzlingly the wheels sweep
Around their axle !   Then these gleaming **reins,**
How lithe !   When this thy chariot attains
Its airy goal, haply some bower veils

Those twilight eyes?   Those eyes!—my spirit
    fails;
Dear goddess, help! or the wide gaping air
Will gulf me—help!"—At this, with madden'd
    stare,
And lifted hands, and trembling lips, he stood;
Like old Deucalion mountain'd o'er the flood,
Or blind Orion hungry for the morn.
And, but from the deep cavern there was borne
A voice, he had been froze to senseless stone;
Nor sigh of his, nor plaint, nor passion'd moan
Had more been heard.   Thus swell'd it forth
    " Descend,
Young mountaineer! descend where alleys bend
Into the sparry hollows of the world!
Oft hast thou seen bolts of the thunder hurl'd
As from thy threshold; day by day hast been
A little lower than the chilly sheen
Of icy pinnacles, and dipp'dst thine arms
Into the deadening ether that still charms
Their marble being: now, as deep profound
As those are high, descend!   He ne'er is crown'd
With immortality, who fears to follow
Where airy voices lead: so through the hollow,
The silent mysteries of earth, descend!"

He heard but the last words, nor could contend
One moment in reflection: for he fled
Into the fearful deep, to hide his head
From the clear moon, the trees, and coming mad-
    ness.

'Twas far too strange, and wonderful for sadness;
Sharpening, by degrees, his appetite
To dive into the deepest.   Dark, nor light,
The region; nor bright, nor sombre wholly,
But mingled up; a gleaming melancholy;
A dusky empire and its diadems;

One faint eternal eventide of gems.
Ay, millions sparkled on a vein of gold,
Along whose track the prince quick footsteps told,
With all its lines abrupt and angular :
Out-shooting sometimes, like a meteor star,
Through a vast antre ; then the metal woof
Like vulcan's rainbow, with some monstrous roof
Curves hugely : now, far in the deep abyss,
It seems an angry lightning, and doth hiss
Fancy into belief : anon it leads
Through winding passages, where sameness breeds
Vexing conceptions of some sudden change ;
Whether to silver grots, or giant range
Of sapphire columns, or fantastic bridge
Athwart a flood of crystal.   On a ridge
Now fareth he, that o'er the vast beneath
Towers like an ocean-cliff, and whence he seeth
A hundred waterfalls, whose voices come
But as the murmuring surge.   Chilly and numb
His bosom grew, when first he, far away,
Described an orbed diamond, set to fray
Old Darkness from his throne : 'twas like the sun
Uprisen o'er chaos : and with such a stun
Came the amazement, that, absorb'd in it,
He saw not fiercer wonders — past the wit
Of any spirit to tell, but one of those
Who, when this planet's sphering time doth close,
Will be its high remembrancers : who they ?
The mighty ones who have made eternal day
For Greece and England.   While astonishment
With deep-drawn sighs was quieting, he went
Into a marble gallery, passing through
A mimic temple, so complete and true
In sacred custom, that he well nigh fear'd
To search it inwards ; whence far off appear'd,
Through a long pillar'd vista, a fair shrine,
And, just beyond, on light tiptoe divine,
A quiver'd Dian.   Stepping awfully,

The youth approach'd ; oft turning his veil'd eye
Down sidelong aisles, and into niches old :
And, when more near against the marble cold
He had touch'd his forehead, he began to thread
All courts and passages, where silence dead,
Roused by his whispering footsteps, murmur'd faint
And long he traversed to and fro, to acquaint
Himself with every mystery, and awe ;
Till, weary, he sat down before the maw
Of a wide outlet, fathomless and dim,
To wild uncertainty and shadows grim.
There, when new wonders ceased to float before,
And thoughts of self came on, how crude and sore
The journey homeward to habitual self !
A mad pursuing of the fog-born elf,
Whose flitting lantern, through rude nettle-brier,
Cheats us into a swamp, into a fire,
Into the bosom of a hated thing.

What misery most drowningly doth sing
In lone Endymion's ear, now he has caught
The goal of consciousness ?   Ah, 'tis the thought,
The deadly feel of solitude · for lo !
He cannot see the heavens, nor the flow
Of rivers, nor hill-flowers running wild
In pink and purple chequer, nor, up-piled,
The cloudy rack slow journeying in the west,
Like herded elephants: nor felt, nor prest
Cool grass, nor tasted the fresh slumberous air;
But far from such companionship to wear
An unknown time, surcharged with grief, away,
Was now his lot.   And must he patient stay,
Tracing fantastic figures with his spear ?
" No ! " exclaim'd he, " why should I tarry here ? "
No! loudly echoed times innumerable.
At which he straightway started, and 'gan tell
His paces back into the temple's chief ;
Warming and glowing strong in the belief

Of help from Dian : so that when again
He caught her airy form, thus did he plain,
Moving more near the while : " O Haunter chaste
Of river sides, and woods, and heathy waste,
Where with thy silver bow and arrows keen
Art thou now forested ?   O woodland Queen,
What smoothest air thy smoother forehead woos ?
Where dost thou listen to the wide halloos
Of thy disparted nymphs ?   Through what dark tree
Glimmers thy crescent ?   Wheresoe'er it be,
'Tis in the breath of heaven : thou dost taste
Freedom as none can taste it, nor dost waste
Thy loveliness in dismal elements ;
But, finding in our green earth sweet contents,
There livest blissfully.   Ah, if to thee
It feels Elysian, how rich to me,
An exiled mortal, sounds its pleasant name !
Within my breast there lives a choking flame —
O let me cool it zephyr-boughs among !
A homeward fever parches up my tongue —
O let me slake it at the running springs !
Upon my ear a noisy nothing rings —
O let me once more hear the linnet's note !
Before mine eyes thick films and shadows float —
O let me 'noint them with the heaven's light !
Dost thou now lave thy feet and ankles white ?
O think how sweet to me the freshening sluice !
Dost thou now please thy thirst with berry-juice ?
O think how this dry palate would rejoice !
If in soft slumber thou dost hear my voice,
O think how I should love a bed of flowers ! —
Young goddess ! let me see my native bowers !
Deliver me from this rapacious deep !"

   Thus ending loudly, as he would o'erleap
His destiny, alert he stood : but when
Obstinate silence came heavily again,
Feeling about for its old couch of space

And airy cradle, lowly bow'd his face,
Desponding, o'er the marble floor's cold thrill.
But 'twas not long, for, sweeter than the rill
To its old channel, or a swollen tide
To margin sallows, were the leaves he spied,
And flowers, and wreaths, and ready myrtle crowns
Upheaping through the slab: refreshment drowns
itself, and strives its own delights to hide —
Nor in one spot alone; the floral pride
In a long whispering birth enchanted grew
Before his footsteps; as when heaved anew
Old ocean rolls a lengthen'd wave to the shore,
Down whose green back the short-lived foam, all
          hoar,
Bursts gradual, with a wayward indolence.

Increasing still in heart, and pleasant sense,
Upon his fairy journey on he hastes;
So anxious for the end, he scarcely wastes
One moment with his hand among the sweets ·
Onward he goes — he stops — his bosom beats
As plainly in his ear as the faint charm
Of which the throbs were born. This still alarm,
This sleepy music, forced him walk tiptoe:
For it came more softly than the east could blow
Arion's magic to the Atlantic isles;
Or than the west, made jealous by the smiles
Of throned Apollo, could breathe back the lyre
To seas Ionian and Tyrian.

O did he ever live, that lonely man,
Who loved — and music slew not? 'Tis the pest
Of love, that fairest joys give most unrest;
That things of delicate and tenderest worth
Are swallow'd all, and made a seared dearth,
By one consuming flame: it doth immerse
And suffocate true blessings in a curse.
Half-happy, by comparison of bliss,

Is miserable. 'Twas even so with this
Dew-dropping melody, in the Carian's ear;
First heaven, then hell, and then forgotten clear
Vanish'd in elemental passion.

And down some swart abysm he had gone,
Had not a heavenly guide benignant led
To where thick myrtle branches, 'gainst his head
Brushing, awaken'd: then the sounds again
Went noiseless as a passing noontide rain
Over a bower, where little space he stood,
For as the sunset peeps into a wood,
So saw he panting light, and towards it went
Through winding alleys; and lo, wonderment!
Upon soft verdure saw, one here, one there,
Cupids a-slumbering on their pinions fair.

After a thousand mazes overgone,
At last, with sudden step, he came upon
A chamber, myrtle-wall'd, embower'd high,
Full of light, incense, tender minstrelsy,
And more of beautiful and strange beside ·
For on a silken couch of rosy pride,
In midst of all, there lay a sleeping youth
Of fondest beauty; fonder, in fair sooth,
Than sighs could fathom, or contentment reach
And coverlids gold-tinted like the peach,
Or ripe October's faded marigolds,
Fell sleek about him in a thousand folds —
Not hiding up an Apollonian curve
Of neck and shoulder, nor the tenting swerve
Of knee from knee, nor ankles pointing light;
But rather, giving them to the fill'd sight
Officiously. Sideway his face reposed
On one white arm, and tenderly unclosed,
By tenderest pressure, a faint damask mouth
To slumbery pout; just as the morning south
Disparts a dew-lipp'd rose. Above his head,

Four lily stalks did their white honours **wed**
To make a coronal; and round him **grew**
All tendrils green, of every bloom and hue.
Together intertwined and trammell'd fresh ·
The vine of glossy sprout; the ivy mesh,
Shading its Ethiop berries; and woodbine,
Of velvet-leaves and bugle-blooms divine;
Convolvulus in streaked vases flush;
The creeper, mellowing for an autumn blush;
And virgin's bower, trailing airily;
With others of the sisterhood   Hard by,
Stood serene Cupids watching silently.
One, kneeling to a lyre, touch'd the strings,
Muffling to death the pathos with his wings ·
And, ever and anon, uprose to look
At the youth's slumber; while another **took**
A willow bough, distilling odorous dew,
And shook it on his hair; another flew
In through the woven roof, and fluttering-**wise**
Rain'd violets upon his sleeping eyes.

At these enchantments, and yet many **more**,
The breathless Latmian wonder'd o'er and o'**er**;
Until impatient in embarrassment,
He forthright pass'd, and lightly treading **went**
To that same feather'd lyrist, who straightway,
Smiling, thus whisper'd: " Though from upper **day**
Thou art a wanderer, and thy presence here
Might seem unholy, be of happy cheer!
For 'tis the nicest touch of human honour,
When some ethereal and high-favouring **donor**
Presents immortal bowers to mortal sense;
As now 'tis done to thee, Endymion.   **Hence**
Was I in no wise startled.   So recline
Upon these living flowers.   Here is **wine**,
Alive with sparkles — never, I aver,
Since Ariadne was a vintager,
So cool a purple: taste these juicy **pears,**

Sent me by sad Vertumnus, when his fears
Were high about Pomona · here is cream,
Deepening to richness from a snowy gleam;
Sweeter than that nurse Amalthea skimm'd
For the boy Jupiter: and here, undimm'd
By any touch, a bunch of blooming plums
Ready to melt between an infant's gums:
And here is manna pick'd from Syrian trees,
In starlight, by the three Hesperides.
Feast on, and meanwhile I will let thee know
Of all these things around us." He did so,
Still brooding o'er the cadence of his lyre;
And thus: " I need not any hearing tire
By telling how the sea-born goddess pined
For a mortal youth, and how she strove to bind
Him all in all unto her doating self.
Who would not be so prison'd ? but, fond elf,
He was content to let her amorous plea
Faint through his careless arms; content to see
An unseized heaven dying at his feet;
Content, O fool ! to make a cold retreat,
When on the pleasant grass such love, lovelorn,
Lay sorrowing; when every tear was born
Of diverse passion; when her lips and eyes
Were closed in sullen moisture, and quick sighs
Came vex'd and pettish through her nostrils small.
Hush ! no exclaim — yet, justly might'st thou call
Curses upon his head. — I was half glad,
But my poor mistress went distract and mad,
When the boar tusk'd him · so away she flew
To Jove's high throne, and by her plainings drew
Immortal tear-drops down the thunderer's beard;
Whereon, it was decreed he should be rear'd
Each summer-time to life. Lo ! this is he,
That same Adonis, safe in the privacy
Of this still region all his winter-sleep
Ay, sleep; for when our love-sick queen did weep
Over his waned corse, the tremulous shower

Heal'd up the wound, and, with a balmy **power,**
Medicined death to a lengthen'd drowsiness:
The which she fills with visions, and doth **dress**
In all this quiet luxury ; and hath set
Us young immortals, without any let,
To watch his slumber through. 'Tis well nigh
      pass'd,
Even to a moment's filling up, and fast
She scuds with summer breezes, to pant through
The first long kiss, warm firstling, to renew
Embower'd sports in Cytherea's isle.
Look, how those winged listeners all this while
Stand anxious: see ! behold !" — This clamant word
Broke through the careful silence ; for they heard
A rustling noise of leaves, and out there flutter'd
Pigeons and doves : Adonis something mutter'd,
The while one hand, that erst upon his thigh
Lay dormant, moved convulsed and gradually
Up to his forehead.   Then there was a hum
Of sudden voices, echoing, " Come ! come !
Arise ! awake !   Clear summer has forth walk'd
Unto the clover-sward, and she has talk'd
Full soothingly to every nested finch :
Rise, Cupids ! or we'll give the bluebell pinch
To your dimpled arms.   Once more sweet life be-
      gin !"
At this, from every side they hurried in,
Rubbing their sleepy eyes with lazy wrists,
And doubling overhead their little fists
In backward yawns.   But all were soon alive:
For as delicious wine doth, sparkling, dive
.In nectar'd clouds and curls through water fair,
So from the arbour roof down swell'd an air
Odorous and enlivening ; making all
To laugh, and play, and sing, and loudly call
For their sweet queen: when lo ! the **wreathed**
      green
Disparted, and far upward could be seen

Blue heaven, and a silver car. air-borne
Whose silent wheels, fresh wet from clouds of morn,
Spun off a drizzling dew, — which falling chill
On soft Adonis' shoulders, made him still
Nestle and turn uneasily about.
Soon were the white doves plain, with necks
      stretch'd out,
And silken traces lighten'd in descent;
And soon, returning from love's banishment,
Queen Venus leaning downward open-arm'd
Her shadow fell upon his breast, and charm'd
A tumult to his heart, and a new life
Into his eyes. Ah, miserable strife,
But for her comforting! unhappy sight,
But meeting her blue orbs! Who, who can write
Of these-first minutes? The unchariest muse
To embracements warm as theirs makes coy excuse.

O it has ruffled every spirit there,
Saving love's self, who stands superb to share
The general gladness: awfully he stands;
A sovereign quell is in his waving hands;
No sight can bear the lightning of his bow;
His quiver is mysterious, none can know
What themselves think of it; from forth his eyes
There darts strange light of varied hues and dyes
A scowl is sometimes on his brow, but who
Look full upon it feel anon the blue
Of his fair eyes run liquid through their souls.
Endymion feels it, and no more controls
The burning prayer within him; so, bent low,
He had begun a plaining of his woe.
But Venus, bending forward, said: "My child,
Favour this gentle youth; his days are wild
With love — he — but alas! too well I see
Thou know'st the deepness of his misery
Ah! smile not so, my son: I tell thee true,
That when through heavy hours I used to rue

The endless sleep of this new-born Adon',
This stranger aye I pitied.   For upon
A dreary morning once I fled away
Into the breezy clouds, to weep and pray
For this my love : for vexing Mars had teased
Me even to tears : thence, when a little eased,
Down-looking, vacant, through a hazy wood,
I saw this youth as he despairing stood :
Those same dark curls blown vagrant in the wind
Those same full fringed lids a constant blind
Over his sullen eyes : I saw him throw
Himself on wither'd leaves, even as though
Death had come sudden ; for no jot he moved,
Yet mutter'd wildly.   I could hear he loved
Some fair immortal, and that his embrace
Had zoned her through the night.   There is no
   trace
Of this in heaven : I have mark'd each cheek,
And find it is the vainest thing to seek ;
And that of all things 'tis kept secretest.
Endymion ! one day thou wilt be blest :
So still obey the guiding hand that fends
Thee safely through these wonders for sweet ends.
'Tis a concealment needful in extreme ;
And if I guess'd not so, the sunny beam
Thou shouldst mount up to with me   Now adieu
Here must we leave thee." — At these words up flew
The impatient doves, up rose the floating car,
Up went the hum celestial.   High afar
The Latmain saw them minish into nought ;
And, when all were clear vanish'd, still he caught
A vivid lightning from that dreadful bow.
When all was darken'd, with Ætnean throe
The earth closed — gave a solitary moan —
And left him once again in twilight lone.

He did not rave, he did not stare aghast,
For all those visions were o'ergone, and past,

And he in loneliness : he felt assured
Of happy times, when all he had endured
Would seem a feather to the mighty prize.
So, with unusual gladness, on he hies
Through caves, and palaces of mottled ore,
Gold dome, and crystal wall, and turquois floor,
Black polish'd porticos of awful shade,
And, at the last, a diamond balustrade,
Leading afar past wild magnificence.
Spiral through ruggedest loopholes, and thence
Stretching across a void, then guiding o'er
Enormous chasms, where all foam and roar,
Streams subterranean tease their granite beds ;
Then heighten'd just above the silvery heads
Of a thousand fountains, so that he could dash
The waters with his spear ; but at the splash,
Done heedlessly, those spouting columns rose
Sudden a poplar's height, and 'gan to inclose
His diamond path with fretwork streaming round
Alike, and dazzling cool, and with a sound,
Haply, like dolphin tumults, when sweet shells
Welcome the float of Thetis.   Long he dwells
On this delight ; for, every minute's space,
The streams with changed magic interlace :
Sometimes like delicatest lattices,
Cover'd with crystal vines ; then weeping trees,
Moving about as in a gentle wind,
Which, in a wink, to watery gauze refined,
Pour'd into shapes of curtain'd canopies,
Spangled, and rich with liquid broideries
Of flowers, peacocks, swans, and naiads fair.
Swifter than lightning went these wonders rare ;
And then the water, into stubborn streams
Collecting, mimick'd the wrought oaken beams,
Pillars, and frieze, and high fantastic roof,
Of those dusk places in times far aloof
Cathedrals call'd.   He bade a loath farewell
To these founts Protean, passing gulf, and dell,

And torrent, and ten thousand jutting shapes,
Half seen through deepest gloom, and grisly gapes
Blackening on every side, and overhead
A vaulted dome like heaven's far bespread
With starlight gems: ay, all so huge and strange,
The solitary felt a hurried change
Working within him into something dreary, —
Vex'd like a morning eagle, lost and weary,
And purblind amid foggy midnight wolds.
But he revives at once : for who beholds
New sudden things, nor casts his mental slough ?
Forth from a rugged arch, in the dusk below,
Came mother Cybele ! alone — alone —
In sombre chariot; dark foldings thrown
About her majesty, and front death-pale,
With turrets crown'd.   Four maned lions hale
The sluggish wheels; solemn their toothed maws.
Their surly eyes brow-hidden, heavy paws
Uplifted drowsily, and nervy tails
Cowering their tawny brushes   Silent sails
This shadowy queen athwart, and faints away
In another gloomy arch.

                    Wherefore delay,
Young traveller, in such a mournful place ?
Art thou wayworn, or canst not further trace
The diamond path ?   And does it indeed end
Abrupt in middle air ?   Yet earthward bend
Thy forehead, and to Jupiter cloud-borne
Call ardently !   He was indeed wayworn;
Abrupt, in middle air, his way was lost;
To cloud-borne Jove he bow'd, and there crost
Towards him a large eagle, 'twixt whose wings,
Without one impious word, himself he flings,
Committed to the darkness and the gloom:
Down, down, uncertain to what pleasant doom,
Swift as a fathoming plummet down he fell
Through unknown things; till exhaled asphodel

Anu rose, with spicy fannings interbreathed,
Came swelling forth where little caves were
      wreathed
So thick with leaves and mosses, that they seem'd
Large honeycor bs of green, and freshly teem'd
With airs lencious. In the greenest nook
The eagle landed him, and farewell took.

   It was a jasmine bower, all bestrown
With golden moss. His every sense had grown
Ethereal for pleasure ; 'bove his head
Flew a delight half-graspable ; his tread
Was Hesperean ; to his capable ears
Silence was music from the holy spheres ;
A dewy luxury was in his eyes ;
The little flowers felt his pleasant sighs
And stirr'd them faintly. Veruant cave and cell
He wander'd through, oft wondering at such swell
Of sudden exaltation : but, "Alas !"
Said he, " will all this gush of feeling pass
Away in solitude ? And must they wane,
Like melodies upon a sandy plain,
Without an echo ? Then shall I be left
So sad, so melancholy, so bereft !
Yet still I feel immortal ! O my love,
My breath of life, where art thou ? High above,
Dancing before the morning gates of heaven ?
Or keeping watch among those starry seven,
Old Atlas' children ? Ait a maid of the waters,
One of shell-winding Triton's bright-hair'd daugh
      ters ?
Or art, impossible ! a nymph of Dian's,
Weaving a coronal of tender scions
For very idleness ? Where'er thou art,
Methinks it now is at my will tc start
Into thine arms ; to scare Aurora's train,
And snatch thee from the morning ; o'er the main
To scud like a wild bird, and take thee off

From thy sea-foamy cradle; or to doff
Thy shepherd vest, and woo thee 'mid fresh leaves
No, no, too eagerly my soul deceives
Its powerless self: I know this cannot be.
O let me then by some sweet dreaming flee
To her entrancements: hither sleep awhile!
Hither most gentle sleep! and soothing toil
For some few hours the coming solitude."

Thus spake he, and that moment felt endued
With power to dream deliciously; so wound
Through a dim passage, searching till he found
The smoothest mossy bed and deepest, where
He threw himself, and just into the air
Stretching his indolent arms, he took, O bliss!
A naked waist: " Fair Cupid, whence is this?"
A well-known .   sigh'd, " Sweetest, here am I
At which soft ravishment, with doting cry
They trembled to each other. — Helicon!
O fountain'd hill!   Old Homer's Helicon!
That thou wouldst spout a little streamlet o'er
These sorry pages; then the verse would soar
And sing above this gentle pair, like lark
Over his nested young · but all is dark
Around thine aged top, and thy clear fount
Exhales in mists to heaven.   Ay, the count
Of mighty Poets is made up; the scroll
Is folded by the Muses; the bright roll
Is in Apollo's hand. our dazed eyes
Have seen a new tinge in the western skies:
The world has done its duty.   Yet, oh yet,
Although the sun of poesy is set,
These lovers did embrace, and we must weep
That there is no old power left to steep
A quill immortal in their joyous tears.
Long time in silence did their anxious fears
Question that thus it was; long time they lay
Fondling and kissing every doubt away;

Long time ere soft caressing sobs began
To mellow into words, and then there ran
Two bubbling springs of talk from their sweet lips.
" O known Unknown ! from whom my being sips
Such darling essence, wherefore may I not
Be ever in these arms ? in this sweet spot
Pillow my chin for ever ? ever press
These toying hands and kiss their smooth excess ?
Why not for ever and for ever feel
That breath about my eyes ?   Ah, thou wilt steal
Away from me again, indeed, indeed —
Thou wilt be gone away, and wilt not heed
My lonely madness.   Speak, my kindest fair !
Is — is it to be so ?   No !   Who will dare
To pluck thee from me ?   And, of thine own
        will,
Full well I feel thou wouldst not leave me.   Still
Let me entwine thee surer, surer — now
How can we part ?   Elysium !   Who art thou ?
Who, that thou canst not be for ever here,
Or lift me with thee to some starry sphere ?
Enchantress ! tell me by this soft embrace,
By the most soft complexion of thy face,
Those lips, O slippery blisses ! twinkling eyes,
And by these tenderest, milky sovereignties —
These tenderest, and by the nectar-wine,
The passion " —— " O loved Ida the divine !
Endymion ! dearest !   Ah, unhappy me !
His soul will 'scape us — O felicity !
How he does love me !   His poor temples beat
To the very tune of love — how sweet, sweet,
        sweet !
Revive, dear youth, or I shall faint and die ;
Revive, or these soft hours will hurry by
In tranced dullness ; speak, and let that spell
Affright this lethargy !   I cannot quell
Its heavy pressure, and will press at least
My lips to thine, that they may richly feast

Until we taste the life of love again.
What! dost thou move? dost kiss? O bliss! O pain
I love thee, youth, more than I can conceive;
And so long absence from thee doth bereave
My soul of any rest: yet must I hence.
Yet, can I not to starry eminence
Uplift thee; nor for very shame can own
Myself to thee.   Ah, dearest! do not groan,
Or thou wilt force me from this secrecy,
And I must blush in heaven.   O that I
Had done it already! that the dreadful smiles
At my lost brightness, my impassion'd wiles,
Had waned from Olympus' solemn height,
And from all serious Gods; that our delight
Was quite forgotten, save of us alone!
And wherefore so ashamed?   'Tis but to atone
For endless pleasure, by some coward blushes:
Yet must I be a coward!   Horror rushes
Too palpable before me — the sad look
Of Jove — Minerva's start — no bosom shook
With awe of purity — no Cupid pinion
In reverence veil'd — my crystalline dominion
Half lost, and all old hymns made nullity!
But what is this to love?   Oh! I could fly
With thee into the ken of heavenly powers,
So thou wouldst thus, for many sequent hours,
Press me so sweetly.   Now I swear at once
That I am wise, that Pallas is a dunce —
Perhaps her love like mine is but unknown —
Oh! I do think that I have been alone
In chastity! yes, Pallas has been sighing,
While every eye saw me my hair uptying
With fingers cool as aspen leaves.   Sweet love!
I was as vague as solitary dove,
Nor knew that nests were built.   Now a soft kiss —
Ay, by that kiss, I vow an endless bliss,
An immortality of passion's thine:
Ere long I will exalt thee to the shine

Of heaven ambrosial; and we will shade
Ourselves whole summers by a river glade;
And I will tell thee stories of the sky,
And breathe thee whispers of its minstrelsy.
My happy love will overwing all bounds!
O let me melt into thee! let the sounds
Of our close voices marry at their birth;
Let us entwine hoveringly! O dearth
Of human words! roughness of mortal speech!
Lispings empyrean will I sometimes teach
Thine honey'd tongue — lute-breathings which I
     gasp
To have thee understand, now while I clasp
Thee thus, and weep for fondness — I am pain'd
Endymion: woe! woe! is grief contain'd
In the very deeps of pleasure, my sole life?"—
Hereat, with many sobs, her gentle strife
Melted into a languor. He return'd
Entranced vows and tears.

          Ye who have yearn'd
With too much passion, will here stay and pity
For the mere sake of truth; as 'tis a ditty
Not of these days, but long ago 'twas told
By a cavern wind unto a forest old;
And then the forest told it in a dream
To a sleeping lake, whose cool and level gleam
A poet caught as he was journeying
To Phœbus' shrine; and in it he did fling
His weary limbs, bathing an hour's space,
And after, straight in that inspired place
He sang the story up into the air,
Giving it universal freedom. There
Has it been ever sounding for those ears
Whose tips are glowing hot. The legend cheers
Yon sentinel stars; and he who listens to it
Must surely be self-doom'd or he will rue it:
For quenchless burnings come upon the heart,

Made fiercer by a fear lest any part
Should be engulfed in the eddying wind.
As much as here is penn'd doth always find
A resting-place, thus much comes clear and plain ;
Anon the strange voice is upon the wane —
And 'tis but echoed from departing sound,
That the fair visitant at last unwound
Her gentle limbs, and left the youth asleep. —
Thus the tradition of the gusty deep.

    Now turn we to our former chroniclers. —
Endymion awoke, that grief of hers
Sweet paining on his ear : he sickly guess'd
How lone he was once more, and sadly press'd
His empty arms together, hung his head,
And most forlorn upon that widow'd bed
Sat silently.   Love's madness he had known :
Often with more than tortured lion's groan
Moanings had burst from him ; but now that rage
Had pass'd away : no longer did he wage
A rough-voiced war against the dooming stars.
No, he had felt too much for such harsh jars :
The lyre of his soul Æolian tuned
Forgot all violence, and but communed
With melancholy thought · O he had swoon'd
Drunken from pleasure's nipple ! and his love
Henceforth was dove-like — Loth was he to move
From the imprinted couch, and when he did,
'Twas with slow, languid paces, and face hid
In muffling hands So temper'd, out he stray'd
Half seeing visions that might have dismay'd
Alecto's serpents ; ravishments more keen
Than Hermes' pipe, when anxious he did lean
Over eclipsing eyes : and at the last
It was a sounding grotto, vaulted, vast,
O'erstudded with a thousand, thousand pearls,
And crimson-mouthed shells with stubborn curls,
Of every shape and size, even to the bulk

In which whales harbour close, tc brood and sulk
Against an endless storm.   Moreover too,
Fish-semblances, of green and azure hue,
Ready to snort their streams.   In this cool wonder
Endymion sat down, and 'gan to ponder
On all his life : his youth, up to the day
When 'mid acclaim, and feasts, and garlands gay,
He stepp'd upon his shepherd throne : the look
Of his white palace in wild forest nook,
And all the revels he had lorded there.
Each tender maiden whom he once thought fair,
With every friend and fellow-woodlander —
Pass'd like a dream before him.   Then the spur
Of the old bards to mighty deeds : his plans
To nurse the golden age 'mong shepherd clans.
That wondrous night : the great Pan-festival.
His sister's sorrow ; and his wanderings all,
Until into the earth's deep maw he rush'd :
Then all its buried magic, till it flush'd
High with excessive love.   " And now," thought he,
" How long must I remain in jeopardy
Of blank amazements that amaze no more ?
Now I have tasted her sweet soul to the core,
All other depths are shallow : essences,
Once spiritual, are like muddy lees,
Meant but to fertilize my earthly root,
And make my branches lift a golden fruit
Into the bloom of heaven ; other light,
Though it be quick and sharp enough to blight
The Olympian eagle's vision, is dark,
Dark as the parentage of chaos.   Hark !
My silent thoughts are echoing from these shells ;
Or they are but the ghosts, the dying swells
Of noises far away ? — list ! " — Hereupon
He kept an anxious ear.   The humming tone
Came louder, and behold, there as he lay,
On either side outgush'd, with misty spray,
A copious spring ; and both together dash'd

Swift, mad, fantasti? round the rocks, and lash d
Among the conchs and shells of the lofty grot,
Leaving a trickling dew.   At last they shot
Down from the ceiling's height, pouring a noise
As of some breathless raceis whose hopes poise
Upon the last few steps, and with spent force
Along the ground they took a winding course.
Endymion follow'd — for it seem'd that one
Ever pursued, the other strove to shun —
Follow'd their languid mazes, till well nigh
He had left thinking of the mystery, —
And was now rapt in tender hoverings
Over the vanish'd bliss.   Ah! what is it sings
His dream away ?   What melodies are these ?
They sound as through the whispering of trees,
Not native in such barren vaults.   Give ear!

" O Arethusa, peerless nymph! why fear
Such tenderness as mine ?   Great Dian, why,
Why didst thou hear her prayer ?   O that I
Were rippling round her dainty fairness now,
Circling about her waist, and striving how
To entice her to a dive! then stealing in
Between her luscious lips and eyelids thin.
O that her shining hair was in the sun,
And I distilling from it thence to run
In amorous rillets down her shrinking form!
To linger on her lily shoulders, warm
Between her kissing breasts, and every charm
Touch raptured! — see how painfully I flow :
Fair maid, be pitiful to my great woe
Stay, stay thy weary course. and let me lead,
A happy wooer, to the flowery mead
Where all that beauty snared me " — " Cruel god
Desist! or my offended mistress' nod
Will stagnate all thy fountains : — tease me not
With syren words — Ah, have I really got
Such power to madden thee ?   And is it true —

Away, away, or I shall dearly rue
My very thoughts   in mercy then away,
Kindest Alpheus, for should I obey
My own dear will, 'twould be a deadly bane." —
" O, Oread-Queen ! would that thou hadst a pain
Like this of mine, then would I fearless turn
And be a criminal." — " Alas, I burn,
I shudder — gentle river, get thee hence.
Alpheus ! thou enchanter ! every sense
Of mine was once made perfect in these woods.
Fresh breezes, bowery lawns, and innocent floods,
Ripe fruits, and lonely couch, contentment gave ;
But ever since I heedlessly did lave
In thy deceitful stream., a panting glow
Grew strong within me : wherefore serve me so,
And call it love ?   Alas ! 'twas cruelty.
Not once more did I close my happy eyes
Amid the thrush's song.   Away ! avaunt !
O 'twas a cruel thing." — " Now thou dost taunt
So softly, Arethusa, that I think
If thou wast playing on my shady brink,
Thou wouldst bathe once again.   Innocent maid
Stifle thine heart no more ; — nor be afraid
Of angry powers : there are deities
Will shade us with their wings.   Those fitful sighs
'Tis almost death to hear : O let me pour
A dewy balm upon them ! — fear no more,
Sweet Arethusa ! Dian's self must feel,
Sometimes, these very pangs.   Dear maiden, steal
Blushing into my soul, and let us fly
These dreary caverns for the open sky.
I will delight thee all my winding course,
From the green sea up to my hidden source
About Arcadian forests ; and will show
The channels where my coolest waters flow
Through mossy rocks ; where 'mid exuberant green
I roam in pleasant darkness, more unseen
Than Saturn in his exile ; where I brim

Round flowery islands, and take thence a skim
Of mealy sweets, which myriads of bees
Buzz from their honey'd wings : and thou shouldst
　　please
Thyself to choose the richest, where we might
Be incense-pillow'd every summer night.
Doff all sad fears, thou white deliciousness,
And let us Le thus comforted ; unless
Thou couldst rejoice to see my hopeless stream
Hurry distracted from Sol's temperate beam,
And pour to death along some hungry sands."—
" What can I do, Alpheus ?　Dian stands
Severe before me : persecuting fate !
Unhappy Arethusa ! thou wast late
A huntress free in — "　At this, sudden fell
Those two sad streams adown a fearful dell.
The Latmian listen'd, but he heard no more,
Save echo, faint repeating o'er and o'er
The name of Arethusa.　On the verge
Of that dark gulf he wept, and said : " I urge
Thee, gentle Goddess of my pilgrimage,
By our eternal hopes, to soothe, to assuage,
If thou art powerful, these lovers' pains ;
And make them happy in some happy plains."

He turn'd — there was a whelming sound — he
　　stept,
There was a cooler light ; and so he kept
Towards it by a sandy path, and lo !
More suddenly than doth a moment go,
The visions of the earth were gone and fled —
He saw the giant sea above his head.

BOOK III.

THERE are who lord it o'er their fellow-men
With most prevailing tinsel: who unpen
Their baaing vanities, to browse away
The comfortable green and juicy hay
From human pastures; or, O torturing fact!
Who, through an idiot blink, will see unpack'd
Fire-branded foxes to sear up and singe
Our gold and ripe-ear'd hopes   With not one
    tinge
Of sanctuary splendour, not a sight
Able to face an owl's, they still are dight
By the blear-eyed nations in empurpled vests,
And crowns, and turbans.   With unladen breasts,
Save of blown self-applause, they proudly mount
To their spirit's perch, their being's high account,
Their tiptop nothings, their dull skies, their
    thrones —
Amid the fierce intoxicating tones
Of trumpets, shoutings, and belabour'd drums,
And sudden cannon.   Ah! how all this hums,
In wakeful ears, like uproar past and gone —
Like thunder-clouds that spake to Babylon,
And set those old Chaldeans to their tasks. —
Are then regalities all gilded masks?
No there are throned seats unscalable
But by a patient wing, a constant spell,
Or by ethereal things that, unconfined,
Can make a ladder of the eternal wind,
And poise about in cloudy thunder-tents
To watch the abysm-birth of elements.
Ay, 'bove the withering of old-lipp'd Fate
A thousand Powers keep religious state,
In water, fiery realm, and airy bourne;
And, silent as a consecrated urn,
Hold sphery sessions for a season due.

Yet few of these far majesties, ah, few!
Have bared their operations to this globe —
Few, who with gorgeous pageantry enrobe
Our piece of heaven — whose benevolence
Shakes hand with our own Ceres; every sense
Filling with spiritual sweets to plenitude,
As bees gorge full their cells.   And by the feud
'Twixt Nothing and Creation, I here swear,
Eterne Apollo! that thy Sister fair
Is of all these the genther-mightiest.
When thy gold breath is misting in the west,
She unobserved steals unto her throne,
And there she sits most meek and most alone;
As if she had not pomp subservient;
As if thine eye, high Poet! was not bent
Towards her with the Muses in thine heart;
As if the minist'ring stars kept not apart,
Waiting for silver-footed messages.
O Moon! the oldest shades 'mong oldest trees
Feel palpitations when thou lookest in :
O Moon! old boughs lisp forth a holier din
The while they feel thine airy fellowship.
Thou dost bless everywhere, with silver lip
Kissing dead things to life.   The sleeping kine,
Couch'd in thy brightness, dream of fields divine
Innumerable mountains rise, and rise,
Ambitious for the hallowing of thine eyes ·
And yet thy benediction passeth not
One obscure hiding-place, one little spot
Where pleasure may be sent: the nested wren
Has thy fair face within its tranquil ken,
And from beneath a sheltering ivy leaf
Takes glimpses of thee; thou art a relief
To the poor patient oyster, where it sleeps
Within its pearly house; — The mighty deeps,
The monstrous sea is thine — the myriad sea!
O Moon   far spooming Ocean bows to thee,
And Tellus feels her forehead's cumbrous load

Cynthia! where art thou now?　What far abode
Of green or silvery bower doth enshrine
Such utmost beauty?　Alas, thou dost pine
For one as sorrowful: thy cheek is pale
For one whose cheek is pale: thou dost bewail
His tears who weeps for thee!　Where dost thou
　　sigh?
Ah! surely that light peeps from Vesper's eye,
Or, what a thing is love!　'Tis She, but lo!
How changed, how full of ache, how gone in woe!
She dies at the thinnest cloud; her loveliness
Is wan on Neptune's blue: yet there's a stress
Of love-spangles, just off yon cape of trees,
Dancing upon the waves, as if to please
The curly foam with amorous influence.
O, not so idle! for down glancing thence,
She fathoms eddies, and runs wild about
O'erwhelming water-courses; scaring out
The thorny sharks from hiding-holes, and fright'
　　ning
Their savage eyes with unaccustom'd lightning.
Where will the splendour be content to reach?
O love! how potent hast thou been to teach
Strange journeyings!　Wherever beauty dwells,
In gulf or aerie, mountains or deep dells,
In light, in gloom, in star or blazing sun,
Thou pointest out the way, and straight 'tis won.
Amid his toil thou gavest Leander breath;
Thou leddest Orpheus through the gleams of
　　death;
Thou madest Pluto bear thin element:
And now, O winged Chieftain! thou hast sent
A moonbeam to the deep, deep water-world,
To find Endymion.

　　　　　　　　On gold sand impearl'd
With lily shells, and pebbles milky white,
Poor Cynthia greeted him, and soothed her light

Against his pallid face : he felt the charm
To breathlessness, and suddenly a warm
Of his heart's blood : 'twas very sweet ; he stay'd
His wandering steps, and half-entranced laid
His head upon a tuft of straggling weeds,
To taste the gentle moon, and fieshening beads,
Lash'd from the crystal roof by fishes' tails.
And so he kept, until the rosy veils
Mantling the east, by Aurora's peering hand
Were lifted from the water's breast, and fann'd
Into sweet air ; and sober'd morning came
Meekly through billows : — when like taper-flame
Left sudden by a dallying breath of air,
He rose in silence, and once more 'gan fare
Along his fated way.

                    Far had he roam'd,
With nothing save the hollow vast, that foam'd
Above, around, and at his feet ; save things
More dead than Morpheus' imaginings :
Old rusted anchors, helmets, breastplates large
Of gone sea-warriors ; brazen beaks and targe ;
Rudders that for a hundred years had lost
The sway of human hand ; gold vase emboss'd
With long-forgotten story, and wherein
No reveller had ever dipp'd a chin
But those of Saturn's vintage ; mouldering scrolls,
Writ in the tongue of heaven, by those souls
Who first were on the earth ; and sculptures
        rude
In ponderous stone, developing the mood
Of ancient Nox ; — then skeletons of man,
Of beast, behemoth, and leviathan,
And elephant, and eagle, and huge jaw
Of nameless monster.   A cold leaden awe
These secrets struck into him ; and unless
Dian had chased away that heaviness,
He might have died . but now, with cheered feel,

He onward kept; wooing these thoughts to steal
About the labyrinth in his soul of love.

" What is there in thee, Moon ! that thou shouldst
　　move
My heart so potently ?　When yet a child
I oft have dried my tears when thou hast smiled.
Thou seem'dst my sister : hand in hand we went
From eve to morn across the firmament.
No apples would I gather from the tree,
Till thou hadst cool'd their cheeks deliciously :
No tumbling water ever spake romance,
But when my eyes with thine thereon could dance ı
No woods were green enough, no bower divine,
Until thou liftedst up thine eyelids fine :
In sowing-time ne'er would I dibble take,
Or drop a seed, till thou wast wide awake ;
And, in the summer-tide of blossoming,
No one but thee hath heard me blithely sing
And mesh my dewy flowers all the night.
No melody was like a passing spright
If it went not to solemnize thy reign
Yes, in my boyhood, every joy and pain
By thee were fashion'd to the self-same end ;
And as I grew in years, still didst thou blend
With all my ardours ; thou wast the deep glen ;
Thou wast the mountain-top — the sage's pen —
The poet's harp — the voice of friends — the sun
Thou wast the river — thou wast glory won ;
Thou wast my clarion's blast — thou wast my
　　steed —
My goblet full of wine — my topmost deed : —
Thou wast the charm of women, lovely Moon
O what a wild and harmonized tune
My spirit struck from all the beautiful !
On some bright essence could I lean, and lull
Myself to immortality : I prest
Nature's soft pillow in a wakeful rest.

But gentle Orb! there came a nearer bliss —
My strange love came — Felicity's abyss!
She came, and thou didst fade, and fade away.
Yet not entirely; no, thy starry sway
Has been an under-passion to this hour.
Now I begin to feel thine orby power.
Is coming fresh upon me: O be kind!
Keep back thine influence, and do not blind
My sovereign vision. — Dearest love, forgive
That I can think away from thee and live! —
Pardon me, airy planet, that I prize
One thought beyond thine argent luxuries!
How far beyond!"   At this a surprised start
Frosted the springing verdure of his heart;
For as he lifted up his eyes to swear
How his own goddess was past all things fair,
He saw far in the concave green of the sea
An old man sitting calm and peacefully.
Upon a weeded rock this old man sat,
And his white hair was awful, and a mat
Of weeds were cold beneath his cold thin feet;
And, ample as the largest winding-sheet,
A cloak of blue wrapp'd up his aged bones,
O'erwrought with symbols by the deepest groans
Of ambitious magic: every ocean-form
Was woven in with black distinctness; storm,
And calm, and whispering, and hideous roar
Were emblem'd in the woof; with every shape
That skims, or dives, or sleeps, 'twixt cape and
        cape.
The gulphing whale was like a dot in the spell,
Yet look upon it, and 'twould size and swell
To its huge self; and the minutest fish
Would pass the very hardest gazer's wish,
And show his little eye's anatomy.
Then there was pictured the regality
Of Neptune; and the sea-nymphs round his state,
In beauteous vassalage, look up and wait.

Beside this old man lay a pearly wand,
And in his lap a book, the which he conn'd
So steadfastly, that the new denizen
Had time to keep him in amazed ken,
To mark these shadowings, and stand in awe.

The old man raised his hoary head and saw
The wilder'd stranger — seeming not to see,
His features were so lifeless.   Suddenly
He woke as from a trance; his snow-white brows
Went arching up, and like two magic ploughs
Furrow'd deep wrinkles in his forehead large,
Which kept as fixedly as rocky marge,
Till round his wither'd lips had gone a smile.
Then up he rose, like one whose tedious toil
Had watch'd for years in forlorn hermitage,
Who had not from mid-life to utmost age
Eased in one accent his o'erburden'd soul,
Even to the trees.   He rose: he grasp'd his stole,
With convulsed clenches waving it abroad,
And in a voice of solemn joy, that awed
Echo into oblivion, he said: —

" Thou art the man !   Now shall I lay my head
In peace upon my watery pillow : now
Sleep will come smoothly to my weary brow.
O Jove ! I shall be young again, be young !
O shell-borne Neptune, I am pierced and stung
With new-born life !   What shall I do ?   Where go,
When I have cast this serpent-skin of woe ? —
I'll swim to the syrens, and one moment listen
Their melodies, and see their long hair glisten;
Anon upon that giant's arm I'll be,
That writhes about the roots of Sicily :
To northern seas I'll in a twinkling sail,
And mount upon the snortings of a whale
To some black cloud ; thence down I'll madly sweep
On forked lightning, to the deepest deep,

Where through some sucking pool I will be hurl'd
With rapture to the other side of the world!
O, I am full of gladness! Sisters three,
I bow full-hearted to your old decree!
Yes, every god be thank'd, and power benign,
For I no more shall wither, droop, and pine.
Thou art the man!" Endymion started back
Dismay'd; and like a wretch from whom the rack
Tortures hot breath, and speech of agony,
Mutter'd: " What lonely death am I to die
In this cold region? Will he let me freeze,
And float my brittle limbs o'er polar seas?
Or will he touch me with his searing hand,
And leave a black memorial on the sand?
Or tear me piecemeal with a bony saw,
And keep me as a chosen food to draw
His magian fish through hated fire and flame?
O misery of hell! resistless, tame,
Am I to be burn'd up? No, I will shout,
Until the gods through heaven's blue look out! —
O Tartarus! but some few days agone
Her soft arms were entwining me, and on
Her voice I hung like fruit among green leaves:
Her lips were all my own, and — ah, ripe sheaves
Of happiness! ye on the stubble droop,
But never may be garner'd. I must stoop
My head, and kiss death's foot. Love! love, fare
            well!
Is there no hope from thee? This horrid spell
Would melt at thy sweet breath. — By Dian's hind
Feeding from her white fingers, on the wind
I see thy streaming hair! and now, by Pan,
I care not for this old mysterious man!"

He spake, and walking to that aged form,
Look'd high defiance. Lo! his heart 'gan warm
With pity, for the gray-haired creature wept.
Had he then wrong'd a heart where sorrow kept?

Had he, though blindly contumelious, brought
Rheum to kind eyes, a sting to human thought,
Convulsion to a mouth of many years?
He had in truth; and he was ripe for tears.
The penitent shower fell, as down he knelt
Before that care-worn sage, who trembling felt
About his large dark locks, and faltering spake:

"Arise, good youth, for sacred Phœbus' sake!
I know thine inmost bosom, and I feel
A very brother's yearning for thee steal
Into mine own: for why? thou openest
The prison-gates that have so long oppress'd
My weary watching.   Though thou know'st it not,
Thou art commission'd to this fated spot
For great enfranchisement.   O weep no more!
I am a friend to love, to loves of yore:
Ay, hadst thou never loved an unknown power,
I had been grieving at this joyous hour
But even now, most miserable old,
I saw thee, and my blood no longer cold
Gave mighty pulses: in this tottering case
Grew a new heart, which at this moment plays
As dancingly as thine.   Be not afraid,
For thou shalt hear this secret all display'd,
Now as we speed towards our joyous task."

So saying, this young soul in age's mask
Went forward with the Carian side by side:
Resuming quickly thus; while ocean's tide
Hung swollen at their backs, and jewell'd sands
Took silently their foot-prints.

                              "My soul stands
Now past the midway from mortality,
And so I can prepare without a sigh
To tell thee briefly all my joy and pain.
I was a fisher once, upon this main,

And my boat danced in every creek and bay;
Rough billows were my home by night and day, —
The sea-gulls not more constant: for I had
No housing from the storm and tempests mad,
But hollow rocks, — and they were palaces
Of silent happiness, of slumberous ease:
Long years of misery have told me so.
Ay, thus it was one thousand years ago.
One thousand years ! — Is it then possible
To look so plainly through them ? to dispel
A thousand years with backward glance sublime ?
To breathe away as 'twere all scummy slime
From off a crystal pool, to see its deep,
And one's own image from the bottom peep ?
Yes: now I am no longer wretched thrall,
My long captivity and moanings all
Are but a slime, a thin-pervading scum,
The which I breathe away, and thronging come
Like things of yesterday my youthful pleasures.

"I touch'd no lute, I sang not, trod no measures
I was a lonely youth on desert shores.
My sports were lonely, 'mid continuous roars,
And craggy isles, and seamews' plaintive cry
Plaining discrepant between sea and sky.
Dolphins were still my playmates; shapes unseen
Would let me feel their scales of gold and green,
Nor be my desolation ; and, full oft,
When a dread waterspout had rear'd aloft
Its hungry hugeness, seeming ready ripe
To burst with hoarsest thunderings, and wipe
My life away like a vast sponge of fate,
Some friendly monster, pitying my sad state,
Has dived to its foundations, gulf'd it down,
And left me tossing safely.   But the crown
Of all my life was utmost quietude :
More did I love to lie in cavern rude,
Keeping in wait whole days for Neptune's voice,

And if it came at last, hark, and rejoice !
There blush'd no summer eve but I would steer
My skiff along green shelving coasts, to hear
The shepherd's pipe come clear from aery steep,
Mingled with ceaseless bleatings of his sheep :
And never was a day of summer shine,
But I beheld its birth upon the brine :
For I would watch all night to see unfold
Heaven's gates, and Æthon snort his morning **gold**
Wide o'er the swelling streams : and constantly
At brim of day-tide, on some grassy lea,
My nets would be spread out, and I at rest.
The poor folk of the sea-country I blest
With daily boon of fish most delicate :
They knew not whence this bounty, and elate
Would strew sweet flowers on a sterile beach.

" Why was I not contented ?   Wherefore reach
At things which, but for thee, O Latmian !
Had been my dreary death !   Fool ! I began
To feel distemper'd longings · to desire
The utmost privilege that ocean's sire
Could grant in benediction · to be free
Of all his kingdom.   Long in misery
I wasted, ere in one extremest fit
I plunged for life or death.   To interknit
One's senses with so dense a breathing stuff
Might seem a work of pain ; so not enough
Can I admire how crystal-smooth it felt,
And buoyant round my limbs.   At first I dwelt
Whole days and days in sheer astonishment ;
Forgetful utterly of self-intent ;
Moving but with the mighty ebb and flow.
Then, like a new-fledged bird that first doth show
His spreaded feathers to the morrow chill,
I tried in fear the pinions of my will.
'Twas freedom ! and at once I visited
The ceaseless wonders of this ocean-bed.

No need to tell thee of them, for I see
That thou hast been a witness — it must be
For these I know thou canst not feel a drouth,
By the melancholy corners of that mouth.
So I will in my story straightway pass
To more immediate matter.   Woe, alas!
That love should be my bane!   Ah, Scylla fair!
Why did poor Glaucus ever — ever dare
To sue thee to his heart?   Kind stranger-youth!
I loved her to the very white of truth,
And she would not conceive it.   Timid thing!
She fled me swift as sea-bird on the wing,
Round every isle, and point, and promontory,
From where large Hercules wound up his story
Far as Egyptian Nile.   My passion grew
The more, the more I saw her dainty hue
Gleam delicately through the azure clear:
Until 'twas too fierce agony to bear;
And in that agony, across my grief
It flash'd, that Circe might find some relief —
Cruel enchantress!   So above the water
I rear'd my head, and look'd for Phœbus' daughter
Æœa's isle was wondering at the moon: —
It seem'd to whirl around me, and a swoon
Left me dead-drifting to that fatal power.

  "When I awoke, 'twas in a twilight bower;
Just when the light of morn, with hum of bees,
Stole through its verdurous matting of fresh trees
How sweet, and sweeter! for I heard a lyre,
And over it a sighing voice expire.
It ceased — I caught light footsteps; and anon
The fairest face that morn e'er look'd upon
Push'd through a screen of roses.   Starry Jove!
With tears, and smiles, and honey-words she wove
A net whose thraldom was more bliss than all
The range of flower'd Elysium.   Thus did fall
The dew of her rich speech: 'Ah! art awake?

O let me hear thee speak, for Cupid's sake!
I am so oppress'd with joy! Why, I have shed
An urn of tears, as though thou wert cold dead;
And now I find thee living, I will pour
From these devoted eyes their silver store,
Until exhausted, of the latest drop,
So it will pleasure thee, and force thee stop
Here, that I too may live: but if beyond
Such cool and sorrowful offerings, thou art fond
Of soothing warmth, of dalliance supreme;
If thou art ripe to taste a long love-dream;
If smiles, if dimples, tongues for ardour mute,
Hang in thy vision like a tempting fruit,
O let me pluck it for thee!' Thus she link'd
Her charming syllables, till indistinct
Their music came to my o'er-sweeten'd soul;
And then she hover'd over me, and stole
So near, that if no nearer it had been
This furrow'd visage thou hadst never seen.

 "Young man of Latmos! thus particular
Am I, that thou may'st plainly see how far
This fierce temptation went. and thou may'st not
Exclaim, How, then, was Scylla quite forgot?

 " Who could resist? Who in this universe?
She did so breathe ambrosia; so immerse
My fine existence in a golden clime.
She took me like a child of suckling time,
And cradled me in roses. Thus condemn'd,
The current of my former life was stemm'd,
And to this arbitrary queen of sense
I bow'd a tranced vassal: nor would thence
Have moved, even though Amphion's harp had
        woo'd
Me back to Scylla o'er the billows rude.
For as Apollo each eve doth devise
A new apparelling for western skies

So every eve, nay, every spendthrift hour
Shed balmy consciousness within that bower.
And I was free of haunts umbrageous;
Could wander in the mazy forest-house
Of squirrels, foxes shy, and antler'd deer,
And birds from coverts innermost and drear
Warbling for very joy mellifluous sorrow —
To me new-born delights!

　　　　　　　" Now let me borrow
ror moments few, a temperament as stern
As Pluto's sceptre, that my words not burn
These uttering lips, while I in calm speech tell
How specious heaven was changed to real hell.

　" One morn she left me sleeping : half awake
I sought for her smooth arms and lips, to slake
My greedy thirst with nectarous camel-draughts;
But she was gone.　Whereat the barbed shafts
Of disappointment stuck in me so sore,
That out I ran and search'd the forest o'er.
Wandering about in pine and cedar gloom
Damp awe assail'd me, for there 'gan to boom
A sound of moan, an agony of sound,
Sepulchral from the distance all around.
Then came a conquering earth-thunder, and rum
　　　　bled
That fierce complain to silence : while I stumbled
Down a precipitous path, as if impell'd.
I came to a dark valley. — Groanings swell'd
Poisonous about my ears, and louder grew,
The nearer I approach'd a flame's gaunt blue,
That glared before me through a thorny brake.
This fire, like the eye of gordian snake,
Bewitch'd me towards; and I soon was near
A sight too fearful for the feel of fear:
In thicket hid I cursed the haggard scene —
The banquet of my arms, my arbour queen,

Seated upon an uptorn forest root;
And all around her shapes, wizard and brute,
Laughing, and wailing, grovelling, serpenting,
Showing tooth, tusk, and venom-bag, and sting.
O such deformities! old Charon's self,
Should he give up awhile his penny pelf,
And take a dream 'mong rushes Stygian,
It could not be so fantasied. Fierce, wan,
And tyrannizing was the lady's look,
As over them a gnarled staff she shook.
Ofttimes upon the sudden she laugh'd out,
And from a basket emptied to the rout
Clusters of grapes, the which they raven'd quick
And roar'd for more; with many a hungry lick
About their shaggy jaws. Avenging, slow,
Anon she took a branch of mistletoe,
And emptied on't a black dull-gurgling phial:
Groan'd one and all, as if some piercing trial
Was sharpening for their pitiable bones.
She lifted up the charm: appealing groans
From their poor breasts went suing to her ear
In vain; remorseless as an infant's bier
She whisk'd against their eyes the sooty oil.
Whereat was heard a noise of painful toil,
Increasing gradual to a tempest rage,
Shrieks, yells, and groans of torture-pilgrimage;
Until their grieved bodies 'gan to bloat
And puff from the tail's end to stifled throat:
Then was appalling silence: then a sight
More wildering than all that hoarse affright;
For the whole herd, as by a whirlwind writhen,
Went through the dismal air like one huge Python
Antagonizing Boreas, — and so vanish'd,
Yet there was not a breath of wind: she banish'd
These phantoms with a nod. Lo! from the dark
Came waggish fauns, and nymphs, and satyrs stark,
With dancing and loud revelry, — and went
Swifter than centaurs after rapine bent. —

Sighing an elephant appear'd and bow'd
Before the fierce witch, speaking thus aloud
In human accent : ' Potent goddess ! chief
Of pains resistless ! make my being brief,
Or let me from this heavy prison fly :
Or give me to the air, or let me die !
I sue not for my happy crown again ;
I sue not for my phalanx on the plain ;
I sue not for my lone, my widow'd wife :
I sue not for my ruddy drops of life,
My children fair, my lovely girls and boys
I will forget them ; I will pass these joys ;
Ask nought so heavenward, so too — too high
Only I pray, as fairest boon, to die,
Or be deliver'd from this cumbrous flesh,
From this gross, detestable, filthy mesh,
And merely given to the cold bleak air.
Have mercy, Goddess ! Circe, feel my prayer !

" That curst magician's name fell icy numb
Upon my wild conjecturing : truth had come
Naked and sabre-like against my heart.
I saw a fury whetting a death-dart ;
And my slain spirit, overwrought with fright,
Fainted away in that dark lair of night.
Think, my deliverer, how desolate
My waking must have been ! disgust and hate,
And terrors manifold divided me
A spoil amongst them. I prepared to flee
Into the dungeon core of that wild wood :
I fled three days — when lo ! before me stood
Glaring the angry witch. O Dis, even now,
A clammy dew is beading on my brow,
At mere remembering her pale laugh, and curse,
' Ha ! ha ! Sir Dainty ! there must be a nurse
Made of rose-leaves and thistle-down, express,
To cradle thee, my sweet, and lull thee : yes,
I am too flinty-hard for thy nice touch :

My tenderest squeeze is but a giant's clutch.
So, fairy-thing, it shall have lullabies
Unheard of yet; and it shall still its cries
Upon some breast more lily-feminine.
Oh, no — it shall not pine, and pine, and pine
More than one pretty, trifling thousand years;
And then 'twere pity, but fate's gentle shears
Cut short its immortality.   Sea-flirt!
Young dove of the waters! truly I'll not hurt
One hair of thine: see how I weep and sigh,
That our heart-broken parting is so nigh.
And must we part?   Ah, yes, it must be so.
Yet ere thou leavest me in utter woe,
Let me sob over thee my last adieus,
And speak a blessing· Mark me ! thou hast **thews**
Immortal, for thou art of heavenly race:
But such a love is mine, that here I chase
Eternally away from thee all bloom
Of youth, and destine thee towards a tomb.
Hence shalt thou quickly to the watery vast;
And there, ere many days be overpast,
Disabled age shall seize thee; and even **then**
Thou shalt not go the way of aged men;
But live and wither, cripple and still breathe
Ten hundred years: which gone, I then **bequeath**
Thy fragile bones to unknown burial.
Adieu, sweet love, adieu!' — As shot stars **fall**,
She fled ere I could groan for mercy.   Stung
And poison'd was my spirit: despair sung
A war-song of defiance 'gainst all hell.
A hand was at my shoulder to compel
My sullen steps; another 'fore my eyes
Moved on with pointed finger.   In this **guise**
Enforced, at the last by ocean's foam
I found me; by my fresh, my native **home,**
Its tempering coolness, to my life akin,
Came salutary as I waded in;
And, with a blind voluptuous rage, I gave

Battle to the swollen billow-ridge, and drave
Large froth before me, while there yet remain'd
Hale strength, nor from my bones all marrow
          drain'd.

" Young lover, I must weep — such hellish spite
With dry check who can tell ?   While thus my
          might
Proving upon this element, dismay'd,
Upon a dead thing's face my hand I laid ;
I look'd — 'twas Scylla !   Cursed, cursed Circe '
O vulture-witch, hast never heard of mercy !
Could not thy harshest vengeance be content,
But thou must nip this tender innocent
Because I loved her ? — Cold, O cold indeed
Were her fair limbs, and like a common weed
The sea-swell took her hair   Dead as she was
I clung about her waist, nor ceased to pass
Fleet as an arrow through unfathom'd brine,
Until there shone a fabric crystalline,
Ribb'd and inlaid with coral, pebble, and pearl
Headlong I darted ; at one eager swirl
Gain'd its bright portal, enter'd, and behold .
'Twas vast, and desolate, and icy-cold ;
And all around — But wherefore this to thee
Who in few minutes more thyself shalt see ? —
I left poor Scylla in a niche and fled.
My fever'd parchings up, my scathing dread
Met palsy half way : soon these limbs became
Gaunt, wither'd, sapless, feeble, cramp'd, and lame

" Now let me pass a cruel, cruel space,
Without one hope, without one faintest trace
Of mitigation, or redeeming bubble
Of colour'd phantasy : for I fear 'twould trouble
Thy brain to loss of reason : and next tell
How a restoring chance came down to quell
One half of the witch in me.

" On a day,
Sitting upon a rock above the spray,
I saw grow up from the horizon's brink
A gallant vessel : soon she seem'd to sink
Away from me again, as though her course
Had been resumed in spite of hindering force --
So vanish'd : and not long, before arose
Dark clouds, and muttering of winds morose,
Old Æolus would stifle his mad spleen,
But could not ; therefore, all the billows green
Toss'd up the silver spume against the clouds.
The tempest came : I saw that vessel's shrouds
In perilous bustle ; while upon the deck
Stood trembling creatures   I beheld the wreck ;
The final gulfing ; the poor struggling souls ;
I heard their cries amid loud thunder-rolls.
O they had all been saved but crazed eld
Annull'd my vigorous cravings ; and thus quell'd
And curb'd, think on't, O Latmian ! did I sit
Writhing with pity, and a cursing fit
Against that hell-born Circe.   The crew had **gone,**
By one and one, to pale oblivion ;
And I was gazing on the surges prone,
With many a scalding tear, and many a groan,
When at my feet emerged an old man's hand,
Grasping this scroll, and this same slender wand.
I knelt with pain — reach'd out my hand — had
      grasp'd
These treasures — touch'd the knuckles — they un
      clasp'd —
I caught a finger : but the downward weight
O'erpower'd me — it sank.   Then 'gan abate
The storm, and through chill aguish gloom **outburst**
The comfortable sun.   I was athirst
To search the book, and in the warming air
Parted its dripping leaves with eager care.
Strange matters did it treat of, and drew **on**
My soul page after page, till well nigh won

Into forgetfulness; when, stupefied,
I read these words, and read again, and tried
My eyes against the heavens, and read again.
O what a load of misery and pain
Each Atlas-line bore off! — a shine of hope
Came gold around me, cheering me to cope
Strenuous with hellish tyranny.   Attend!
For thou hast brought their promise to an end.

"'In the wide sea there lives a forlorn wretch,
Doom'd with enfeebled carcase to outstretch
His loathed existence through ten centuries,
And then to die alone.   Who can devise
A total opposition?   No one.   So
One million times ocean must ebb and flow,
And he oppressed.   Yet he shall not die,
These things accomplish'd: — If he utterly
Scans all the depths of magic, and expounds
The meanings of all motions, shapes, and sounds;
If he explores all forms and substances
Straight homeward to their symbol-essences;
He shall not die.   Moreover, and in chief,
He must pursue this task of joy and grief
Most piously; — all lovers tempest-tost,
And in the savage overwhelming lost,
He shall deposit side by side, until
Time's creeping shall the dreary space fulfil.
Which done, and all these labours ripened,
A youth, by heavenly power loved and led,
Shall stand before him; whom he shall direct
How to consummate all.   The youth elect
Must do the thing, or both will be destroy'd.'"

"Then," cried the young Endymion, overjoy'd,
"We are twin brothers in this destiny!
Say, I entreat thee, what achievement high
Is, in this restless world, for me reserved.
What! if from thee my wandering feet had
        swerved.

Had we both perish'd ?" — " Look !" the sage re-
    plied,
" Dost thou not mark a gleaming through the tide,
Of divers brilliances ? 'tis the edifice
I told thee of, where lovely Scylla lies ;
And where I have enshrined piously
All lovers, whom fell storms have doom'd to die
Throughout my bondage."   Thus discoursing, on
They went till unobscured the porches shone ;
Which hurryingly they gain'd, and enter'd straight
Sure never since king Neptune held his state
Was seen such wonder underneath the stars.
Turn to some level plain where haughty Mars
Has legion'd all his battle ; and behold
How every soldier, with firm foo , doth hold
His even breast ; see, many steeled squares,
And rigid ranks of iron — whence who dares
One step ? Imagine further, line by line,
These warrior thousands on the field supine : —
So in that crystal place, in silent rows,
Poor lovers lay at rest from joys and woes.
The stranger from the mountains, breathless, traced
Such thousands of shut eyes in order placed ;
Such ranges of white feet, and patient lips
All ruddy, — for here death no blossom nips.
He mark'd their brows and foreheads ; saw their
    hair
Put sleekly on one side with nicest care ;
And each one's gentle wrists, with reverence,
Put cross-wise to its heart.

                " Let us commence
(Whisper'd the guide, stuttering with joy) even
    now."
He spake, and, trembling like an aspen-bough
Began to tear his scroll in pieces small.
Uttering the while some mumblings funeral.
He tore it into pieces small as snow

That drifts unfeather'd when bleak northerns
     blow ;
And having done it, took his dark blue cloak
And bound it round Endymion : then struck
His wand against the empty air times nine.
" What more there is to do, young man, is thine :
But first a little patience ; first undo
This tangled thread, and wind it to a clue.
Ah, gentle ! 'tis as weak as spider's skein ;
And shouldst thou break it — What, is it done so
     clean ?
A power overshadows thee !   Oh, brave !
The spite of hell is tumbling to its grave.
Here is a shell ; 'tis pearly blank to me,
Nor mark'd with any sign or charactery —
Canst thou read aught ?   O read for pity's sake !
Olympus ! we are safe !   Now, Carian, break
This wand against yon lyre on the pedestal."

   'Twas done : and straight with sudden swell and
     fall
Sweet music breathed her soul away, and sigh'd
A lullaby to silence. — " Youth ! now strew
These minced leaves on me, and passing through
Those files of dead, scatter the same around,
And thou wilt see the issue." — 'Mid the sound
Of flutes and viols, ravishing his heart,
Endymion from Glaucus stood apart,
And scatter'd in his face some fragments light.
How lightning-swift the change ! a youthful wight
Smiling beneath a coral diadem,
Out-sparkling sudden like an upturn'd gem,
Appear'd, and, stepping to a beauteous corse,
Kneel'd down beside it, and with tenderest force
Press'd its cold hand, and wept — and Scylla
     sigh'd !
Endymion, with quick hand, the charm applied —
The nymph arose   he left them to their joy,

And onward went upon his high employ,
Showering those powerful fragments on the dead,
And, as he pass'd, each lifted up its head,
As doth a flower at Apollo's touch
Death felt it to his inwards; 'twas too much:
Death fell a-weeping in his charnel-house.
The Latmian persevered along, and thus
All were reanimated.   There arose
A noise of harmony, pulses and throes
Of gladness in the air — while many, who
Had died in mutual arms devout and true,
Sprang to each other madly; and the rest
Felt a high certainty of being blest.
They gazed upon Endymion.   Enchantment
Grew drunken, and would have its head and bent.
Delicious symphonies, like airy flowers,
Budded, and swell'd, and, full-blown, shed **full**
            showers
Of light, soft, unseen leaves of sounds divine.
The two deliverers tasted a pure wine
Of happiness, from fairy press oozed out.
Speechless they eyed each other, and about
The fair assembly wander'd to and fro,
Distracted with the richest overflow
Of joy that ever pour'd from heaven.

———— " Away ! "
Shouted the new-born god; " Follow, and pay
Our piety to Neptunus supreme ! " —
Then Scylla, blushing sweetly from her dream,
They led on first, bent to her meek surprise,
Through portal columns of a giant size
Into the vaulted, boundless emerald.
Joyous all follow'd, as the leader call'd,
Down marble steps ; pouring as easily
As hour-glass sand — and fast, as you might see
Swallows obeying the south summer's call,
Or swans upon a gentle waterfall.

8

Thus went that beautiful multitude, nor **far,**
Ere from among some rocks of glittering spar,
Just within ken, they saw descending thick
Another multitude.   Whereat more quick
Moved either host.   On a wide sand they met,
And of those numbers every eye was wet;
For each their old love found.   A murmuring **rose**
Like what was never heard in all the throes
Of wind and waters : 'tis past human wit
To tell; 'tis dizziness to think of it.

This mighty consummation made, the host
Moved on for many a league, and gain'd and **lost**
Huge sea-marks; vanward swelling in array,
And from the rear diminishing away,
Till a faint dawn surprised them.   Glaucus cried,
" Behold ! behold, the palace of his pride !
God Neptune's palaces."   With noise increased,
They shoulder'd on towards that brightening **east.**
At every onward step proud domes arose
In prospect, diamond gleams and golden glows
Of amber 'gainst their faces levelling.
Joyous, and many as the leaves in spring,
Still onward; still the splendour gradual swell'd.
Rich opal domes were seen, on high upheld
By jasper pillars, letting through their shafts
A blush of coral.   Copious wonder-draughts
Each gazer drank; and deeper drank more **near**
For what poor mortals fragment up, as **mere**
As marble was their lavish, to the vast
Of one fair palace, that far, far surpass'd,
Even for common bulk, those olden three,
Memphis, and Babylon, and Nineveh.

As large, as bright, as colour'd as the **bow**
Of Iris, when unfading it doth show
Beyond a silvery shower, was the arch
Through which this Paphian army took its **march.**

Into the outer courts of Neptune's state
Whence could be seen, direct, a golden gate,
To which the leaders sped ; but not half raught
Ere it burst open swift as fairy thought,
And made those dazzled thousands veil their eyes
Like callow eagles at the first sunrise.
Soon with an eagle nativeness their gaze
Ripe from hue-golden swoons took all the blaze,
And then, behold ! large Neptune on his throne
Of emerald deep : yet not exalt alone ;
At his right hand stood winged Love, and on
His left sat smiling Beauty's paragon.

Far as the mariner on highest mast
Can see all round upon the calmed vast,
So wide was Neptune's hall : and as the blue
Doth vault the waters, so the waters drew
Their doming curtains, high, magnificent,
Awed from the throne aloof ;— and when storm-rent
Disclosed the thunder-gloomings in Jove's air ;
But soothed as now, flash'd sudden everywhere,
Noiseless, sub-marine cloudlets, glittering
Death to a human eye : for there did spring
From natural west, and east, and south, and north,
A light as of four sunsets, blazing forth
A gold-green zenith 'bove the Sea-God's head.
Of lucid depth the floor, and far outspread
As breezeless lake, on which the slim canoe
Of feather'd Indian darts about, as through
The delicatest air : air verily,
But for the portraiture of clouds and sky :
This palace floor breath-air, — but for the amaze
Of deep-seen wonders motionless, — and blaze
Of the dome pomp, reflected in extremes,
Globing a golden sphere.

They stood in dreams
Till Triton blew his horn.   The palace rang ;

The Nereids danced; the Syrens faintly sang;
And the great Sea-King bow'd his dripping head.
Then Love took wing, and from his pinions shed
On all the multitude a nectarous dew.
The ooze-born Goddess beckoned and drew
Fair Scylla and her guides to conference;
And when they reach'd the throned eminence
She kiss'd the sea-nymph's cheek, who sat her down
A toying with the doves. Then, " Mighty crown
And sceptre of this kingdom!" Venus said,
" Thy vows were on a time to Nais paid:
Behold!" — Two copious tear-drops instant fell
From the God's large eyes; he smiled delectable,
And over Glaucus held his blessing hands. —
" Endymion! Ah! still wandering in the bands
Of love? Now this is cruel. Since the hour
I met thee in earth's bosom, all my power
Have I put forth to serve thee. What, not yet
Escaped from dull mortality's harsh net?
A little patience, youth! 'twill not be long,
Or I am skilless quite: an idle tongue,
A humid eye, and steps luxurious,
Where these are new and strange, are ominous.
Ay, I have seen these signs in one of heaven,
When others were all blind; and were I given
To utter secrets, haply I might say
Some pleasant words: but Love will have his day
So wait awhile expectant. Pr'ythee soon,
Even in the passing of thine honey-moon,
Visit my Cytherea: thou wilt find
Cupid well-natured, my Adonis kind;
And pray persuade with thee — Ah, I have done,
All blisses be upon thee, my sweet son!" —
Thus the fair Goddess: while Endymion
Knelt to receive those accents halcyon.

Meantime a glorious revelry began
Before the Water-Monarch. Nectar ran

in courteous fountains to all cups outreach'd ;
And plunder'd vines, teeming exhaustless, pleach'd
New growth about each shell and pendent lyre ;
The which, in entangling for their fire,
Pull'd down fresh foliage and coverture
For dainty toy.   Cupid, empire-sure,
Flutter'd and laugh'd, and oft-times through the
   throng
Made a delighted way.   Then dance, and song,
And garlanding, grew wild; and pleasure reign'd.
In harmless tendril they each other chain'd,
And strove who should be smother'd deepest in
Fresh crush of leaves.

      O 'tis a very sin
For one so weak to venture his poor verse
In such a place as this.   O do not curse,
High Muses ! let him hurry to the ending.

 All suddenly were silent.   A soft blending
Of dulcet instruments came charmingly ;
And then a hymn.

      " King of the stormy sea !
Brother of Jove, and co-inheritor
Of elements !   Eternally before
Thee the waves awful bow.   Fast, stubborn rock,
At thy fear'd trident shrinking, doth unlock
Its deep foundations, hissing into foam.
All mountain-rivers lost, in the wide home
Of thy capacious bosom ever flow.
Thou frownest, and old Æolus thy foe
Skulks to his cavern, 'mid the gruff complaint
Of all his rebel tempests.   Dark clouds faint
When, from thy diadem, a silver gleam
Slants over blue dominion.   Thy bright team
Gulfs in the morning light, and scuds along
To bring thee nearer to that golden song

Apollo singeth, while his chariot
Waits at the doors of heaven.   Thou art not
For scenes like this: an empire stern hast thou,
And it hath furrow'd that large front : yet now,
As newly come of heaven, dost thou sit
To blend and interknit
Subdued majesty with this glad time.
O shell-born King sublime !
We lay our hearts before thee evermore —
We sing, and we adore !

      " Breathe softly, flutes
Be tender of your strings, ye soothing lutes;
Nor be the trumpet heard ! O vain, O vain
Not flowers budding in an April rain,
Nor breath of sleeping dove, nor river's flow —
No, nor the Æolian twang of Love's own bow,
Can mingle music fit for the soft ear
Of goddess Cytherea !
Yet deign, white Queen of Beauty, thy fair eyes
On our soul's sacrifice.

      " Bright-winged Child !
Who has another care when thou hast smiled ?
Unfortunates on earth, we see at last
All death-shadows, and glooms that overcast
Our spirits, fann'd away by thy light pinions.
O sweetest essence ! sweetest of all minions !
God of warm pulses, and dishevell'd hair,
And panting bosoms bare !
Dear unseen light in darkness ! eclipser
Of light in light ! delicious poisoner !
Thy venom'd goblet will we quaff until
We fill — we fill !
And by thy Mother's lips —— "

      Was heard no more
For clamour, when the golden palace-door

Open'd again, and from without, in shone
A new magnificence.   On oozy throne
Smooth-moving came Oceanus the old,
To take a latest glimpse at his sheepfold,
Before he went into his quiet cave
To muse for ever — Then, a lucid wave,
Scoop'd from its trembling sisters of mid-sea,
Afloat, and pillowing up the majesty
Of Doris, and the Ægean seer, her spouse —
Next, on a dolphin, clad in laurel boughs,
Theban Amphion leaning on his lute :
His fingers went across it — All were mute
To gaze on Amphitrite, queen of pearls,
And Thetis pearly too. —

                       The palace **whirls**
Around giddy Endymion ; seeing he
Was there far strayed from mortality.
He could not bear it — shut his eyes in **vain ;**
Imagination gave a dizzier pain
" O I shall die ! sweet Venus, be my stay !
Where is my lovely mistress ?   Well-away !
I die — I hear her voice — I feel my wing — "
At Neptune's feet he sank.   A sudden ring
Of Nereids were about him, in kind strife
To usher back his spirit into life :
But still he slept.   At last they interwove
Their cradling arms, and purposed to **convey**
Towards a crystal bower far away.

    Lo ! while slow carried through the **pitying**
            crowd,
To his inward senses these words spake aloud ;
Written in star-light on the dark above :
" Dearest Endymion ! my entire love !
How have I dwelt in fear of fate ; 'tis done —
Immortal bliss for me too hast thou won.
Arise then ! for the hen-dove shall not **hatch**

Her ready eggs, before I'll kissing snatch
Thee into endless heaven. Awake! awake!"

The youth at once arose. a placid lake
Came quiet to his eyes; and forest green,
Cooler than all the wonder he had seen,
Lull'd with its simple song his fluttering breast
How happy once again in grassy nest!

———◆———

BOOK IV.

MUSE of my native land! loftiest Muse!
O first-born on the mountains! By the hues
Of heaven on the spiritual air begot.
Long didst thou sit alone in northern grot,
While yet our England was a wolfish den;
Before our forests heard the talk of men;
Before the first of Druids was a child;—
Long didst thou sit amid our regions wild,
Rapt in a deep prophetic solitude.
There came an eastern voice of solemn mood:—
Yet wast thou patient. Then sang forth the Nine,
Apollo's garland:— yet didst thou divine
Such home-bred glory, that they cried in vain,
" Come hither, Sister of the Island!" Plain
Spake fair Ausonia; and once more she spake
A higher summons:— still didst thou betake
Thee to thy native hopes. O thou hast won
A full accomplishment! The thing is done,
Which undone, these our latter days had risen
On barren souls. Great Muse, thou know'st what
    prison
Of flesh and bone, curbs, and confines, and frets
Our spirits' wings: despondency besets
Our pillows; and the fresh to-morrow morn
Seems to give forth its light in very scorn

Of our dull, uninspired, snail-paced lives.
Long have I said, how happy he who shrives
To thee!   But then I thought on poets gone,
And could not pray: — nor can I now — so on
I move to the end in lowliness of heart. —

"Ah, woe is me! that I should fondly part
From my dear native land!   Ah, foolish maid!
Glad was the hour, when, with thee, myriads bade
Adieu to Ganges and their pleasant fields!
To one so friendless the clear freshet yields
A bitter coolness; the ripe grape is sour:
Yet I would have, great gods! but one short hour
Of native air — let me but die at home."

Endymion to heaven's airy dome
Was offering up a hecatomb of vows,
When these words reach'd him.   Whereupon he bows
His head through thorny-green entanglement
Of underwood, and to the sound is bent,
Anxious as hind towards her hidden fawn.

"Is no one near to help me?   No fair dawn
Of life from charitable voice?   No sweet saying
To set my dull and sadden'd spirit playing?
No hand to toy with mine?   No lips so sweet
That I may worship them?   No eyelids meet
To twinkle on my bosom?   No one dies
Before me, till from these enslaving eyes
Redemption sparkles! — I am sad and lost."

Thou, Carian lord, hadst better have been tost
Into a whirlpool.   Vanish into air,
Warm mountaineer! for canst thou only bear
A woman's sigh alone and in distress?
See not her charms!   Is Phœbe passionless?
Phœbe is fairer far — O gaze no more: —
Yet if thou wilt behold all beauty's store,

Behold her panting in the forest grass !
Do not those curls of glossy jet surpass
For tenderness the arms so idly lain
Amongst them ?   Feelest not a kindred pain,
To see such lovely eyes in swimming search
After some warm delight, that seems to perch
Dovelike in the dim cell lying beyond
Their upper lids ? — Hist !

                 " O for Hermes' wand
To touch this flower into human shape !
That woodland Hyacinthus could escape
From his green prison, and here kneeling down
Call me his queen, his second life's fair crown !
Ah me, how I could love ! — My soul doth melt
For the unhappy youth — Love !   I have felt
So faint a kindness, such a meek surrender
To what my own full thoughts had made too tender
That but for tears my life had fled away !
Ye deaf and senseless minutes of the day,
And thou, old forest, hold ye this for true,
There is no lightning, no authentic dew
But in the eye of love : there's not a sound,
Melodious howsoever, can confound
The heavens and earth in one to such a death
As doth the voice of love : there's not a breath
Will mingle kindly with the meadow air,
Till it has panted round, and stolen a share
Of passion from the heart ! " —

                     Upon a bough
He leant, wretched.   He surely cannot now
Thirst for another love : O impious,
That he can even dream upon it thus !
Thought he, " Why am I not as are the dead,
Since to a woe like this I have been led
Through the dark earth, and through the wondrous
      sea ?

Goddess ! I love thee not the less: from **thee**
By Juno's smile I turn not — no, no, no —
While the great waters are at ebb and **flow,** —
I have a triple soul ! O fond pretence —
For both, for both my love is so immense,
I feel my heart is cut in twain for them."

And so he groan'd, as one by beauty **slain.**
The lady's heart beat quick, and he could **see**
Her gentle bosom heave tumultuously.
He sprang from his green covert: there she **lay,**
Sweet as a musk-rose upon new-made hay ;
With all her limbs on tremble, and her **eyes**
Shut softly up alive. To speak he tries :
" Fair damsel, pity me ! forgive that I
Thus violate thy bower's sanctity !
O pardon me, for I am full of grief —
Grief born of thee, young angel ! fairest **thief !**
Who stolen hast away the wings wherewith
   was to top the heavens. Dear maid, **sith**
Thou art my executioner, and I feel
Loving and hatred, misery and weal,
Will in a few short hours be nothing **to me,**
And all my story that much passion slew **me ;**
Do smile upon the evening of my days ;
And, for my tortured brain begins to craze,
Be thou my nurse ; and let me understand
How dying I shall kiss that lily hand. —
Dost weep for me ! Then should I be **content.**
Scowl on, ye fates ! until the firmament
Outblackens Erebus, and the full-cavern'd **earth**
Crumbles into itself. By the cloud-girth
Of Jove, those tears have given me a thirst
To meet oblivion." — As her heart would **burst**
The maiden sobb'd awhile, and then replied :
" Why must such desolation betide
As that thou speakest of ? Are not these **green**
   nooks

Empty of all misfortune ?   Do the brooks
Utter a gorgon voice ?   Does yonder thrush,
Schooling its half-fledged little ones to brush
About the dewy forest, whisper tales ? —
Speak not of grief, young stranger, or cold snails
Will slime the rose to night.   Though if thou wilt,
Methinks 'twould be a guilt — a very guilt —
Not to companion thee, and sigh away
The light — the dusk — the dark — till break of
    day ! "
" Dear lady," said Endymion, " 'tis past:
I love thee ! and my days can never last.
That I may pass in patience still speak ·
Let me have music dying, and I seek
No more delight — I bid adieu to all.
Didst thou not after other climates call,
And murmur about Indian streams ? " — Then she,
Sitting beneath the midmost forest tree,
For pity sang this roundelay ——

      " O Sorrow !
       Why dost borrow
The natural hue of health, from vermeil lips ? —
       To give maiden blushes
       To the white rose bushes ?
Or is it thy dewy hand the daisy tips ?

      " O Sorrow !
       Why dost borrow
The lustrous passion from a falcon-eye ? —
       To give the glowworm light ?
       Or, on a moonless night,
To tinge, on syren shores, the salt sea-spry ?

      " O Sorrow !
       Why dost borrow
The mellow ditties from a mourning tongue ? —
       To give at evening pale

Unto the nightingale,
That thou mayst listen the cold dews among?

" O Sorrow !
Why dost borrow
Heart's lightness from the merriment of May ?
A lover would not tread
A cowslip on the head,
Though he should dance from eve till peep of
day —
Nor any drooping flower
Held sacred for thy bower,
Wherever he may sport himself and play.

" To Sorrow,
I bade good morrow,
And thought to leave her far away behind;
But cheerly, cheerly,
She loves me dearly;
She is so constant to me, and so kind:
I would deceive her,
And so leave her,
But ah ! she is so constant and so kind.

" Beneath my palm-trees, by the river side,
I sat a weeping: in the whole world wide
There was no one to ask me why I wept —
And so I kept
Brimming the water-lily cups with tears
Cold as my fears.
Beneath my palm-trees, by the river side,
I sat a weeping: what enamour'd bride,
Cheated by shadowy wooer from the clouds,
But hides and shrouds
Beneath dark palm-trees by a river side?

' And as I sat, over the light blue hills
There came a noise of revellers: the rills

Into the wide stream came of purple hue —
    'Twas Bacchus and his crew !
The earnest trumpet spake, and silver thrills
From kissing cymbals made a merry din —
    'Twas Bacchus and his kin !
Like to a moving vintage down they came,
Crown'd with green leaves, and faces all on
    flame ;
All madly dancing through the pleasant valley,
    To scare thee, Melancholy !
O then, O then, thou wast a simple name !
And I forgot thee, as the berried holly
By shepherds is forgotten, when in June,
Tall chestnuts keep away the sun and moon —
    I rush'd into the folly !

" Within his car, aloft, young Bacchus stood,
Trifling his ivy-dart, in dancing mood,
    With sidelong laughing ;
And little rills of crimson wine imbrued
His plump white arms, and shoulders, enough white
    For Venus' pearly bite ;
And near him rode Silenus on his ass,
Pelted with flowers as he on did pass
    Tipsily quaffing.

" Whence came ye, merry Damsels ! whence
    came ye,
So many, and so many, and such glee ?
Why have ye left your bowers desolate,
    Your lutes, and gentler fate ?
' We follow Bacchus ! Bacchus on the wing,
    A conquering !
Bacchus, young Bacchus ! good or ill betide,
We dance before him thorough kingdoms wide : —
Come hither, lady fair, and joined be
    To our wild minstrelsy !'

" Whence came ye, jolly Satyrs! whence came ye,
So many, and so many, and such glee?
Why have ye left your forest haunts, why left
     Your nuts in oak-tree cleft? —
' For wine, for wine we left our kernel tree ;
For wine we left our heath, and yellow brooms,
     And cold mushrooms ;
For wine we follow Bacchus through the earth ;
Great god of breathless cups and chirping mirth !
Come hither, lady fair, and joined be
     To our mad minstrelsy !'

" Over wide streams and mountains great we went,
And, save when Bacchus kept his ivy tent,
Onward the tiger and the leopard pants,
     With Asian elephants :
Onward these myriads — with song and dance,
With zebras striped, and sleek Arabians' prance,
Web-footed alligators, crocodiles,
Bearing upon their scaly backs, in files,
Plump infant laughers mimicking the coil
Of seamen, and stout galley-rowers' toil :
With toying oars and silken sails they glide,
     Nor care for wind and tide.
Mounted on panthers' furs and lions' manes,
From rear to van they scour about the plains ;
A three days' journey in a moment done ;
And always, at the rising of the sun,
About the wilds they hunt with spear and horn,
     On spleenful unicorn.

" I saw Osirian Egypt kneel adown
     Before the vine-wreath crown !
I saw parch'd Abyssinia rouse and sing
     To the silver cymbals' ring !
I saw the whelming vintage hotly pierce
     Old Tartary the fierce !
The kings of Ind their jewel-sceptres vail,

And from their treasures scatter pearled hail;
Great Brahma from his mystic heaven groans,
    And all his priesthood moans,
Before young Bacchus' eye-wink turning pale
Into these regions came I, following him,
Sick-hearted, weary — so I took a whim
To stray away into these forests drear,
    Alone, without a peer:
And I have told thee all thou mayest hear.

    " Young Stranger!
    I've been a ranger
In search of pleasure throughout every clime
    Alas! 'tis not for me:
    Bewitch'd I sure must be,
To lose in grieving all my maiden prime.

    " Come then, Sorrow,
    Sweetest Sorrow!
Like an own babe I nurse thee on my breast
    I thought to leave thee,
    And deceive thee,
But now of all the world I love thee best.

    " There is not one,
    No, no, not one
But thee to comfort a poor lonely maid;
    Thou art her mother,
    And her brother,
Her playmate, and her wooer in the shade."

O what a sigh she gave in finishing,
And look, quite dead to every worldly thing
Endymion could not speak, but gazed on her
And listen'd to the wind that now did stir
About the crisped oaks full drearily,
Yet with as sweet a softness as might be
Remember'd from its velvet summer song.

At last he said "Poor lady! how thus long
Have I been able to endure that voice?
Fair Melody! kind Syren! I've no choice
I must be thy sad servant evermore:
I cannot choose but kneel here and adore.
Alas, I must not think — by Phœbe, no!
Let me not think, soft Angel! shall it be so?
Say, beautifullest, shall I never think?
O thou couldst foster me beyond the brink
Of recollection! make my watchful care
Close up its bloodshot eyes, nor see despair!
Do gently murder half my soul, and I
Shall feel the other half so utterly! —
I'm giddy at that cheek so fair and smooth;
O let it blush so ever: let it soothe
My madness! let it mantle rosy warm
With the tinge of love, panting in safe alarm.
This cannot be thy hand, and yet it is;
And this is sure thine other softling — this
Thine own fair bosom, and I am so near!
Wilt fall asleep? O let me sip that tear!
And whisper one sweet word that I may know
This is this world — sweet dewy blossom!" —Woe
WOE! WOE TO THAT ENDYMION! WHERE IS
  HE? —
Even these words went echoing dismally
Through the wide forest — a most fearful tone,
Like one repenting in his latest moan;
And while it died away a shade pass'd by,
As of a thunder-cloud. When arrows fly
Through the thick branches, poor ring-doves sleek
  forth
Their timid necks and tremble; so these both
Leant to each other trembling, and sat so
Waiting for some destruction — when lo!
Foot-feather'd Mercury appear'd sublime
Beyond the tall tree tops; and in less time
than shoots the slanted hail-storm, down he dropp'd

Towards the ground; but rested not, nor stopp d
One moment from his home : only the sward
He with his wand light touch'd, and heavenward
Swifter than sight was gone — even before
The teeming earth a sudden witness boie
Of his swift magic.   Diving swans appear
Above the crystal circlings white and clear ;
And catch the cheated eye in wild surprise,
How they can dive in sight and unseen rise —
So from the turf outsprang two steeds jet-black,
Each with large dark blue wings upon his back
The youth of Caria placed the lovely dame
On one, and felt himself in spleen to tame
The other's fierceness.   Through the air they flew
High as the eagles.   Like two drops of dew
Exhaled to Phœbus' lips, away they are gone,
Far from the earth away — unseen, alone,
Among cool clouds and winds, but that the free
The buoyant life of song can floating be
Above their heads, and follow them untired.
Muse of my native land ! am I inspired ?
This is the giddy air, and I must spread
Wide pinions to keep here ; nor do I dread
Or height, or depth, or width, or any chance
Precipitous · I have beneath my glance
Those towering horses and their mournful freight.
Could I thus sail, and see, and thus await
Fearless for power of thought, without thine aid ?
There is a sleepy dusk, an odorous shade
From some approaching wonder, and behold
Those winged steeds, with snorting nostrils bold
Snuff at its faint extreme, and seem to tire,
Dying to embers from their native fire !

  There curl'd a purple mist around them ; soon,
It seem'd as when around the pale new moon
Sad Zephyr droops the clouds like weeping willow
'Twas Sleep slow journeying with head on pillow

For the first time, since he came nigh dead-born
From the old womb of night, his cave forlorn
Had he left more forlorn; for the first time,
He felt aloof the day and morning's prime —
Because into his depth Cimmerian
There came a dream, showing how a young man,
Ere a lean bat could plump its wintry skin,
Would at high Jove's empyreal footstool win
An immortality, and how espouse
Jove's daughter, and be reckon'd of his house.
Now was he slumbering towards heaven's gate,
That he might at the threshold one hour wait
To hear the marriage melodies, and then
Sink downward to his dusky cave again:
His litter of smooth semilucent mist,
Diversely tinged with rose and amethyst,
Puzzled those eyes that for the centre sought;
And scarcely for one moment could be caught
His sluggish form reposing motionless.
Those two on winged steeds, with all the stress
Of vision search'd for him, as one would look
Athwart the sallows of a river nook
To catch a glance at silver-throated eels, —
Or from old Skiddaw's top, when fog conceals
His rugged forehead in a mantle pale,
With an eye-guess towards some pleasant vale,
Descry a favourite hamlet faint and far.

These raven horses, though they foster'd are
Of earth's splenetic fire, dully drop
Their full-vein'd ears, nostrils blood wide, and stop
Upon the spiritless mist have they outspread
Their ample feathers, are in slumber dead, —
And on those pinions, level in mid-air,
Endymion sleepeth and the lady fair.
Slowly they sail, slowly as icy isle
Upon a calm sea drifting: and meanwhile
The mournful wanderer dreams. Behold! he walks

On heaven's pavement, brotherly ne talks
To divine powers· from his hand full fain
Juno's proud birds are pecking pearly grain
He tries the nerve of Phœbus' golden bow,
And asketh where the golden apples grow:
Upon his arm he braces Pallas' shield,
And strives in vain to unsettle and wield
A Jovian thunderbolt· arch Hebe brings
A full-brimm'd goblet, dances lightly, sings
And tantalizes long; at last he drinks,
And lost in pleasure, at her feet he sinks,
Touching with dazzled lips her starlight hand.
He blows a bugle, — an ethereal band
Are visible above· the Seasons four, —
Green-kirtled Spring, flush Summer, golden store
In Autumn's sickle, Winter frosty hoar,
Join dance with shadowy Hours, while still the blast,
In swells unmitigated, still doth last
To sway their floating morris.   " Whose is this ?
Whose bugle ? " he inquires: they smile — " O Dis
Why is this mortal here ?   Dost thou not know
Its mistress' lips ?   Not thou ? — 'Tis Dian's : lo !
She rises crescented ! "   He looks, 'tis she,
His very goddess : good-bye earth, and sea,
And air, and pains, and care, and suffering ;
Good-bye to all but love !   Then doth he spring
Towards her, and awakes — and, strange, o'erhead,
Of those same fragrant exhalations bred,
Beheld awake his very dream : the gods
Stood smiling , merry Hebe laughs and nods ;
And Phœbe bends towards him crescented.
O state perplexing !   On the pinion bed,
Too well awake, he feels the panting side
Of his delicious lady.   He who died
For soaring too audacious in the sun,
Where that same treacherous wax began to run,
Felt not more tongue-tied than Endymion
His heart leapt up as to its rightful throne,

To that fair-shadow'd passion pulsed its **way** —
Ah, what perplexity ! Ah, well a-day !
So fond, so beauteous was his bed-fellow,
He could not help but kiss her · then he **grew**
Awhile forgetful of all beauty save
Young Phœbe's, golden-hair'd ; and so 'gan **crave**
Forgiveness yet he turn'd once more to look
At the sweet sleeper, — all his soul was shook, —
She press'd his hand in slumber ; so once **more**
He could not help but kiss her and adore.
At this the shadow wept, melting away.
The Latmian started up " Bright goddess, **stay !**
Search my most hidden breast ! By truth's **own**
tongue,
I have no dædale heart , why is it wrung
To desperation ? Is there nought for me,
Upon the bourne of bliss, but misery ?"

These words awoke the stranger of dark **tresses :**
Her dawning love-look rapt Endymion blesses
With 'haviour soft. Sleep yawn'd from **underneath.**
" Thou swan of Ganges, let us no more breathe
This murky phantasm ' thou contented seem'st
Pillow'd in lovely idleness, nor dream'st
What horrors may discomfort thee and me.
Ah, shouldst thou die from my heart-treachery ! —
Yet did she merely weep — her gentle **soul**
Hath no revenge in it ; as it is whole
In tenderness, would I were whole in love !
Can I prize thee, fair maid, all price above,
Even when I feel as true as innocence !
I do, I do. — What is this soul then ? **Whence**
Came it ? It does not seem my own, and **I**
Have no self-passion or identity.
Some fearful end must be ; where, where **is it ?**
By Nemesis ! I see my spirit flit
Alone about the dark — Forgive me, sweet !
Shall we away ?" He roused the steeds ; **they**
beat

Their wings chivalrous into the clear air,
Leaving old Sleep within his vapoury lair.

The good-night blush of eve was waning slow,
And Vesper, risen star, began to throe
In the dusk heavens silvery, when they
Thus sprang direct towards the Galaxy.
Nor did speed hinder converse soft and strange —
Eternal oaths and vows they interchange,
In such wise, in such temper, so aloof
Up in the winds, beneath a starry roof,
So witless of their doom, that verily
'Tis well nigh past man's search their hearts to see;
Whether they wept, or laugh'd, or grieved, or
    toy'd —
Most like with joy gone mad, with sorrow cloy'd.

Full facing their swift flight, from ebon streak,
The moon put forth a little diamond peak,
No bigger than an unobserved star,
Or tiny point of fairy scimetar;
Bright signal that she only stoop'd to tie
Her silver sandals, ere deliciously
She bow'd into the heavens her timid head.
Slowly she rose, as though she would have fled,
While to his lady meek the Carian turn'd,
To mark if her dark eyes had yet discern'd
This beauty in its birth — Despair! despair!
He saw her body fading gaunt and spare
In the cold moonshine. Straight he seized her wrist
It melted from his grasp; her hand he kiss'd,
And, horror! kiss'd his own — he was alone.
Her steed a little higher soar'd, and then
Dropt hawk-wise to the earth.

                There lies a den,
Beyond the seeming confines of the space
Made for the soul to wander in and trace

Its own existence, of remotest glooms.
Dark regions are around it, where the tombs
Of buried griefs the spirit sees, but scarce
One hour doth linger weeping, for the pierce
Of new-born woe it feels more inly smart:
And in these regions many a venom'd dart
At random flies; they are the proper home
Of every ill: the man is yet to come
Who hath not journey'd in this native hell.
But few have ever felt how calm and well
Sleep may be had in that deep den of all.
There anguish does not sting, nor pleasure pall;
Woe-hurricanes beat ever at the gate,
Yet all is still within and desolate.
Beset with painful gusts, within ye hear
No sound so loud as when on curtain'd bier
The death-watch tick is stifled.   Enter none
Who strive therefore; on the sudden it is won
Just when the sufferer begins to burn,
Then it is free to him; and from an urn,
Still fed by melting ice, he takes a draught —
Young Semele such richness never quaff'd
In her maternal longing.   Happy gloom!
Dark Paradise! where pale becomes the bloom
Of health by due; where silence dreariest
Is most articulate; where hopes infest;
Where those eyes are the brightest far that keep
Their lids shut longest in a dreamless sleep.
O happy spirit-home!   O wondrous soul!
Pregnant with such a den to save the whole
In thine own depth.   Hail, gentle Carian!
For, never since thy griefs and woes began,
Hast thou felt so content: a grievous feud
Hath led thee to this Cave of Quietude.
Ay, his lull'd soul was there, although upborne
With dangerous speed: and so he did not mourn
Because he knew not whither he was going.
So happy was he, not the aerial blowing

Of trumpets at clear parley from the east
Could rouse from that fine relish, that high feast.
They stung the feather'd horse ; with fierce alarm
He flapp'd towards the sound   Alas ! no charm
Could lift Endymion's head, or he had view'd
A skyey mask, a pinion'd multitude, —
And silvery was its passing : voices sweet
Warbling the while as if to lull and greet
The wanderer in his path.   Thus warbled they,
While past the vision went in bright array.

   " Who, who from Dian's feast would be **away** ?
For all the golden bowers of the day
Are empty left ?   Who, who away would be
From Cynthia's wedding and festivity ?
Not Hesperus : lo ! upon his silver wings
He leans away for highest heaven and sings,
Snapping his lucid fingers merrily ! —
Ah, Zephyrus ! art here, and Flora too ?
Ye tender bibbers of the rain and dew,
Young playmates of the rose and daffodil,
Be careful, ere ye enter in, to fill
      Your baskets high
With fennel green, and balm, and golden pines,
Savory latter-mint, and columbines,
Cool parsley, basil sweet, and sunny thyme ;
Yea, every flower and leaf of every clime,
All gather'd in the dewy morning · hie
      Away ! fly, fly ! —
Crystalline brother of the belt of heaven,
Aquarius ! to whom king Jove has given
Two liquid pulse streams 'stead of feather'd wings,
Two fanlike fountains, — thine illuminings
      For Dian play :
Dissolve the frozen purity of air ;
Let thy white shoulders silvery and bare
Show cold through watery pinions ; make more
      bright

The Star-Queen's crescent on her marriage night
     Haste, haste away!
Castor has tamed the planet Lion, see!
And of the Bear has Pollux mastery:
A third is in the race! who is the third,
Speeding away swift as the eagle bird?
     The ramping Centaur!
The Lion's mane 's on end: the Bear how fierce!
The Centaur's arrow ready seems to pierce
Some enemy: far forth his bow is bent
Into the blue of heaven. He'll be shent,
     Pale unrelentor,
When he shall hear the wedding lutes a playing. —
Andromeda! sweet woman! why delaying
So timidly among the stars · come hither!
Join this bright throng, and nimbly follow whither
     They all are going
Danae's Son, before Jove newly bow'd,
Has wept for thee, calling to Jove aloud.
Thee, gentle lady, did he disenthrall ·
Ye shall for ever live and love, for all
     Thy tears are flowing —
By Daphne's fright, behold Apollo!" —

                      More
Endymion heard not: down his steed him bore,
Prone to the green head of a misty hill.

  His first touch of the earth went nigh to kill.
" Alas!" said he, " were I but always borne
'Through dangerous winds, had but my footsteps
     worn
A path in hell, for ever would I bless
Horrors which nourish an uneasiness
For my own sullen conquering; to him
Who lives beyond earth's boundary, grief is dim,
Sorrow is but a shadow · now I see
The grass; I feel the solid ground — Ah, me!

It is thy voice — divinest! Where? — who? whe
Left thee so quiet on this bed of dew?
Behold upon this happy earth we are;
Let us aye love each other; let us fare
On forest-fruits, and never, never go
Among the abodes of mortals here below,
Or be by phantoms duped. O destiny!
Into a labyrinth now my soul would fly,
But with thy beauty will I deaden it.
Where didst thou melt to? By thee will I sit
For ever: let our fate stop here — a kid
I on this spot will offer: Pan will bid
Us live in peace, in love and peace among
His forest wildernesses I have clung
To nothing, loved a nothing, nothing seen
Or felt but a great dream! Oh, I have been
Presumptuous against love, against the sky,
Against all elements, against the tie
Of mortals each to each, against the blooms
Of flowers, rush of rivers, and the tombs
Of heroes gone! Against his proper glory
Has my own soul conspired: so my story
Will I to children utter, and repent.
There never lived a mortal man, who bent
His appetite beyond his natural sphere,
But starved and died. My sweetest Indian, here,
Here will I kneel, for thou redeemed hast
My life from too thin breathing: gone and past
Are cloudy phantasms. Caverns lone, farewell!
And air of visions, and the monstrous swell
Of visionary seas! No, never more
Shall airy voices cheat me to the shore
Of tangled wonder, breathless and aghast.
Adieu, my daintiest Dream! although so vast
My love is still for thee. The hour may come
When we shall meet in pure elysium.
On earth I may not love thee, and therefore
Doves will I offer up, and sweetest store

All through ye teeming year : so thou wilt shine
On me, and a this danced fair of mine,
And bless our simple lives. My Indian bliss !
My river-lily bud ! one human kiss !
One sigh of real breath — one gentle squeeze,
Warm as a dove's nest among summer trees,
And warm with dew at ooze from living blood !
Whither didst melt ? Ah, what of that ! — all good
We'll talk about — no more of dreaming. — Now,
Where shall our dwelling be ? Under the brow
Of some steep mossy hill, where ivy dun
Would hide us up, although spring leaves were
    none ;
And where dark yew-trees, as we rustle through,
Will drop their scarlet-berry cups of dew !
O thou would'st joy to live in such a place !
Dusk for our loves, yet light enough to grace
Those gentle limbs on mossy bed reclined :
For by one step the blue sky shouldst thou find,
And by another, in deep dell below,
See, through the trees, a little river go
All in its mid-day gold and glimmering.
Honey from out the gnarled hive I'll bring,
And apples, wan with sweetness, gather thee, —
Cresses that grow where no man may them see,
And sorrel untorn by the dew-claw'd stag :
Pipes will I fashion of the syrinx flag,
That thou mayst always know whither I roam,
When it shall please thee in our quiet home
To listen and think of love. Still let me speak :
Still let me dive into the joy I seek, —
For yet the past doth prison me. The rill,
Thou haply mayst delight in, will I fill
With fairy fishes from the mountain tarn,
And thou shalt feed them from the squirrel's barn
Its bottom will I strew with amber shells,
And pebbles blue from deep enchanted wells.
Its sides I'll plant with dew-sweet eglantine,

And honeysuckles full of clear bee-wine.
I will entice this crystal rill to trace
Love's silver name upon the meadow's face.
I'll kneel to Vesta, for a flame of fire;
And to god Phœbus, for a golden lyre;
To Empress Dian, for a hunting-spear;
To Vesper, for a taper silver-clear,
That I may see thy beauty through the night,
To Flora, and a nightingale shall light
Tame on thy finger; to the River-gods
And they shall bring thee taper fishing-rods
Of gold, and lines of naiads' long bright tress.
Heaven shield thee for thine utter loveliness!
Thy mossy footstool shall the altar be
'Fore which I'll bend, bending, dear love, to thee:
Those lips shall be my Delphos, and shall speak
Laws to my footsteps, colour to my cheek,
Trembling or steadfastness to this same voice,
And of three sweetest pleasurings the choice:
And that affectionate light, those diamond things,
Those eyes, those passions, those supreme pearl
      springs,
Shall be my grief, or twinkle me to pleasure.
Say, is not bliss within our perfect seizure?
Oh that I could not doubt!"

                        The mountaineer
Thus strove by fancies vain and crude to clear
His brier'd path to some tranquillity.
It gave bright gladness to his lady's eye,
And yet the tears she wept were tears of sorrow
Answering thus, just as the golden morrow
Beam'd upward from the valleys of the east:
" O that the flutter of his heart had ceased,
Or the sweet name of love had pass'd away!
Young feather'd tyrant! by a swift decay
Wilt thou devote this body to the earth
And I do think that at my very birth

I lisp'd thy blooming titles inwardly;
For at the first, first dawn and thought of thee,
With uplift hands I bless'd the stars of heaven
Art thou not cruel? ever have I striven
To think thee kind, but ah, it will not do!
When yet a child, I heard that kisses drew
Favour from thee, and so I kisses gave
To the void air, bidding them find out love:
But when I came to feel how far above
All fancy, pride, and fickle maidenhood,
All earthly pleasure, all imagined good,
Was the warm tremble of a devout kiss, —
Even then that moment, at the thought of this,
Fainting I fell into a bed of flowers,
And languish'd there three days.   Ye milder
   powers,
Am I not cruelly wrong'd?   Believe, believe
Me, dear Endymion, were I to weave
With my own fancies garlands of sweet life,
Thou should'st be one of all.   Ah, bitter strife!
I may not be thy love: I am forbidden —
Indeed I am — thwarted, affrighted, chidden,
By things I trembled at, and gorgon wrath.
Twice hast thou ask'd whither I went: henceforth
Ask me no more! I may not utter it,
Nor may I be thy love.   We might commit
Ourselves at once to vengeance: we might die;
We might embrace and die. voluptuous thought!
Enlarge not to my hunger, or I'm caught
In trammels of perverse deliciousness.
No, no, that shall not be: thee will I bless,
And bid a long adieu."

    The Carian
No word return'd: both lovelorn, silent, wan,
Into the valleys green together went.
Far wandering, they were perforce content
To sit beneath a fair lone beechen tree;

Nor at each other gazed, but heavily
Pored on its hazel cirque of shedded leaves

Endymion ! unhappy ! it nigh grieves
Me to behold thee thus in last extreme :
Enskied ere this, but truly that I deem
Truth the best music in a first-born song.
Thy lute-voice'd brother will I sing ere long,
And thou shalt aid — hast thou not aided me ?
Yes, moonlight Emperor ! felicity
Has been thy meed for many thousand years ;
Yet often have I, on the brink of tears,
Mourn'd as if yet thou wert a forester ; —
Forgetting the old tale.

He did not stir
His eyes from the dead leaves, or one small pulse
Of joy he might have felt.   The spirit culls
Unfaded amaranth, when wild it strays
Through the old garden-ground of boyish days.
A little onward ran the very stream
By which he took his first soft poppy dream ;
And on the very bark 'gainst which he leant
A crescent he had carved, and round it spent
His skill in little stars.   The teeming tree
Had swoll'n and green'd the pious charactery,
But not ta'en out.   Why, there was not a slope
Up which he had not fear'd the antelope ;
And not a tree, beneath whose rooty shade
He had not with his tamed leopards play'd ;
Nor could an arrow light, or javelin,
Fly in the air where his had never been —
And yet he knew it not

O treachery !
Why does his lady smile, pleasing her eye
With all his sorrowing ?   He sees her not.
But who so stares on him ?   His sister sure

Peona of the woods! — Can she endure ? —
Impossible — how dearly they embrace !
His lady smiles; delight is in her face ;
It is no treachery.

      " Dear brother mine !
Endymion, weep not so!   Why should'st thou pine
When all great Latmos so exalt will be ?
Thank the great gods, and look not bitterly;
And speak not one pale word, and sigh no more.
Sure I will not believe thou hast such store
Of grief, to last thee to my kiss again.
Thou surely canst not bear a mind in pain,
Come hand in hand with one so beautiful.
Be happy both of you! for I will pull
The flowers of autumn for your coronals.
Pan's holy priest for young Endymion calls ;
And when he is restored, thou, fairest dame,
Shalt be our queen.   Now, is it not a shame
To see ye thus, — not very, very sad ?
Perhaps ye are too happy to be glad:
O feel as if it were a common day ;
Free-voiced as one who never was away.
No tongue shall ask, whence come ye ? but ye
  shall
Be gods of your own rest imperial.
Not even I, for one whole month will pry
Into the hours that have pass'd us by,
Since in my arbour I did sing to thee.
O Hermes! on this very night will be
A hymning up to Cynthia, queen of light;
For the soothsayers old saw yesternight
Good visions in the air, — whence will befall,
As say these sages, health perpetual
To shepherds and their flocks; and furthermore,
In Dian's face they read the gentle lore :
Therefore for her these vesper-carols are.
Our friends will all be there from nigh and far

Many upon thy death have ditties made ,
And many, even now, their foreheads shade
With cypress, on a day of sacrifice.
New singing for our maids shalt thou devise,
And pluck the sorrow from our huntsmen's brows,
Tell me, my lady-queen, how to espouse
This wayward brother to his rightful joys !
His eyes are on thee bent, as thou didst poise
His fate most goddess-like.   Help me, I pray,
To lure — Endymion, dear brother, say
What ails thee ? "   He could bear no more, and so
Bent his soul fiercely like a spiritual bow,
And twang'd it inwardly, and calmly said :
" I would have thee my only friend, sweet maid !
My only visitor ! not ignorant though,
That those deceptions which for pleasure go
'Mong men, are pleasures real as real may be :
But there are higher ones I may not see,
If impiously an earthly realm I take.
Since I saw thee, I have been wide awake
Night after night, and day by day, until
Of the empyrean I have drunk my fill.
Let it content thee, Sister, seeing me
More happy than betides mortality.
A hermit young, I'll live in mossy cave,
Where thou alone shalt come to me, and lave
Thy spirit in the wonders I shall tell.
Through me the shepherd realm shall prosper well
For to thy tongue will I all health confide.
And for my sake, let this young maid abide
With thee as a dear sister.   Thou alone,
Peona, mayst return to me.   I own
This may sound strangely : but when, dearest girl
Thou seest it for my happiness, no pearl
Will trespass down those cheeks.   Companion fair
Wilt be content to dwell with her, to share
This sister's love with me ? "   Like one resign'd
And bent by circumstances. and thereby blind

In self-commitment, thus, that meek unknown
" Ay, but a buzzing by my ears has flown,
Of jubilee to Dian — truth I heard !
Well then, I see there is no little bird,
Tender soever, but is Jove's own care.
Long have I sought for rest, and unaware,
Behold I find it ! so exalted too !
So after my own heart ! I knew, I knew
There was a place untenanted in it ;
In that same void white Chastity shall sit,
And monitor me nightly to lone slumber.
With sanest lips I vow me to the number
Of Dian's sisterhood ; and kind lady,
With thy good help, this very night shall see
My future days to her fane consecrate."

As feels a dreamer what doth most create
His own particular fright, so these three felt
Or like one who, in after ages, knelt
To Lucifer or Baal, when he'd pine
After a little sleep : or when in mine
Far under-ground, a sleeper meets his friend
Who know him not. Each diligently bends
Towards common thoughts and things for very
        fear ;
Striving their ghastly malady to cheer,
By thinking it a thing of yes and no,
That housewives talk of. But the spirit-blow
Was struck, and all were dreamers. At the last
Endymion said : " Are not our fates all cast ?
Why stand we here ? Adieu, ye tender pair !
Adieu !" Whereat those maidens, with wild stare
Walk'd dizzily away. Pained and hot
His eyes went after them, until they got
Near to a cypress grove, whose deadly maw,
In one swift moment, would what then he saw
Engulf for ever. " Stay," he cried, " ah, stay !
Turn damsels ! hist ! one word I have to say :

Sweet Indian, I would see thee once again.
It is a thing I dote on : so I'd fain,
Peona, ye should hand in hand repair,
Into those holy groves that silent are
Behind great Dian's temple.　I'll be yon,
At Vesper's earliest twinkle — they are gone —
But once, once, once again —"　At this he prest
His hands against his face, and then did rest
His head upon a mossy hillock green
And so remain'd as he a corpse had been
All the long day; save when he scantly lifted
His eyes abroad, to see how shadows shifted
With the slow move of time, — sluggish and weary
Until the poplar tops, in journey dreary,
Had reach'd the river's brim.　Then up he rose,
And, slowly as that very river flows,
Walk'd towards the temple-grove with this lamen'
"Why such a golden eve?　The breeze is sent
Careful and soft, that not a leaf may fall
Before the serene father of them all
Bows down his summer head below the west.
Now am I of breath, speech, and speed possest,
But at the setting I must bid adieu
To her for the last time.　Night will strew
On the damp grass myriads of lingering leaves,
And with them shall I die ; nor much it grieves
To die, when summer dies on the cold sward.
Why, I have been a butterfly, a lord
Of flowers, garlands, love-knots, silly posies,
Groves, meadows, melodies, and arbour-roses;
My kingdom's at its death, and just it is
That I should die with it: so in all this
We miscall grief, bale, sorrow, heart-break, woe,
What is there to plain of?　By Titan's foe
I am but rightly served"　So saying, he
Tripp'd lightly on, in sort of deathful glee;
Laughing at the clear stream and setting sun,
As though they jests had been ·　or had he done

His laugh at nature's holy countenance,
Until that grove appear'd, as if perchance,
And then his tongue with sober seemlihed
Gave utterance as he enter'd : " Ha ! " he **said,**
" King of the butterflies ; but by this gloom,
And by old Rhadamanthus' tongue of doom,
This dusk religion, pomp of solitude,
And the Promethean clay by thief endued,
By old Saturnus' forelock, by his head
Shook with eternal palsy, I did wed
Myself to things of light from infancy ;
And thus to be cast out, thus lorn to die,
Is sure enough to make a mortal man
Grow impious." So he inwardly began
On things for which no wording can be found ;
Deeper and deeper sinking, until drown'd
Beyond the reach of music : for the choir
Of Cynthia he heard not, though rough brier
Nor muffling thicket interposed to dull
The Vesper hymn, far swollen, soft and full,
Through the dark pillars of those sylvan aisles.
He saw not the two maidens, nor their smiles,
Wan as primroses gather'd at midnight
By chilly-finger'd spring. Unhappy wight !
" Endymion ! " said Peona, " we are here !
What wouldst thou ere we all are laid on bier ? "
Then he embraced her, and his lady's hand
Press'd, saying · " Sister, I would have **command,**
If it were heaven's will, on our sad fate "
At which that dark-eyed stranger stood elate
And said, in a new voice, but sweet as love,
To Endymion's amaze : " By Cupid's dove,
And so thou shalt ! and by the lily truth
Of my own breast thou shalt, beloved youth ! "
And as she spake, into her face there came
Light, as reflected from a silver flame ·
Her long black hair swell'd ampler, in **display**
Full golden ; in her eyes a brighter day

Dawn'd blue, and full of love.   Aye, he beheld
Phœbe, his passion! joyous she upheld
Her lucid bow, continuing thus: "Drear, drear
Has our delaying been; but foolish fear
Withheld me first; and then decrees of fate;
And then 'twas fit that from this mortal state
Thou   shouldst, my love, by some   unlook'd-for
       change
Be spiritualized.   Peona, we shall range
These forests, and to thee they safe shall be
As was thy cradle; hither shalt thou flee
To meet us many a time."   Next Cynthia bright
Peona kiss'd, and bless'd with fair good night:
Her brother kiss'd her too, and knelt adown
Before his goddess, in a blissful swoon.
She gave her fair hands to him, and behold,
Before three swiftest kisses he had told,
They vanished far away! — Peona went
Home through the gloomy wood in wonderment.

LAMIA.

PART I.

UPON a time, before the faery broods
    Drove Nymph and Satyr from the prosperous
       woods,
Before King Oberon's bright diadem,
Sceptre, and mantle, clasp'd with dewy gem,
Frighted away the Dryads and the Fauns
From rushes green, and brakes, and cowslipp'd
       lawns,
The ever-smitten Hermes empty left
His golden throne, bent warm on amorous theft :
From high Olympus had he stolen light,
On this side of Jove's clouds, to escape the sight
Of his great summoner, and made retreat
Into a forest on the shores of Crete.
For somewhere in that sacred island dwelt
A nymph, to whom all hoofed Satyrs knelt ;
At whose white feet the languid Tritons pour'd
Pearls, while on land they wither'd and adored
Fast by the springs where she to bathe was wont,
And in those meads where sometimes she might
       haunt,
Were strewn rich gifts, unknown to any Muse,
Though Fancy's casket were unlock'd to choose.
Ah, what a world of love was at her feet !
So Hermes thought, and a celestial heat
Burn'd from his winged heels to either ear,
That from a whiteness, as the lily clear,
Blush'd into roses 'mid his golden hair,
Fallen in jealous curls about his shoulders bare
From vale to vale, from wood to wood, he flew,

Breathing upon the flowers his passion new,
And wound with many a river to its head,
To find where this sweet nymph prepared her
     secret bed:
In vain; the sweet nymph might nowhere be found,
And so he rested, on the lonely ground,
Pensive, and full of painful jealousies
Of the Wood-Gods, and even the very trees.
There as he stood, he heard a mournful voice,
Such as once heard, in gentle heart, destroys
All pain but pity: thus the lone voice spake:
" When from this wreathed tomb shall I awake!
When move in a sweet body fit for life,
And love, and pleasure, and the ruddy strife
Of hearts and lips! Ah, miserable me!"
The God, dove-footed, glided silently
Round bush and tree, soft-brushing, in his speed,
The taller grasses and full-flowering weed,
Until he found a palpitating snake,
Bright, and cirque-couchant in a dusky brake.

    She was a gordian shape of dazzling hue,
Vermilion-spotted, golden, green, and blue;
Striped like a zebra, freckled like a pard,
Eyed like a peacock, and all crimson barr'd;
And full of silver moons, that, as she breathed,
Dissolved, or brighter shone, or interwreathed
Their lustres with the gloomier tapestries —
So rainbow-sided, touch'd with miseries,
She seem'd at once, some penanced lady elf,
Some demon's mistress, or the demon's self.
Upon her crest she wore a wannish fire
Sprinkled with stars, like Ariadne's tiar:
Her head was serpent, but ah, bitter-sweet!
She had a woman's mouth with all its pearls com-
     plete:
And for her eyes — what could such eyes do there
But weep, and weep, that they were born so fair?

As Proserpine still weeps for her Sicilian air.
Her throat was serpent, but the words she spake
Came, as through bubbling honey, for Love's sake,
And thus; while Hermes on his pinions lay,
Like a stoop'd falcon ere he takes his prey:

"Fair Hermes! crown'd with feathers, fluttering
    light,
I had a splendid dream of thee last night·
I saw thee sitting, on a throne of gold,
Among the Gods, upon Olympus old,
The only sad one; for thou didst not hear
The soft, lute-finger'd Muses chanting clear,
Nor even Apollo when he sang alone,
Deaf to his throbbing throat's long, long melodious
    moan.
I dreamt I saw thee, robed in purple flakes,
Break amorous through the clouds, as morning
    breaks,
And, swiftly as a bright Phœbean dart,
Strike for the Cretan isle; and here thou art!
Too gentle Hermes, hast thou found the maid?"
Whereat the star of Lethe not delay'd
His rosy eloquence, and thus inquired:
"Thou smooth-lipp'd serpent, surely high-inspired!
Thou beauteous wreath, with melancholy eyes,
Possess whatever bliss thou canst devise,
Telling me only where my nymph is fled, —
Where she doth breathe!" "Bright planet, thou
    hast said,"
Return'd the snake, "but seal with oaths, fair God!"
"I swear," said Hermes, "by my serpent rod,
And by thine eyes, and by thy starry crown!"
Light flew his earnest words, among the blossoms
    blown.
Then thus again the brilliance feminine:
"Too frail of heart! for this lost nymph of thine,
Free as the air, invisibly, she strays

About these thornless wilds; her pleasant days
She tastes unseen; unseen her nimble feet
Leave traces in the grass and flowers sweet:
From weary tendrils, and bow'd branches green,
She plucks the fruit unseen, she bathes unseen:
And by my power is her beauty veil'd
To keep it unaffronted, unassail'd
By the love-glances of unlovely eyes,
Of Satyrs, Fauns, and blear'd Silenus' sighs.
Pale grew her immortality, for woe
Of all these lovers, and she grieved so
I took compassion on her, bade her steep
Her hair in weird syrops, that would keep
Her loveliness invisible, yet free
To wander as she loves, in liberty.
Thou shalt behold her, Hermes, thou alone,
If thou wilt, as thou swearest, grant my boon!"
Then, once again, the charmed God began
An oath, and through the serpent's ears it ran
Warm, tremulous, devout, psalterian.
Ravish'd she lifted her Circean head,
Blush'd a live damask, and swift-lisping said,
" I was a woman, let me have once more
A woman's shape, and charming as before.
I love a youth of Corinth — O the bliss!
Give me my woman's form, and place me where he is
Stoop, Hermes, let me breathe upon thy brow,
And thou shalt see thy sweet nymph even now."
The God on half-shut feathers sank serene,
She breathed upon his eyes, and swift was seen
Of both the guarded nymph near-smiling on the
     green.
It was no dream; or say a dream it was,
Real are the dreams of Gods, and smoothly pass
Their pleasures in a long immortal dream.
One warm, flush'd moment, hovering, it might seem
Dash'd by the wood-nymph's beauty, so he burn'd
Then, lighting on the printless verdure, turn'd

To the swoon'd serpent, and with languid arm,
Delicate, put to proof the lithe Caducean charm
So done, upon the nymph his eyes he bent
Full of adoring tears and blandishment,
And towards her stept · she, like a moon in wane,
Faded before him, cower'd, nor could restrain
Her fearful sobs, self-folding like a flower
That faints into itself at evening hour :
But the God fostering her chilled hand,
She felt the warmth, her eyelids open'd bland,
And, like new flowers at morning song of bees,
Bloom'd, and gave up her honey to the lees.
Into the green-recessed woods they flew ;
Nor grew they pale, as mortal lovers do.

Left to herself, the serpent now began
To change ; her elfin blood in madness ran,
Her mouth foam'd, and the grass, therewith besprent,
Wither'd at dew so sweet and virulent ;
Her eyes in torture fix'd, and anguish drear,
Hot, glazed, and wide, with lid-lashes all sear,
Flash'd phosphor and sharp sparks, without one
    cooling tear.
The colours all inflamed throughout her train,
She writhed about, convulsed with scarlet pain :
A deep volcanian yellow took the place
Of all her milder-mooned body's grace ;
And, as the lava ravishes the mead,
Spoilt all her silver mail, and golden brede ·
Made gloom of all her frecklings, streaks and bars
Eclipsed her crescents, and lick'd up her stars .
So that, in moments few, she was undrest
Of all her sapphires, greens, and amethyst,
And rubious-argent : of all these bereft,
Nothing but pain and ugliness were left.
Still shone her crown, that vanish'd, also she
Melted and disappear'd as suddenly ;
And in the air, her new voice luting soft,

Cried, "Lycius! gentle Lycius!" — borne aloft
With the bright mists about the mountains hoar
These words dissolved: Crete's forests heard no
    more.

    Whither fled Lamia, now a lady bright,
A full-born beauty new and exquisite?
She fled into that valley they pass o'er
Who go to Corinth from Cenchreas' shore;
And rested at the foot of those wild hills,
The rugged founts of the Peræan rills,
And of that other ridge whose barren back
Stretches, with all its mist and cloudy rack,
South-westward to Cleone   There she stood
About a young bird's flutter from a wood,
Fair, on a sloping green of mossy tread,
By a clear pool, wherein she passioned
To see herself escaped from so sore ills,
While her robes flaunted with the daffodils.

    Ah, happy Lycius! — for she was a maid
More beautiful than ever twisted braid,
Or sigh'd, or blush'd, or on spring-flower'd lea
Spread a green kirtle to the minstrelsy:
A virgin purest lipp'd, yet in the lore
Of love deep learned to the red heart's core:
Not one hour old, yet of sciential brain
To unperplex bliss from its neighbour pain,
Define their pettish limits, and estrange
Their points of contact, and swift counterchange
Intrigue with the specious chaos, and dispart
Its most ambiguous atoms with sure art;
As though in Cupid's college she had spent
Sweet days a lovely graduate, still unshent,
And kept his rosy terms in idle languishment.

    Why this fair creature chose so fairily
By the wayside to linger, we shall see ·

But first 'tis fit to tell how she could muse
And dream, when in the serpent prison-house,
Of all she list, strange or magnificent ·
How, ever, where she will'd, her spirit went;
Whether to faint Elysium, or where
Down through tress-lifting waves the Nereids fair
Wind into Thetis' bower by many a pearly stair;
Or where God Bacchus drains his cups divine,
Stretch'd out, at ease, beneath a glutinous pine;
Or where in Pluto's gardens palatine
Mulciber's columns gleam in far piazzian line.
And sometimes into cities she would send
Her dream, with feast and rioting to blend;
And once, while among mortals dreaming **thus,**
She saw the young Corinthian Lycius
Charioting foremost in the envious race,
Like a young Jove with calm uneager face,
And fell into a swooning love of him
Now on the moth-time of that evening dim
He would return that way, as well she knew,
To Corinth from the shore; for freshly blew
The eastern soft wind, and his galley now
Grated the quay-stones with her brazen **prow**
In port Cenchreas, from Egina isle
Fresh anchor'd; whither he had been awhile
To sacrifice to Jove, whose temple there
Waits with high marble doors for blood **and in-**
        cense rare.
Jove heard his vows, and better'd his desire;
For by some freakful chance he made retire
From his companions, and set forth to walk,
Perhaps grown wearied of their Corinth talk :
Over the solitary hills he fared,
Thoughtless, at first, but ere eve's star **appear'd**
His phantasy was lost, where reason fades,
In the calm'd twilight of Platonic shades.
Lamia beheld him coming, near, more **near —**
Close to her passing, in indifference drear,

His silent sandals swept the mossy green;
So neighbour'd to him, and yet so unseen
She stood: he pass'd, shut up in mysteries,
His mind wrapp'd like his mantle, while her eyes
Follow'd his steps, and her neck regal white
Turn'd — syllabling thus, " Ah, Lycius bright !
And will you leave me on the hills alone ?
Lycius, look back ! and be some pity shown."
He did ; not with cold wonder fearingly,
But Orpheus-like at an Eurydice ,
For so delicious were the words she sung,
It seem'd he had loved them a whole summer long
And soon his eyes had drunk her beauty up,
Leaving no drop in the bewildering cup,
And still the cup was full, — while he, afraid
Lest she should vanish ere his lips had paid
Due adoration, thus began to adore ,
Her soft look growing coy, she saw his chain so
      sure :
" Leave thee alone ! Look back ! Ah, Goddess, see
Whether my eyes can ever turn from thee !
For pity do not this sad heart belie —
Even as thou vanishest so I shall die.
Stay ! though a Naiad of the rivers, stay !
To thy far wishes will thy streams obey :
Stay ! though the greenest woods be thy domain,
Alone they can drink up the morning rain :
Though a descended Pleiad, will not one
Of thine harmonious sisters keep in tune
Thy spheres, and as thy silver proxy shine ?
So sweetly to these ravish'd ears of mine
Came thy sweet greeting, that if thou shouldst
      fade,
Thy memory will waste me to a shade . —
For pity do not melt !" — " If I should stay,"
Said Lamia, " here, upon this floor of clay,
And pain my steps upon these flowers too rough.
What canst thou say or do of charm enough

To dull the nice remembrance of my home ?
Thou canst not ask me with thee here to roam
Over these hills and vales, where no joy is, —
Empty of immortality and bliss !
Thou art a scholar, Lycius, and must know
That finer spirits cannot breathe below
In human climes, and live : Alas ! poor youth,
What taste of purer air hast thou to soothe
My essence ? What serener palaces,
Where I may all my many senses please,
And by mysterious sleights a hundred thirsts ap
      pease,
It cannot be — Adieu ! " So said, she rose
Tiptoe with white arms spread. He, sick to lose
The amorous promise of her lone complain,
Swoon'd murmuring of love, and pale with pain
The cruel lady, without any show
Of sorrow for her tender favourite's woe,
But rather, if her eyes could brighter be,
With brighter eyes and slow amenity,
Put her new lips to his, and gave afresh
The life she had so tangled in her mesh ·
And as he from one trance was wakening
Into another, she began to sing,
Happy in beauty, life, and love, and everything,
A song of love, too sweet for earthly lyres,
While, like held breath, the stars drew in their
      panting fires.
And then she whisper'd in such trembling tone,
As those who, safe together met alone
For the first time through many anguish'd days,
Use other speech than looks ; bidding him raise
His drooping head. and clear his soul of doubt,
For that she was a woman, and without
Any more subtle fluid in her veins
Than throbbing blood, and that the self-same pains
Inhabited her frail-strung heart as his.
And next she wonder'd how his eyes could miss

Her face so long in Corinth, where, she **said,**
She dwelt but half retired, and there had **led**
Days happy as the gold coin could invent
Without the aid of love; yet in content
Till she saw him, as once she pass'd him by,
Where 'gainst a column he leant thoughtfully
At Venus' temple porch, 'mid baskets heap'd
Of amorous herbs and flowers, newly reap'd
Late on that eve, as 'twas the night before
The Adonian feast; whereof she saw no more,
But wept alone those days, for why should **she**
     adore?
Lycius from death awoke into amaze,
To see her still, and singing so sweet lays;
Then from amaze into delight he fell
To hear her whisper woman's lore so **well;**
And every word she spake enticed him **on**
To unperplex'd delight and pleasure **known.**
Let the mad poets say whate'er they please
Of the sweets of Fairies, Peris, Goddesses,
There is not such a treat among them all,
Haunters of cavern, lake, and waterfall,
As a real woman, lineal indeed
From Pyrrha's pebbles or old Adam's seed.
Thus gentle Lamia judged, and judged aright,
That Lycius could not love in half a fright,
So threw the goddess off, and won his heart
More pleasantly by playing woman's part,
With no more awe than what her beauty gave,
That, while it smote, still guaranteed to save.
Lycius to all made eloquent reply,
Marrying to every word a twin-born sigh;
And last, pointing to Corinth, ask'd her sweet,
If 'twas too far that night for her soft feet.
The way was short, for Lamia's eagerness
Made, by a spell, the triple league decrease
To a few paces; not at all surmised
By blinded Lycius, so in her comprised

They pass'd the city gates, he knew not how,
So noiseless, and he never thought to know.

As men talk in a dream, so Corinth all,
Throughout her palaces imperial,
And all her populous streets and temples lewd,
Mutter'd, like tempest in the distance brew'd,
To the wide-spreaded night above her towers.
Men, women, rich and poor, in the cool hours,
Shuffled their sandals o'er the pavement white,
Companion'd or alone; while many a light
Flared, here and there, from wealthy festivals,
And threw their moving shadows on the walls,
Or found them cluster'd in the corniced shade
Of some arch'd temple door, or dusky colonnade

Muffling his face, of greeting friends in fear,
Her fingers he press'd hard, as one came near
With curl'd gray beard, sharp eyes, and smooth
        bald crown,
Slow-stepp'd, and robed in philosophic gown
Lycius shrank closer, as they met and past,
Into his mantle, adding wings to haste,
While hurried Lamia trembled: "Ah," said he,
" Why do you shudder, love, so ruefully ?
Why does your tender palm dissolve in dew ?"
" I'm wearied," said fair Lamia: " tell me who
Is that old man ? I cannot bring to mind
His features: — Lycius ! wherefore did you blind
Yourself from his quick eyes ?" Lycius replied,
" 'Tis Apollonius sage, my trusty guide
And good instructor; but to-night he seems
The ghost of folly haunting my sweet dreams."

While yet he spake they had arrived before
A pillar'd porch, with lofty portal door,
Where hung a silver lamp whose phosphor glow
Reflected in the slabbed steps below,

Mild as a star in water; for so new
And so unsullied was the marble hue,
So through the crystal polish, liquid fine,
Ran the dark veins, that none but feet divine
Could e'er have touch'd there.   Sounds Æolian
Breathed from the hinges, as the ample span
Of the wide doors disclosed a place unknown
Some time to any, but those two alone.
And a few Persian mutes, who that same year
Were seen about the markets · none knew where
They could inhabit; the most curious
Were foil'd, who watch'd to trace them to their
    house :
And but the flitter-winged verse must tell,
For truth's sake what woe afterwards befell,
'Twould humour many a heart to leave them thus,
Shut from the busy world of more incredulous.

———◆———

PART II.

LOVE in a hut, with water and a crust,
Is — Love, forgive us ! — cinders, ashes, dust;
Love in a palace is perhaps at last
More grievous torment than a hermit's fast : —
That is a doubtful tale from faery land,
Hard for the non-elect to understand.
Had Lycius lived to hand his story down,
He might have given the moral a fresh frown,
Or clench'd it quite : but too short was their bliss
To breed distrust and hate, that make the soft
    voice hiss.
Besides, there, nightly, with terrific glare,
Love, jealous grown of so complete a pair,
Hover'd and buzz'd his wings, with fearful roar,
Above the lintel of their chamber door,
And down the passage cast a glow upon the floor

For all this came a ruin: side by side
They were enthroned, in the even tide,
Upon a couch, near to a curtaining
Whose airy texture, from a golden string,
Floated into the room, and let appear
Unveil'd the summer heaven, blue and clear,
Betwixt two marble shafts:— there they reposed,
Where use had made it sweet, with eyelids closed,
Saving a tithe which love still open kept,
That they might see each other while they almost
    slept;
When from the slope side of a suburb hill,
Deafening the swallow's twitter, came a thrill
Of trumpets — Lycius started — the sounds fled,
But left a thought, a buzzing in his head.
For the first time, since first he harbour'd in
That purple-lined palace of sweet sin,
His spirit pass'd beyond its golden bourn
Into the noisy world almost forsworn.
The lady, ever watchful, penetrant,
Saw this with pain, so arguing a want
Of something more, more than her empery
Of joys; and she began to moan and sigh
Because he mused beyond her, knowing well
That but a moment's thought is passion's passing
    bell.
" Why do you sigh, fair creature?" whisper'd he.
" Why, do you think?" return'd she tenderly:
" You have deserted me; where am I now?
Not in your heart while care weighs on your brow
No, no, you have dismiss'd me; and I go
From your breast houseless: ay, it must be so."
He answer'd, bending to her open eyes,
Where he was mirror'd small in paradise, —
' My silver planet, both of eve and morn!
Why will you plead yourself so sad forlorn,
While I am striving how to fill my heart
With deeper crimson, and a double smart?

How to entangle, trammel up and snare
Your soul in mine, and labyrinth you there,
Like the hid scent in an unbudded rose ?
Ay, a sweet kiss — you see your mighty woes.
My thoughts ! shall I unveil them ? Listen then
What mortal hath a prize, that other men
May be confounded and abash'd withal,
But lets it sometimes pace abroad majestical,
And triumph, as in thee I should rejoice
Amid the hoarse alarm of Corinth's voice.
Let my foes choke, and my friends shout afar,
While through the thronged streets your bridal car
Wheels round its dazzling spokes." — The lady's
    cheek
Trembled ; she nothing said, but, pale and meek,
Arose and knelt before him, wept a rain
Of sorrows at his words ; at last with pain
Beseeching him, the while his hand she wrung,
To change his purpose. He thereat was stung,
Perverse, with stronger fancy to reclaim
Her wild and timid nature to his aim ;
Besides, for all his love, in self despite,
Against his better self, he took delight
Luxurious in her sorrows, soft and new.
His passion, cruel grown, took on a hue
Fierce and sanguineous as 'twas possible
In one whose brow had no dark veins to swell.
Fine was the mitigated fury, like
Apollo's presence when in act to strike
The serpent — Ha ! the serpent ! certes, she
Was none. She burnt, she loved the tyranny,
And, all subdued, consented to the hour
When to the bridal he should lead his paramour.
Whispering in midnight silence, said the youth,
" Sure some sweet name thou hast, though, by my
    truth,
I have not ask'd it, ever thinking thee
Not mortal, but of heavenly progeny,

As still I do.   Hast any mortal name,
Fit appellation for this dazzling frame ?
Or friends or kinsfolk on the citied earth,
To share our marriage feast and nuptial mirth ?"
" I have no friends," said Lamia, " no, not one ;
My presence in wide Corinth hardly known ·
My parents' bones are in their dusty urns
Sepulchred, where no kindled incense burns,
Seeing all their luckless race are dead, save me,
And I neglect the holy rite for thee.
Even as you list invite your many guests ;
But if, as now it seems, your vision rests
With any pleasure on me, do not bid
Old Apollonius — from him keep me hid."
Lycius, perplex'd at words so blind and blank,
Made close inquiry ; from whose touch she shrank
Feigning a sleep ; and he to the dull shade
Of deep sleep in a moment was betray'd.

It was the custom then to bring away
The bride from home at blushing shut of day,
Veil'd, in a chariot, heralded along
By strewn flowers, torches, and a marriage song,
With other pageants : but this fair unknown
Had not a friend.   So being left alone,
(Lycius was gone to summon all his kin,)
And knowing surely she could never win
His foolish heart from its mad pompousness,
She set herself, high-thoughted, how to dress
The misery in fit magnificence
She did so, but 'tis doubtful how and whence
Came, and who were her subtle servitors.
About the halls, and to and from the doors,
There was a noise of wings, till in short space
The glowing banquet-room shone with wide-arched
          grace.
A haunting music, sole perhaps and lone
Supportress of the faery-roof, made moan

Throughout, as fearful the whole charm might fade
Fresh carved cedar, mimicking a glade
Of palm and plantain, met from either side,
High in the midst, in honour of the bride :
Two palms and then two plantains, and so on
From either side their stems branch'd one to one
All down the aisled place ; and beneath all
There ran a stream of lamps straight on from wall
    to wall.
So canopied, lay an untasted feast
Teeming with odours.   Lamia, regal drest,
Silently paced about, and as she went,
In pale contented sort of discontent,
Mission'd her viewless servants to enrich
The fretted splendour of each nook and niche.
Between the tree-stems marbled plain at first,
Came jasper panels ; then, anon, there burst
Forth creeping imagery of slighter trees,
And with the larger wove in small intricacies.
Approving all, she faded at self-will,
And shut the chamber up, close, hush'd and still,
Complete and ready for the revels rude,
When dreadful guests would come to spoil her soli
    tude.

    The day appear'd, and all the gossip rout.
O senseless Lycius ! Madman ! wherefore flout
The silent-blessing fate, warm cloister'd hours,
And show to common eyes these secret bowers ?
The herd approach'd ; each guest, with busy brain
Arriving at the portal, gazed amain,
And enter'd marvelling : for they knew the street,
Remember'd it from childhood all complete
Without a gap, yet ne'er before had seen
That royal porch, that high-built fair demesne ;
So in they hurried all, mazed, curious and keen
Save one, who look'd thereon with eye severe,
And with calm-planted steps walk'd in austere

'Twas Apollonius: something too he laugh'd,
As though some knotty problem, that had daft
His patient thought, had now begun to thaw,
And solve and melt: — 'twas just as he foresaw.

He met within the murmurous vestibule
His young disciple. " 'Tis no common rule,
Lycius," said he, " for uninvited guest
To force himself upon you, and infest
With an unbidden presence the bright throng
Of younger friends; yet must I do this wrong,
And you forgive me." Lycius blush'd and led
The old man through the inner doors broad-spread
With reconciling words and courteous mien
Turning into sweet milk the sophist's spleen.

Of wealthy lustre was the banquet-room,
Fill'd with pervading brilliance and perfume:
Before each lucid panel fuming stood
A censer fed with myrrh and spiced wood,
Each by a sacred tripod held aloft,
Whose slender feet wide-swerved upon the soft
Wool-woofed carpets: fifty wreaths of smoke
From fifty censers their light voyage took
To the high roof, still mimick'd as they rose
Along the mirror'd walls by twin-clouds odorous.
Twelve sphered tables by silk seats insphered,
High as the level of a man's breast rear'd
On libbard's paws, upheld the heavy gold
Of cups and goblets and the store thrice told
Of Ceres' horn, and, in huge vessels, wine
Came from the gloomy tun with merry shine.
Thus loaded with a feast the tables stood,
Each shrining in the midst the image of a God.

When in an antechamber every guest
Had felt the cold full sponge to pleasure press'd,
By ministering slaves, upon his hands and feet,

And fragrant oils with ceremony meet
Pour'd on his hair, they all moved to the feast
In white robes, and themselves in order placed
Around the silken couches, wondering
Whence all this mighty cost and blaze of wealth
      could spring

    Soft went the music the soft air along,
While fluent Greek a vowel'd under-song
Kept up among the guests, discoursing low
At first, for scarcely was the wine at flow;
But when the happy vintage touch'd their brains,
Louder they talk, and louder come the strains
Of powerful instruments: — the gorgeous dyes,
The space, the splendour of the draperies,
The roof of awful richness, nectarous cheer,
Beautiful slaves, and Lamia's self, appear,
Now, when the wine has done its rosy deed,
And every soul from human trammels freed,
No more so strange; for merry wine, sweet wine,
Will make Elysian shades not too fair, too divine.
Soon was God Bacchus at meridian height;
Flush'd were their cheeks, and bright eyes double
      bright:
Garlands of every green, and every scent
From vales deflower'd, or forest-trees branch-rent,
In baskets of bright osier'd gold were brought
High as the handles heap'd, to suit the thought
Of every guest: that each, as he did please,
Might fancy-fit his brows, silk-pillow'd at his ease.

    What wreath for Lamia? What for Lycius?
What for the sage, old Apollonius?
Upon her aching forehead be there hung
The leaves of willow and of adder's tongue;
And for the youth, quick, let us strip for him
The thyrsus, that his watching eyes may swim
Into forgetfulness; and. for the sage,

Let spear-grass and the spiteful thistle wage
War on his temples. Do not all charms fly
At the mere touch of cold philosophy?
There was an awful rainbow once in heaven:
We know her woof, her texture; she is given
In the dull catalogue of common things.
Philosophy will clip an Angel's wings,
Conquer all mysteries by rule and line,
Empty the haunted air, and gnomed mine —
Unweave a rainbow, as it erewhile made
The tender-person'd Lamia melt into a shade.

By her glad Lycius sitting, in chief place,
Scarce saw in all the room another face,
Till, checking his love trance, a cup he took
Full brimm'd, and opposite sent forth a look
'Cross the broad table, to beseech a glance
From his old teacher's wrinkled countenance,
And pledge him. The bald-head philosopher
Had fix'd his eye, without a twinkle or a stir,
Full on the alarmed beauty of the bride,
Brow-beating her fair form, and troubling her sweet
    pride.
Lycius then press'd her hand, with devout touch,
As pale it lay upon the rosy couch:
'Twas icy, and the cold ran through his veins;
Then sudden it grew hot, and all the pains
Of an unnatural heat shot to his heart.
" Lamia, what means this? Wherefore dost thou
    start?
Know'st thou that man?" Poor Lamia answer'd
    not.
He gazed into her eyes, and not a jot
Own'd they the lovelorn piteous appeal:
More, more he gazed: his human senses reel:
Some hungry spell that loveliness absorbs:
There was no recognition in those orbs
" Lamia!" he cried — and no soft-toned reply.

The many heard, and the loud revelry
Grew hush : the stately music no more breathes ;
The myrtle sicken'd in a thousand wreaths.
By faint degrees, voice, lute, and pleasure ceased ;
A deadly silence step by step increased,
Until it seem'd a horrid presence there,
And not a man but felt the terror in his hair.
" Lamia !" he shriek'd ; and nothing but the shriek
With its sad echo did the silence break.
'' Begone, foul dream !" he cried, gazing again
In the bride's face, where now no azure vein
Wander'd on fair-spaced temples ; no soft bloom
Misted the cheek ; no passion to illume
The deep-recessed vision : — all was blight ;
Lamia, no longer fair, there sat a deadly white.
" Shut, shut those juggling eyes, thou ruthless man
Turn them aside, wretch ! or the righteous ban
Of all the Gods, whose dreadful images
Here represent their shadowy presences,
May pierce them on the sudden with the thorn
Of painful blindness ; leaving thee forlorn,
In trembling dotage to the feeblest fright
Of conscience, for their long-offended might,
For all thine impious proud-heart sophistries,
Unlawful magic, and enticing lies
Corinthians ! look upon that gray-beard wretch !
Mark how, possess'd, his lashless eyelids stretch
Around his demon eyes ! Corinthians, see !
My sweet bride withers at their potency."
" Fool !" said the sophist, in an under-tone
Gruff with contempt ; which a death-nighing moan
From Lycius answer'd, as heart-struck and lost,
He sank supine beside the aching ghost.
" Fool ! Fool !" repeated he, while his eyes still
Relented not, nor moved ; " from every ill
Of life have I preserved thee to this day,
And shall I see thee made a serpent's prey ? "
Then Lamia breathed death-breath ; the sophist's eye,

Like a sharp spear, went through her utterly,
Keen, cruel, perceant, stinging : she, as well
As her weak hand could any meaning tell,
Motion'd him to be silent ; vainly so,
He look'd and look'd again a level — No !
" A serpent ! " echoed he ; no sooner said,
Than with a frightful scream she vanished :
And Lycius' arms were empty of delight,
As were his limbs of life, from that same night.
On the high couch he lay ! — his friends came
       round —
Supported him — no pulse or breath they found,
And, in its marriage robe, the heavy body wound.*

* " Philostratus, in his fourth book, *de Vita Apollonii*, hath
a memorable instance in this kind, which I may not omit, of one
Menippus Lycius, a young man twenty-five years of age, that,
going betwixt Cenchreas and Corinth, met such a phantasm in
the habit of a fair gentlewoman, which, taking him by the hand,
carried him home to her house, in the suburbs of Corinth, and
told him she was a Phœnician by birth, and if he would tarry
with her, he should hear her sing and play, and drink such wine
as never any drank, and no man should molest him : but she,
being fair and lovely, would die with him, that was fair and lovely
to behold. The young man, a philosopher, otherwise staid and
discreet, able to moderate his passions, though not this of love,
tarried with her awhile to his great content, and at last married
her, to whose wedding, amongst other guests, came Apollonius ;
who, by some probable conjectures, found her out to be a serpent,
a lamia ; and that all her furniture was, like Tantalus' gold,
described by Homer, no substance, but mere illusions. When
she saw herself descried, she wept, and desired Apollonius to be
silent, but he would not be moved, and thereupon she, plate,
house, and all that was in it, vanished in an instant ; many thou
sands took notice of this fact, for it was done in the midst of
Greece." — BURTON's *Anatomy of Melancholy*, Part 3, Sect. 2
Memb. I Subs. I

ISABELLA, OR THE POT OF BASIL;

A STORY FROM BOCCACCIO

———◆———

I.

FAIR ISABEL, poor simple Isabel !
  Lorenzo, a young palmer in Love's eye !
 They could not in the self-same mansion dwell
Without some stir of heart, some malady ;
They could not sit at meals but feel how well
  It soothed each to be the other by ;
They could not, sure, beneath the same roof sleep,
But to each other dream, and nightly weep.

II.

With every morn their love grew tenderer,
  With every eve deeper and tenderer still ;
He might not in house, field, or garden stir,
  But her full shape would all his seeing fill ;
And his continual voice was pleasanter
  To her, than noise of trees or hidden rill ;
Her lute-string gave an echo of his name,
She spoilt her half-done broidery with the same.

III.

He knew whose gentle hand was at the latch,
  Before the door had given her to his eyes ;
And from her chamber-window he would catch
  Her beauty farther than the falcon spies ;

And constant as her vespers would he watch,
　Because her face was turn'd to the same skies;
And with sick longing all the night outwear,
To hear her morning-step upon the stair.

IV.

A whole long month of May in this sad plight
　Made their cheeks paler by the break of June
" To-morrow will I bow to my delight,
　To-morrow will I ask my lady 's boon." —
" O may I never see another night,
　Lorenzo, if thy lips breathe not love's tune." -
So spake they to their pillows; but, alas,
Honeyless days and days did he let pass;

V.

Until sweet Isabella's untouch'd cheek
　Fell sick within the rose's just domain,
Fell thin as a young mother's, who doth seek
　By every lull to cool her infant's pain:
" How ill she is!" said he, " I may not speak,
　And yet I will, and tell my love all plain:
If looks speak love-laws, I will drink her tears,
And at the least 'twill startle off her cares."

VI.

So said he one fair morning, and all day
　His heart beat awfully against his side;
And to his heart he inwardly did pray
　For power to speak; but still the ruddy tide
Stifled his voice, and pulsed resolve away —
　Fever'd his high conceit of such a bride,
Yet brought him to the meekness of a child:
Alas! when passion is both meek and wild!

VII.

So once more he had waked and anguished
   A dreary night of love and misery.
If Isabel's quick eye had not been wed
   To every symbol on his forehead high;
She saw it waxing very pale and dead,
   And straight all flush'd; so, lisped tenderly,
"Lorenzo!" — here she ceased her timid quest,
But in her tone and look he read the rest.

VIII.

"O Isabella! I can half perceive
   That I may speak my grief into thine ear,
If thou didst ever anything believe,
   Believe how I love thee, believe how near
My soul is to its doom: I would not grieve
   Thy hand by unwelcome pressing, would not fear
Thine eyes by gazing; but I cannot live
Another night, and not my passion shrive.

IX.

"Love! thou art leading me from wintry cold,
   Lady! thou leadest me to summer clime,
And I must taste the blossoms that unfold
   In its ripe warmth this gracious morning time.'
So said, his erewhile timid lips grew bold,
   And poesied with hers in dewy rhyme:
Great bliss was with them, and great happiness
Grew, like a lusty flower in June's caress.

X.

Parting they seem'd to tread upon the air,
   Twin roses by the zephyr blown apart
Only to meet again more close, and share

The inward fragrance of each other's heart.
She, to her chamber gone, a ditty fair
  Sang, of delicious love and honey'd dart;
He with light steps went up a western hill.
And bade the sun farewell, and joy'd his fill.

XI.

All close they met again, before the dusk
  Had taken from the stars its pleasant veil
All close they met, all eves, before the dusk
  Had taken from the stars its pleasant veil,
Close in a bower of hyacinth and musk,
  Unknown of any, free from whispering tale.
Ah! better had it been for ever so,
Than idle ears should pleasure in their woe.

XII.

Were they unhappy then? — It cannot be —
  Too many tears for lovers have been shed,
Too many sighs give we to them in fee,
  Too much of pity after they are dead,
Too many doleful stories do we see,
  Whose matter in bright gold were best be read
Except in such a page where Theseus' spouse
Over the pathless waves towards him bows.

XIII.

But, for the general award of love,
  The little sweet doth kill much bitterness;
Though Dido silent is in under-grove,
  And Isabella's was a great distress,
Though young Lorenzo in warm Indian clove
  Was not embalm'd, this truth is not the less —
Even bees, the little almsmen of spring-bowers,
Know there is richest juice in poison-flowers.

XIV.

With her two brothers this fair lady dwelt,
　　Enriched from ancestral merchandise,
And for them many a weary hand did swelt
　　In torched mines and noisy factories,
And many once proud-quiver'd loins did melt
　　In blood from stinging whip; with hollow eyes
Many all day in dazzling river stood,
To take the rich-ored driftings of the flood.

XV.

For them the Ceylon diver held his breath,
　　And went all naked to the hungry shark;
For them his ears gush'd blood; for them in death
　　The seal on the cold ice with piteous bark
Lay full of darts; for them alone did seethe
　　A thousand men in troubles wide and dark:
Half-ignorant, they turn'd an easy wheel,
That set sharp racks at work, to pinch and peel.

XVI.

Why were they proud? Because their marble founts
　　Gush'd with more pride than do a wretch's tears?
Why were they proud? Because fair orange-mounts
　　Were of more soft ascent than lazar stairs?
Why were they proud? Because red-lined accounts
　　Were richer than the songs of Grecian years?
Why were they proud? again we ask aloud,
Why in the name of Glory were they proud?

XVII.

Yet were these Florentines as self-retired
　　In hungry pride and gainful cowardice,
As two close Hebrews in that land inspired,

Paled in and vineyarded from beggar-spies;
The hawks of ship-mast forests — the untired
  And pannier'd mules for ducats and old lies —
Quick cat's-paws on the generous stray-away, —
Great wits in Spanish, Tuscan, and Malay.

XVIII.

How was it these same ledger-men could spy
  Fair Isabella in her downy nest?
How could they find out in Lorenzo's eye
  A straying from his toil?   Hot Egypt's pest
Into their vision covetous and sly!
  How could these money-bags see east and west!
Yet so they did — and every dealer fair
Must see behind, as doth the hunted hare.

XIX.

O eloquent and famed Boccaccio!
  Of thee we now should ask forgiving boon,
And of thy spicy myrtles as they blow,
  And of thy roses amorous of the moon,
And of thy lilies, that do paler glow
  Now they can no more hear thy ghittern's tune,
For venturing syllables that ill beseem
The quiet glooms of such a piteous theme.

XX.

Grant thou a pardon here, and then the tale
  Shall move on soberly, as it is meet;
There is no other crime, no mad assail
  To make old prose in modern rhyme more sweet
But it is done — succeed the verse or fail —
  To honour thee, and thy gone spirit greet,
To stead thee as a verse in English tongue,
An echo of thee in the north-wind sung.

XXI

These brethren having found by many signs
  What love Lorenzo for their sister had,
And how she loved him too, each unconfines
  His bitter thoughts to other, well nigh mad
That he, the servant of their trade designs,
  Should in their sister's love be blithe and glad
When 'twas their plan to coax her by degrees
To some high noble and his olive-trees.

XXII.

And many a jealous conference had they,
  And many times they bit their lips alone,
Before they fix'd upon a surest way
  To make the youngster for his crime atone ,
And at the last, these men of cruel clay
  Cut mercy with a sharp knife to the bone.
For they resolved in some forest dim
To kill Lorenzo, and there bury him.

XXIII.

So on a pleasant morning, as he leant
  Into the sun-rise, o'er the balustrade
Of the garden-terrace, towards him they bent
  Their footing through the dews ; and to him said
" You seem there in the quiet of content,
  Lorenzo, and we are most loth to invade
Calm speculation , but if you are wise,
Bestride your steed while cold is in the skies.

XXIV.

" To-day we purpose, ay, this hour we mount
  To spur three leagues towards the Appenine ;

Come down, we pray thee, ere the hot sun count
    His dewy rosary on the eglantine."
Lorenzo, courteously as he was wont,
    Bow'd a fair greeting to these serpents' whine ;
And went in haste, to get in readiness,
With belt, and spur, and bracing huntsman's dress

XXV.

And as he to the court-yard pass'd along,
    Each third step did he pause, and listen'd oft
If he could hear his lady's matin-song,
    Or the light whisper of her footstep soft ;
And as he thus over his passion hung,
    He heard a laugh full musical aloft ;
When, looking up, he saw her features bright
Smile through an in-door lattice all delight.

XXVI.

" Love, Isabel ! " said he, " I was in pain
    Lest I should miss to bid thee a good morrow :
Ah ! what if I should lose thee, when so fain
    I am to stifle all the heavy sorrow
Of a poor three hours' absence ? but we'll gain
    Out of the amorous dark what day doth borrow
Good bye ! I'll soon be back." — "Good bye ! " said
        she
And as he went she chanted merrily.

XXVII.

So the two brothers and their murder'd man
    Rode past fair Florence, to where Arno's stream
Gurgles through straighten'd banks, and still doth
        fan
    Itself with dancing bulrush, and the bream
Keeps head against the freshets.   Sick and wan

12

The brothers' faces in the ford did seem,
Lorenzo's flush with love.   They pass'd the **water**
Into a forest quiet for the slaughter.

XXVIII.

There was Lorenzo slain and buried in,
   There in that forest did his great love cease;
Ah when a soul doth thus its freedom win,
   It aches in loneliness — is ill at peace
As the break-covert bloodhounds of such sin:
   They dipp'd their swords in the water, and did
      tease
Their horses homeward, with convulsed spur,
Each richer by his being a murderer.

XXIX.

They told their sister how, with sudden speed,
   Lorenzo had ta'en ship for foreign lands,
Because of some great urgency and need
   In their affairs, requiring trusty hands.
Poor girl! put on thy stifling widow's weed,
   And 'scape at once from Hope's accursed bands
To-day thou wilt not see him, nor to-morrow,
And the next day will be a day of sorrow.

XXX.

She weeps alone for pleasures not to be;
   Sorely she wept until the night came on,
And then, instead of love, O misery!
   She brooded o'er the luxury alone:
His image in the dusk she seem'd to see,
   And to the silence made a gentle moan,
Spreading her perfect arms upon the air,
And on her couch low murmuring, "Where? O
      where?"

XXXI.

But Selfishness, Love's cousin, held not long
 Its fiery vigil in her single breast ;
She fretted for the golden hour, and hung
 Upon the time with feverish unrest —
Not long ; for soon into her heart a throng
 Of higher occupants, a richer zest,
Came tragic ; passion not to be subdued,
And sorrow for her love in travels rude.

XXXII.

In the mid days of autumn, on their eves
 The breath of Winter comes from far away,
And the sick west continually bereaves
 Of some gold tinge, and plays a roundelay
Of death among the bushes and the leaves,
 To make all bare before he dares to stray
From his north cavern. So sweet Isabel
By gradual decay from beauty fell,

XXXIII.

Because Lorenzo came not. Oftentimes
 She ask'd her brothers, with an eye all pale,
Striving to be itself, what dungeon climes
 Could keep him off so long ? They spake a tale
Time after time, to quiet her. Their crimes
 Came on them, like a smoke from Hinnom's vale ;
And every night in dreams they groan'd aloud,
To see their sister in her snowy shroud.

XXXIV.

And she had died in drowsy ignorance,
 But for a thing more deadly dark than all ,

It came like a fierce potion, drunk by chance,
   Which saves a sick man from the feather'd pall
For some few gasping moments; like a lance,
   Waking an Indian from his cloudy hall
With cruel pierce, and bringing him again
Sense of the gnawing fire at heart and brain.

XXXV.

It was a vision.   In the drowsy gloom,
   The dull of midnight, at her couch's foot
Lorenzo stood, and wept: the forest tomb
   Had marr'd his glossy hair which once could
      shoot
Lustre into the sun, and put cold doom
   Upon his lips, and taken the soft lute
From his lorn voice, and past his loamed ears
Had made a miry channel for his tears.

XXXVI.

Strange sound it was, when the pale shadow spake
   For there was striving, in its piteous tongue,
To speak as when on earth it was awake,
   And Isabella on its music hung:
Languor there was in it, and tremulous shake,
   As in a palsied Druid's harp unstrung;
And through it moan'd a ghostly under-song,
Like hoarse night-gusts sepulchral briars among.

XXXVII.

Its eyes, though wild, were still all dewy bright
   With love, and kept all phantom fear aloof
From the poor girl by magic of their light,
   The while it did unthread the horrid woof
Of the late dark'n'd time — the murderous spite
   Of pride and avarice — the dark pine roof

In the forest — and the sodden turfed dell,
Where, without any word, from stabs he fell

XXXVIII.

Saying moreover, " Isabel, my sweet !
 Red whortleberries droop above my head,
And a large flint-stone weighs upon my feet ;
 Around me beeches and high chestnuts shed
Their leaves and prickly nuts ; a sheepfold bleat
 Comes from beyond the river to my bed :
Go, shed one tear upon my heather-bloom,
And it shall comfort me within the tomb.

XXXIX.

" I am a shadow now, alas ! alas !
 Upon the skirts of human nature dwelling
Alone : I chant alone the holy mass,
 While little sounds of life are round me knell
  ing,
And glossy bees at noon do fieldward pass,
 And many a chapel bell the hour is telling,
Paining me through : those sounds grow strange to
  me,
And thou art distant in Humanity.

XL.

" I know what was, I feel full well what is,
 And I should rage, if spirits could go mad ;
Though I forget the taste of earthly bliss,
 That paleness warms my grave, as though I
  had
A seraph chosen from the bright abyss
 To be my spouse : thy paleness makes me glad
Thy beauty grows upon me, and I feel
A greater love through all my essence steal."

XLI.

The Spirit mourn'd " Adieu ! " — dissolved and left
   The atom darkness in a slow turmoil;
As when of healthful midnight sleep bereft,
   Thinking on rugged hours and fruitless toil,
We put our eyes into a pillowy cleft,
   And see the spangly gloom froth up and boil:
It made sad Isabella's eyelids ache,
And in the dawn she started up awake;

XLII

" Ha ! ha ! " said she, " I knew not this hard life,
   I thought the worst was simple misery;
I thought some Fate with pleasure or with strife
   Portion'd us — happy days, or else to die;
But there is crime — a brother's bloody knife !
   Sweet Spirit, thou hast school'd my infancy:
I'll visit thee for this, and kiss thine eyes,
And greet thee morn and even in the skies."

XLIII.

When the full morning came, she had devised
   How she might secret to the forest hie;
How she might find the clay, so dearly prized,
   And sing to it one latest lullaby;
How her short absence might be unsurmised,
   While she the inmost of the dream would try
Resolved, she took with her an aged nurse,
And went into that dismal forest-hearse.

XLIV.

See, as they creep along the river side,
   How she doth whisper to that aged dame,

And, after looking round the champaign wide,
　Shows her a knife. — " What feverous hectic
　　flame
Burns in thee, child ? — what good can thee betide
　That thou shouldst smile again ?" — The evening
　　came,
And they had found Lorenzo's earthy bed ;
The flint was there, the berries at his head.

XLV.

Who hath not loiter'd in a green churchyard,
　And let his spirit, like a demon mole,
Work through the clayey soil and gravel hard,
　To see skull, coffin'd bones, and funeral stole ;
Pitying each form that hungry Death hath marr'd,
　And filling it once more with human soul ?
Ah ! this is holiday to what was felt
When Isabella by Lorenzo knelt.

XLVI.

She gazed into the fresh-thrown mould, as though
　One glance did fully all its secrets tell ;
Clearly she saw, as other eyes would know
　Pale limbs at bottom of a crystal well ;
Upon the murderous spot she seem'd to grow,
　Like to a native lily of the dell :
Then with her knife, all sudden she began
To dig more fervently than misers can.

XLVII.

Soon she turn'd up a soiled glove, whereon
　Her silk had play'd in purple phantasies ;
She kiss'd it with a lip more chill than stone,
　And put it in her bosom, where it dries
And freezes utterly unto the bone

Those dainties made to still an infant's cries:
Then 'gan she work again; nor stay'd her care,
But to throw back at times her veiling hair.

XLVIII.

That old nurse stood beside her wondering,
   Until her heart felt pity to the core
At sight of such a dismal labouring,
   And so she kneeled, with her locks all hoar,
And put her lean hands to the horrid thing:
   Three hours they labour'd at this travail sore,
At last they felt the kernel of the grave,
And Isabella did not stamp and rave.

XLIX.

Ah! wherefore all this wormy circumstance?
   Why linger at the yawning tomb so long?
O for the gentleness of old Romance,
   The simple plaining of a minstrel's song!
Fair reader, at the old tale take a glance,
   For here, in truth, it doth not well belong
To speak:— O turn thee to the very tale,
And taste the music of that vision pale.

L.

With duller steel than the Persèan sword
   They cut away no formless monster's head,
But one, whose gentleness did well accord
   With death, as life. The ancient harps have said,
Love never dies, but lives, immortal Lord:
   If Love impersonate was ever dead,
Pale Isabella kiss'd it, and low moan'd
'Twas love; cold,— dead indeed, but not dethron d

LI.

In anxious secrecy they took it home,
  And then the prize was all for Isabel:
She calm'd its wild hair with a golden comb,
  And all around each eye's sepulchral cell
Pointed each fringed lash; the smeared loam
  With tears, as chilly as a dripping well,
She drench'd away: and still she comb'd and kept
Sighing all day — and still she kiss'd and wept.

LII.

Then in a silken scarf, — sweet with the dews
  Of precious flowers pluck'd in Araby,
And divine liquids come with odorous ooze
  Through the cold serpent-pipe refreshfully, —
She wrapp'd it up; and for its tomb did choose
  A garden-pot, wherein she laid it by,
And cover'd it with mould, and o'er it set
Sweet Basil, which her tears kept ever wet.

LIII.

And she forgot the stars, the moon, and sun,
  And she forgot the blue above the trees,
And she forgot the dells where waters run,
  And she forgot the chilly autumn breeze;
She had no knowledge when the day was done,
  And the new morn she saw not: but in peace
Hung over her sweet Basil evermore,
And moisten'd it with tears unto the core.

LIV.

And so she ever fed it with thin tears,
  Whence thick, and green, and beautiful it grew,

So that it smelt more balmy than its peers
  Of Basil-tufts in Florence; for it drew
Nurture besides, and life, from human fears,
  From the fast mouldering head there shut from
      view:
So that the jewel, safely casketed,
Came forth, and in perfumed leaflets spread.

LV.

O Melancholy, linger here awhile!
  O Music, Music, breathe despondingly!
O Echo, Echo, from some sombre isle,
  Unknown, Lethean, sigh to us — O sigh!
Spirits in grief, lift up your heads, and smile;
  Lift up your heads, sweet Spirits, heavily,
And make a pale light in your cypress glooms,
Tinting with silver wan your marble tombs.

LVI.

Moan hither, all ye syllables of woe,
  From the deep throat of sad Melpomene!
Through bronzed lyre in tragic order go,
  And touch the strings into a mystery;
Sound mournfully upon the winds and low;
  For simple Isabel is soon to be
Among the dead: She withers, like a palm
Cut by an Indian for his juicy balm.

LVII.

O leave the palm to wither by itself;
  Let not quick Winter chill its dying hour! —
It may not be — those Baälites of pelf,
  Her brethren, noted the continual shower
From her dead eyes; and many a curious elf,
  Among her kindred, wonder'd that such dower

Of youth and beauty should be thrown aside
By one mark'd out to be a Noble's bride.

LVIII

And, furthermore, her brethren wonder'd much
   Why she sat drooping by the Basil green,
And why it flourish'd, as by magic touch;
   Greatly they wonder'd what the thing might
      mean ·
They could not surely give belief. that such
   A very nothing would have power to wean
Her from her own fair youth, and pleasures gay,
And even remembrance of her love's delay.

LIX.

Therefore they watch'd a time when they might sift
   This hidden whim; and long they watch'd in vain
For seldom did she go to chapel-shrift,
   And seldom felt she any hunger-pain:
And when she left, she hurried back, as swift
   As bird on wing to breast its eggs again:
And, patient as a hen-bird, sat her there
Beside her Basil, weeping through her hair

LX.

Yet they contrived to steal the Basil-pot,
   And to examine it in secret place:
The thing was vile with green and livid spot,
   And yet they knew it was Lorenzo's face:
The guerdon of their murder they had got,
   And so left Florence in a moment's space,
Never to turn again. — Away they went,
With blood upon their heads, to banishment

LXI.

O Melancholy, turn thine eyes away !
  O Music, Music, breathe despondingly !
O Echo, Echo, on some other day,
  From isles Lethean, sigh to us — O sigh !
Spirits of grief, sing not your " Well-a-way ! "
  For Isabel, sweet Isabel, will die ;
Will die a death too lone and incomplete,
Now they have ta'en away her Basil sweet.

LXII.

Piteous she look'd on dead and senseless things,
  Asking for her lost Basil amorously :
And with melodious chuckle in the strings
  Of her lorn voice, she oftentimes would cry
After the Pilgrim in his wanderings,
  To ask him where her Basil was ; and why
'Twas hid from her : " For cruel 'tis," said she,
" To steal my Basil-pot away from me."

LXIII.

And so she pined, and so she died forlorn,
  Imploring for her Basil to the last.
No heart was there in Florence but did mourn
  In pity of her love, so overcast.
And a sad ditty of this story borne
  From mouth to mouth through all the country
      pass'd :
Still is the burthen sung — " O cruelty,
To steal my Basil-pot away from me ! "

THE EVE OF ST. AGNES.

I.

ST. AGNES' EVE — Ah, bitter chill it was
The owl, for all his feathers, was a-cold;
The hare limp'd trembling through the frozen
    grass,
And silent was the flock in woolly fold:
Numb were the Beadsman's fingers while he told
His rosary, and while his frosted breath,
Like pious incense from a censer old,
Seem'd taking flight for heaven without a death,
Past the sweet Virgin's picture, while his prayer he
    saith.

II.

His prayer he saith, this patient, holy man;
Then takes his lamp, and riseth from his knees,
And back returneth, meagre, barefoot, wan,
Along the chapel aisle by slow degrees:
The sculptured dead, on each side seem to freeze,
Emprison'd in black, purgatorial rails:
Knights, ladies, praying in dumb orat'ries,
He passeth by; and his weak spirit fails
To think how they may ache in icy hoods and mails.

III.

Northward he turneth through a little door,
And scarce three steps, ere Music's golden tongue
Flatter'd to tears this aged man and poor;
But no — already had his death-bell rung;

The joys of all his life were said and sung.
His was harsh penance on St. Agnes' Eve:
Another way he went, and soon among
Rough ashes sat he for his soul's reprieve,
And all night kept awake, for sinner's sake to grieve

IV.

That ancient Beadsman heard the prelude soft ;
And so it chanced, for many a door was wide,
From hurry to and fro.   Soon, up aloft,
The silver, snarling trumpets 'gan to chide :
The level chambers, ready with their pride,
Were glowing to receive a thousand guests :
The carved angels, ever eager-eyed,
Stared, where upon their heads the cornice rests,
With hair blown back, and wings put cross-wise on
        their breasts.

V

At length burst in the argent revelry,
With plume, tiara, and all rich array,
Numerous as shadows haunting fairily
The brain, new-stuff'd, in youth, with triumpas
        gay
Of old romance.   These let us wish away,
And turn, sole-thoughted, to one Lady there,
Whose heart had brooded, all that wintry day,
On love, and wing'd St. Agnes' saintly care,
As she had heard old dames full many times declare

VI.

They told her how, upon St. Agnes' Eve,
Young virgins might have visions of delight,
And soft adorings from their loves receive
Upon the honev'd middle of the night,

If ceremonies due they did aright ;
As, supperless to bed they must retire,
And couch supine their beauties, lily white ;
Nor look behind, nor sideways, but require
Of Heaven with upward eyes for all that they desire

VII.

Full of this whim was thoughtful Madeline :
The music, yearning like a God in pain,
She scarcely heard : her maiden eyes divine,
Fix'd on the floor, saw many a sweeping train
Pass by — she heeded not at all : in vain
Came many a tiptoe, amorous cavalier,
And back retired ; not cool'd by high disdain,
But she saw not : her heart was otherwhere ;
She sigh'd for Agnes' dreams, the sweetest of the
    year.

VIII.

She danced along with vague, regardless eyes,
Anxious her lips, her breathing quick and short :
The hallow'd hour was near at hand : she sighs
Amid the timbrels, and the throng'd resort
Of whisperers in anger, or in sport ;
'Mid looks of love, defiance, hate, and scorn,
Hoodwink'd with faery fancy ; all amort,
Save to St. Agnes and her lambs unshorn,
And all the bliss to be before to-morrow morn.

IX.

So, purposing each moment to retire,
She linger'd still. Meantime, across the moors,
Had come young Porphyro, with heart on fire
For Madeline. Beside the portal doors,
Buttress'd from moonlight, stands he, and implores
All saints to give him sight of Madeline,

But for one moment in the tedious hours,
　That he might gaze and worship all unseen ;
Perchance speak, kneel, touch, kiss — in sooth such
　　　things have been.

X.

He ventures in : let no huzz'd whisper tell :
All eyes be muffled, or a hundred swords
Will storm his heart, Love's feverous citadel :
For him, those chambers held barbarian hordes
Hyena foemen, and hot-blooded lords,
Whose very dogs would execrations howl
Against his lineage : not one breast affords
Him any mercy, in that mansion foul,
Save one old beldame, weak in body and in soul.

XI.

Ah, happy chance ! the aged creature came,
Shuffling along with ivory-headed wand,
To where he stood, hid from the torch's flame,
Behind a broad hall-pillar, far beyond
The sound of merriment and chorus bland :
He startled her ; but soon she knew his face,
And grasp'd his fingers in her palsied hand,
Saying, " Mercy, Porphyro ! hie thee from this
　　　place ;
They are all here to-night, the whole blood-thirsty
　　　race !

XII.

" Get hence ! get hence ! there's dwarfish Hilde
　　　brand ,
He had a fever late, and in the fit
He cursed thee and thine, both nouse and land :
Then there's that old Lord Maurice, not a whit
More tame for his gray hairs — Alas me ! flit !

Flit like a ghost away." — "Ah, Gossip dear,
We're safe enough ; here in this arm-chair sit,
And tell me how " — " Good Saints ! not here,
    not here ;
Follow me, child, or else these stones will be thy
    bier."

XIII.

He follow'd through a lowly arched way,
Brushing the cobwebs with his lofty plume
And as she mutter'd " Well-a — well-a-day !"
He found him in a little moonlight room,
Pale, latticed, chill, and silent as a tomb.
" Now tell me where is Madeline," said he,
" O tell me, Angela, by the holy loom
Which none but secret sisterhood may see,
When they St. Agnes' wool are weaving piously'

XIV.

" St. Agnes ! Ah ! it is St. Agnes' Eve —
Yet men will murder upon holy days:
Thou must hold water in a witch's sieve,
And be liege-lord of all the Elves and Fays,
To venture so : it fills me with amaze
To see thee, Porphyro ! St. Agnes' Eve !
God's help ! my lady fair the conjurer plays
This very night : good angels her deceive !
But let me laugh awhile, I 've mickle time to grieve

XV.

Feebly she laugheth in the languid moon,
While Porphyro upon her face doth look,
Like puzzled urchin on an aged crone
Who keepeth closed a wondrous riddle-book,
As spectacled she sits in chimney nook.
But soon his eyes grew brilliant, when she told

His lady's purpose; and he scarce could brook
Tears, at the thought of those enchantments cold
And Madeline asleep in lap of legends old.

XVI.

Sudden a thought came like a full-blown rose,
Flushing his brow, and in his pained heart
Made purple riot: then doth he propose
A stratagem, that makes the beldame start:
"A cruel man and impious thou art:
Sweet lady, let her pray, and sleep and dream
Alone with her good angels, far apart
From wicked men like thee　　Go, Go! I deem
Thou canst not surely be the same that thou didst
　　seem."

XVII.

"I will not harm her, by all saints I swear,"
Quoth Porphyro: "O may I ne'er find grace
When my weak voice shall whisper its last
　　prayer,
If one of her soft ringlets I displace,
Or look with ruffian passion in her face:
Good Angela, believe me by these tears;
Or I will, even in a moment's space,
Awake, with horrid shout, my foemen's ears,
And beard them, though they be more fang'd than
　　wolves and bears."

XVIII.

"Ah! why wilt thou affright a feeble soul?
A poor, weak, palsy-stricken, church-yard thing,
Whose passing-bell may ere the midnight toll;
Whose prayers for thee, each morn and evening,
Were never miss'd." Thus plaining, doth she
　　bring

A gentler speech from burning Porphyro;
So woful, and of such deep sorrowing,
That Angela gives promise she will do
Whatever he shall wish, betide her weal or woe.

XIX.

Which was, to lead him, in close secrecy,
Even to Madeline's chamber, and there hide
Him in a closet, of such privacy
That he might see her beauty unespied,
And win perhaps that night a peerless bride,
While legion'd fairies paced the coverlet,
And pale enchantment held her sleepy-eyed.
Never on such a night have lovers met,
Since Merlin paid his Demon all the monstrous debt.

XX.

"It shall be as thou wishest," said the Dame:
"All cates and dainties shall be stored there
Quickly on this feast-night: by the tambour
    frame
Her own lute thou wilt see: no time to spare,
For I am slow and feeble, and scarce dare
On such a catering trust my dizzy head.
Wait here, my child, with patience kneel in
    prayer
The while: Ah! thou must needs the lady wed,
Or may I never leave my grave among the dead."

XXI.

So saying she hobbled off with busy fear.
The lover's endless minutes slowly pass'd;
The Dame return'd, and whisper'd in his ear
To follow her; with aged eyes aghast
From fright of dim espial.   Safe at last,

Through many a dusky gallery, they gain
The maiden's chamber, silken, hush'd and chaste
Where Porphyro took covert, pleased amain.
His poor guide hurried back with agues in her
    brain.

XXII.

Her faltering hand upon the balustrade,
Old Angela was feeling for the stair,
When Madeline, St Agnes' charmed maid,
Rose, like a mission'd spirit, unaware ·
With silver taper's light, and pious care,
She turn'd, and down the aged gossip led
To a safe level matting. Now prepare,
Young Porphyro, for gazing on that bed ;
She comes, she comes again, like ring-dove fray'd
    and fled.

XXIII.

Out went the taper as she hurried in ;
Its little smoke, in pallid moonshine, died :
She closed the door, she panted, all akin
To spirits of the air, and visions wide.
No utter'd syllable, or, woe betide !
But to her heart, her heart was voluble,
Paining with eloquence her balmy side ;
As though a tongueless nightingale should swell
Her throat in vain, and die, heart-stifled in her dell

XXIV.

A casement high and triple arch'd there was,
All garlanded with carven imageries
Of fruits, and flowers, and bunches of knot-grass
And diamonded with panes of quaint device,
Innumerable of stains and splendid dyes,
As are the tiger-moth's deep-damask'd wings ;
And in the midst, 'mong thousand heraldries,

And twilight saints, and dim emblazonings,
A shielded scutcheon blush'd with blood of queens
    and kings.

XXV.

Full on this casement shone the wintry moon,
And threw warm gules on Madeline's fair breast,
As down she knelt for heaven's grace and boon;
Rose-bloom fell on her hands, together prest,
And on her silver cross soft amethyst,
And on her hair a glory, like a saint:
She seem'd a splendid angel, newly drest,
    Save wings, for heaven: Porphyro grew faint:
She knelt, so pure a thing, so free from mortal
    taint.

XXVI.

Anon his heart revives. her vespers done,
Of all its wreathed pearls her hair she frees;
Unclasps her warmed jewels one by one;
Loosens her fragrant bodice; by degrees
Her rich attire creeps rustling to her knees:
Half-hidden, like a mermaid in sea-weed,
Pensive awhile she dreams awake, and sees,
    In fancy, fair St. Agnes in her bed,
But dares not look behind, or all the charm is fled.

XXVII.

Soon, trembling in her soft and chilly nest,
In sort of wakeful swoon, perplex'd she lay,
Until the poppied warmth of sleep oppress'd
Her soothed limbs, and soul fatigued away;
Flown, like a thought, until the morrow-day;
Blissfully haven'd both from joy and pain;
Clasp'd like a missal where swart Paynims pray
    Blinded alike from sunshine and from rain,
As though a rose should shut, and be a bud again

XXVIII.

Stolen to this paradise, and so entranced,
Porphyro gazed upon her empty dress,
And listen'd to her breathing, if it chanced
To wake into a slumberous tenderness;
Which when he heard, that minute did he bless,
And breathed himself: then from the closet
    crept,
Noiseless as fear in a wide wilderness
And over the hush'd carpet, silent, stept,
And 'tween the curtains peep'd, where, lo!—how
    fast she slept.

XXIX.

Then by the bed-side, where the faded moon
Made a dim, silver twilight, soft he set
A table, and, half anguish'd, threw thereon
A cloth of woven crimson, gold, and jet:—
O for some drowsy Morphean amulet!
The boisterous, midnight, festive clarion,
The kettle-drum, and far-heard clarionet,
Affray his ears, though but in dying tone:—
The hall-door shuts again, and all the noise is gone

'XXX.

And still she slept an azure-lidded sleep,
In blanched linen, smooth, and lavender'd,
While he from forth the closet brought a heap
Of candied apple, quince, and plum, and gourd
With jellies soother than the creamy curd,
And lucent syrops, tinct with cinnamon;
Manna and dates, in argosy transferr'd
From Fez; and spiced dainties, every one,
From silken Samarcand to cedar'd Lebanon.

XXXI.

These delicates he heap'd with glowing **hand**
On golden dishes and in baskets bright
Of wreathed silver : sumptuous they **stand**
In the retired quiet of the night,
Filling the chilly room with perfume light. —
"And now, my love, my seraph fair awake !
Thou art my heaven, and I thine eremite :
Open thine eyes, for meek St. Agnes' sake,
Or I shall drowse beside thee, so my soul **doth**
     ache."

XXXII.

Thus whispering, his warm, unnerved **arm**
Sank in her pillow.   Shaded was her **dream**
By the dusk curtains : — 'twas a midnight **charm**
Impossible to melt as iced stream :
The lustrous salvers in the moonlight **gleam ;**
Broad golden fringe upon the carpet **lies :**
It seem'd he never, never could redeem
From such a steadfast spell his lady's **eyes ;**
So mused awhile, entoil'd in woofed phant~~asies.~~

XXXIII.

Awakening up, he took her hollow lute, —
Tumultuous, — and, in chords that tenderest **be,**
He play'd an ancient ditty, long since mute,
In Provence call'd " La belle dame sans mercy : "
Close to her ear touching the melody ; —
Wherewith disturb'd, she utter'd a soft moan :
He ceased — she panted quick — and **suddenly**
Her blue affrayed eyes wide open shone :
Upon his knees he sank, pale as smooth-sculpt~~ured~~
    ~~stone.~~

XXXIV.

Her eyes were open, but she still beheld,
Now wide awake, the vision of her sleep :
There was a painful change, that nigh expell'd
The blisses of her dream so pure and deep.
At which fair Madeline began to weep,
And moan forth witless words with many a sigh
While still her gaze on Porphyro would keep,
Who knelt, with joined hands and piteous eye,
Fearing to move or speak, she look'd so dream
    ingly.

XXXV

"Ah, Porphyro !" said she, " but even now
Thy voice was at sweet tremble in mine ear,
Made tuneable with every sweetest vow;
And those sad eyes were spiritual and clear.
How changed thou art! how pallid, chill, and
    drear !
Give me that voice again, my Porphyro,
Those looks immortal, those complainings dear!
Oh leave me not in this eternal woe,
For if thou diest, my Love, I know not where to
    go."

XXXVI.

Beyond a mortal man impassion'd far
At these voluptuous accents, he arose,
Ethereal, flush'd, and like a throbbing star
Seen 'mid the sapphire heaven's deep repose :
Into her dream he melted, as the rose
Blendeth its odour with the violet, —
Solution sweet : meantime the frost-wind blows
Like Love's alarum pattering the sharp sleet
Against the window-panes; St. Agnes' moon hath
    set.

XXXVII.

'Tis dark: quick pattereth the flaw-blown sleet
" This is no dream, my bride, my Madeline!"
'Tis dark: the iced gusts still rave and beat:
" No dream, alas! alas! and woe is mine!
Porphyro will leave me here to fade and pine. —
Cruel! what traitor could thee hither bring?
I curse not, for my heart is lost in thine,
Though thou forsakest a deceived thing; —
A dove forlorn and lost with sick unpruned wing "

XXXVIII.

" My Madeline! sweet dreamer! lovely bride
Say, may I be for aye thy vassal blest?
Thy beauty's shield, heart-shaped and vermeil
    dyed?
Ah, silver shrine, here will I take my rest
After so many hours of toil and quest,
A famish'd pilgrim, — saved by miracle.
Though I have found, I will not rob thy nest
Saving of thy sweet self; if thou think'st well
To trust, fair Madeline, to no rude infidel."

XXXIX.

" Hark! 'tis an elfin storm from faery land,
Of haggard seeming, but a boon indeed:
Arise — arise! the morning is at hand; —
The bloated wassailers will never heed:
Let us away, my love, with happy speed;
There are no ears to hear, or eyes to see, —
Drown'd all in Rhenish and the sleepy mead:
Awake! arise! my love, and fearless be,
For o'er the southern moors I have a home for
    thee."

XL.

She hurried at his words, beset with fears,
For there were sleeping dragons all around,
At glaring watch, perhaps, with ready spears —
Down the wide stairs a darkling way they found,
In all the house was heard no human sound.
A chain-droop'd lamp was flickering by each
    door ;
The arras, rich with horseman, hawk, and hound,
Flutter'd in the besieging wind's uproar ;
And the long carpets rose along the gusty floor.

XLI.

They glide, like phantoms, into the wide hall !
Like phantoms to the iron porch they glide,
Where lay the Porter, in uneasy sprawl,
With a huge empty flagon by his side :
The wakeful bloodhound rose, and shook his hide,
But his sagacious eye an inmate owns :
By one, and one, the bolts full easy slide : —
The chains lie silent on the footworn stones ;
The key turns, and the door upon its hinges groans

XLII.

And they are gone : ay, ages long ago
These lovers fled away into the storm.
That night the Baron dreamt of many a woe,
And all his warrior-guests, with shade and form
Of witch, and demon, and large coffin-worm,
Were long be-nightmared.   Angela the old
Died palsy-twitch'd, with meagre face deform,
The Beadsman, after thousand aves told,
For aye unsought-for slept among his ashes cold

HYPERION.

————◆————

BOOK I.

DEEP in the shady sadness of a vale
  Far sunken from the healthy breath of morn,
   Far from the fiery noon, and eve's one star,
Sat gray-hair'd Saturn, quiet as a stone,
Still as the silence round about his lair,
Forest on forest hung about his head
Like cloud on cloud. No stir of air was there,
Not so much life as on a summer's day
Robs not one light seed from the feather'd grass,
But where the dead leaf fell, there did it rest.
A stream went voiceless by, still deaden'd more
By reason of his fallen divinity
Spreading a shade . the Naiad 'mid her reeds
Press'd her cold finger closer to her lips.

  Along the margin-sand large foot-marks went,
No further than to where his feet had stray'd,
And slept there since. Upon the sodden ground
His old right hand lay nerveless, listless, dead,
Unsceptred ; and his realmless eyes were closed ;
While his bow'd head seem'd listening to the Earth,
His ancient mother, for some comfort yet.

  It seem'd no force could wake him from his place
But there came one, who with a kindred hand
Touch'd his wide shoulders, after bending low
With reverence, though to one who knew it not
She was a Goddess of the infant world,

By her in stature the tall Amazon
Had stood a pigmy's height. she would have ta'en
Achilles by the hair and bent his neck ;
Or with a finger stay'd Ixion's wheel.
Her face was large as that of Memphian sphinx,
Pedestall'd haply in a palace-court,
When sages look'd to Egypt for their lore.
But oh how unlike marble was that face :
How beautiful, if sorrow had not made
Sorrow more beautiful than Beauty's self.
There was a listening fear in her regard,
As if calamity had but begun ,
As if the vanward clouds of evil days
Had spent their malice, and the sullen rear
Was with its stored thunder labouring up.
One hand she press'd upon that aching spot
Where beats the human heart, as if just there,
Though an immortal, she felt cruel pain :
The other upon Saturn's bended neck
She laid, and to the level of his ear
Leaning with parted lips, some words she spake
In solemn tenour and deep organ tone :
Some mourning words, which in our feeble tongue
Would come in these like accents ; O how frail
To that large utterance of the early Gods !
" Saturn, look up ! — though wherefore, poor old
     King ?
I have no comfort for thee, no not one :
I cannot say, ' O wherefore sleepest thou ?'
For heaven is parted from thee, and the earth
Knows thee not, thus afflicted, for a God ;
And ocean too, with all its solemn noise,
Has from thy sceptre pass'd ; and all the air
Is emptied of thine hoary majesty.
Thy thunder, conscious of the new command,
Rumbles reluctant o'er our fallen house ,
And thy sharp lightning in unpractised hands
Scorches and burns our once serene domain.

O aching time ! O moments big as years !
All as ye pass swell out the monstrous truth
And press it so upon our weary griefs
That unbelief has not a space to breathe
Saturn, sleep on . — O thoughtless, why did I
Thus violate thy slumbrous solitude ?
Why should I ope thy melancholy eyes ?
Saturn, sleep on ! while at thy feet I weep.

As when, upon a tranced summer-night,
Those green-robed senators of mighty woods,
Tall oaks, branch-charmed by the earnest stars,
Dream, and so dream all night without a stir,
Save from one gradual solitary gust
Which comes upon the silence, and dies off,
As if the ebbing air had but one wave :
So came these words and went ; the while in tears
She touch'd her fair large forehead to the ground,
Just where her falling hair might be outspread
A soft and silken mat for Saturn's feet.
One moon, with alteration slow, had shed
Her silver seasons four upon the night,
And still these two were postured motionless,
Like natural sculpture in cathedral cavern ;
The frozen God still couchant on the earth,
And the sad Goddess weeping at his feet :
Until at length old Saturn lifted up
His faded eyes, and saw his kingdom gone,
And all the gloom and sorrow of the place,
And that fair kneeling Goddess ; and then spake,
As with a palsied tongue, and while his beard
Shook horrid with such aspen-malady :
" O tender spouse of gold Hyperion,
Thea, I feel thee ere I see thy face ;
Look up, and let me see our doom in it ;
Look up, and tell me if this feeble shape
Is Saturn's ; tell me, if thou hear'st the voice
Of Saturn ; tell me, if this wrinkling brow,

Naked and bare of its great diadem,
Peers like the front of Saturn.   Who had power
To make me desolate ? whence came the strength ?
How was it nurtured to such bursting forth,
While Fate seem'd strangled in my nervous grasp ?
But it is so , and I am smother'd up,
And buried from all godlike exercise
Of influence benign on planets pale,
Of admonitions to the winds and seas,
Of peaceful sway above man's harvesting,
And all those acts which Deity supreme
Doth ease its heart of love in.   I am gone
Away from my own bosom: I-have left
My strong identity, my real self,
Somewhere between the throne, and where I sit
Here on this spot of earth.   Search, Thea, search !
Open thine eyes eterne, and sphere them round
Upon all space: space starr'd, and lorn of light:
Space region'd with life-air, and barren void;
Spaces of fire, and all the yawn of hell.
Search, Thea, search ! and tell me if thou seest
A certain shape or shadow, making way
With wings or chariot fierce to repossess
A heaven he lost erewhile: it must — it must
Be of ripe progress — Saturn must be king.
Yes, there must be a golden victory;
There must be Gods thrown down, and trumpets
        blown
Of triumph calm, and hymns of festival
Upon the gold clouds metropolitan,
Voices of soft proclaim, and silver stir
Of strings in hollow shells; and there shall be
Beautiful things made new, for the surprise
Of the sky-children; I will give command.
Thea! Thea! Thea! where is Saturn ? "

    This passion lifted him upon his feet,
And made his hands to struggle in the air,

His Druid locks to shake and ooze with sweat,
His eyes to fever out, his voice to cease.
He stood, and heard not Thea's sobbing deep;
A little time, and then again he snatch'd
Utterance thus: — " But cannot I create ?
Cannot I form ?   Cannot I fashion forth
Another world, another universe,
To overbear and crumble this to nought ?
Where is another chaos ?   Where ? "   That word
Found way unto Olympus, and made quake
The rebel three.   Thea was startled up,
And in her bearing was a sort of hope,
As thus she quick-voiced spake, yet full of awe.

" This cheers our fallen house : come to our
        friends,
O Saturn ! come away, and give them heart ;
I know the covert, for thence came I hither."
Thus brief ; then with beseeching eyes she went
With backward footing through the shade a space
He follow'd, and she turn'd to lead the way
Through aged boughs, that yielded like the mist
Which eagles cleave, upmounting from their nest.

Meanwhile in other realms big tears were shed,
More sorrow like to this, and such like woe,
Too huge for mortal tongue or pen of scribe :
The Titans fierce, self-hid, or prison-bound,
Groan'd for the old allegiance once more,
And listen'd in sharp pain for Saturn's voice.
But one of the whole mammoth-brood still kept
His sovereignty, and rule, and majesty ;
Blazing Hyperion on his orbed fire
Still sat, still snuff'd the incense, teeming up
From man to the sun's God, yet unsecure :
For as among us mortals omens drear
Fright and perplex, so also shudder'd he,
Not at dog's howl, or gloom-bird's hated screech,

Or the familiar visiting of one
Upon the first toll of his passing-bell,
Or prophesyings of the midnight lamp ;
But horrors, portion'd to a giant nerve,
Oft made Hyperion ache.   His palace bright,
Bastion'd with pyramids of glowing gold,
And touch'd with shade of bronzed obelisks,
Glared a blood-red through all its thousand courts,
Arches, and domes, and fiery galleries ;
And all its curtains of Aurorian clouds
Flush'd angerly : while sometimes eagles' wings,
Unseen before by Gods or wondering men,
Darken'd the place ; and neighing steeds were
        heard,
Not heard before by Gods or wondering men.
Also, when he would taste the spicy wreaths
Of incense, breathed aloft from sacred hills,
Instead of sweets, his ample palate took
Savour of poisonous brass and metal sick :
And so, when harbour'd in the sleepy west,
After the full completion of fair day,
For rest divine upon exalted couch,
And slumber in the arms of melody,
He paced away the pleasant hours of ease
With stride colossal, on from hall to hall ;
While far within each aisle and deep recess,
His winged minions in close clusters stood,
Amazed and full of fear ; like anxious men
Who on wide plains gather in panting troops,
When earthquakes jar their battlements and
        towers.
Even now, while Saturn, roused from icy trance,
Went step for step with Thea through the woods,
Hyperion, leaving twilight in the rear,
Came slope upon the threshold of the west ;
Then, as was wont, his palace-door flew ope
In smoothed silence, save what solemn tubes,
Blown by the serious Zephyrs, gave of sweet

And wandering sounds. slow-breathed melodies
And like a rose in vermeil tint and shape,
In fragrance soft, and coolness to the eye,
That inlet to severe magnificence
Stood full blown, for the God to enter in.

He enter'd, but he enter'd full of wrath;
His flaming robes stream'd out beyond his heels,
And gave a roar, as if of earthly fire,
That scared away the meek ethereal Hours
And made their dove-wings tremble   On he flared,
From stately nave to nave, from vault to vault,
Through bowers of fragrant and enwreathed light,
And diamond-paved lustrous long arcades,
Until he reach'd the great main cupola;
There standing fierce beneath, he stampt his foot,
And from the basements deep to the high towers
Jarr'd his own golden region; and before
The quavering thunder thereupon had ceased,
His voice leapt out, despite of godlike curb,
To this result: "O dreams of day and night!
O monstrous forms!   O effigies of pain!
O spectres busy in a cold, cold gloom!
O lank-ear'd Phantoms of black-weeded pools!
Why do I know ye? why have I seen ye? **why**
Is my eternal essence thus distraught
To see and to behold these horrors new?
Saturn is fallen, am I too to fall?
Am I to leave this haven of my rest,
This cradle of my glory, this soft clime,
This calm luxuriance of blissful light,
These crystalline pavilions, and pure fanes,
Of all my lucent empire?   It is left
Deserted, void, nor any haunt of mine.
The blaze, the splendour, and the symmetry,
I cannot see — but darkness, death and **darkness**
Even here, into my centre of repose,
The shady visions come to domineer,

14

Insult, and blind, and stifle up my pomp —
Fall! — No, by Tellus and her briny robes!
Over the fiery frontier of my realms
I will advance a terrible right arm
Shall scare that infant thunderer, rebel Jove,
And bid old Saturn take his throne again "
He spake, and ceased, the while a heavier threa'
Held struggle with his throat, but came not forth
For as in theatres of crowded men
Hubbub increases more they call out " Hush ."
So at Hyperion's words the Phantoms pale
Bestirr'd themselves, thrice horrible and cold ;
And from the mirror'd level where he stood
A mist arose, as from a scummy marsh.
At this, through all his bulk an agony
Crept gradual, from the feet unto the crown,
Like a lithe serpent vast and muscular
Making slow way, with head and neck convulsed
From over-strained might.   Released, he fled
To the eastern gates, and full six dewy hours
Before the dawn in season due should blush,
He breathed fierce breath against the sleepy
        portals,
Clear'd them of heavy vapours, burst them wide
Suddenly on the ocean's chilly streams.
The planet orb of fire, whereon he rode
Each day from east to west the heavens through,
Spun round in sable curtaining of clouds;
Not therefore veiled quite, blindfold, and hid,
But ever and anon the glancing spheres,
Circles, and arcs, and broad-belting colure,
Glow'd through, and wrought upon the muffling dark
Sweet-shaped lightnings from the nadir deep
Up to the zenith — hieroglyphics old,
Which sages and keen-eyed astrologers
Then living on the earth, with labouring thought
Won from the gaze of many centuries:
Now lost, save what we find on remnants huge

Of stone, or marble swart; their import gone,
Their wisdom long since fled   Two wings this orb
Possess'd for glory, two fair argent wings,
Ever exalted at the God's approach
And now, from forth the gloom their plumes immense
Rose, one by one, till all outspreaded were;
While still the dazzling globe maintain'd eclipsed,
Awaiting for Hyperion's command.
Fain would he have commanded, fain took throne
And bid the day begin, if but for change.
He might not: — No, though a primeval God.
The sacred seasons might not be disturb'd.
Therefore the operations of the dawn
Stay'd in their birth, even as here 'tis told.
Those silver wings expanded sisterly,
Eager to sail their orb; the porches wide
Open'd upon the dusk demesnes of night;
And the bright Titan, frenzied with new woes,
Unused to bend, by hard compulsion bent
His spirit to the sorrow of the time;
And all along a dismal rack of clouds,
Upon the boundaries of day and night,
He stretch'd himself in grief and radiance faint
There as he lay, the Heaven with its stars
Look'd down on him with pity, and the voice
Of Cœlus, from the universal space,
Thus whisper'd low and solemn in his ear:
" O brightest of my children dear, earth-born
And sky-engender'd, Son of Mysteries!
All unrevealed even to the powers
Which met at thy creating! at whose joys
And palpitations sweet, and pleasures soft,
I, Cœlus, wonder how they came and whence;
And at the fruits thereof what shapes they be,
Distinct, and visible; symbols divine,
Manifestations of that beauteous life
Diffused unseen throughout eternal space;
Of these new-form'd art thou, oh brightest child!

Of these, thy brethren and the Goddesses
There is sad feud among ye, and rebellion
Of son against his sire.   I saw him fall,
I saw my first-born tumbled from his throne !
To me his arms were spread, to me his voice
Found way from forth the thunders round his head
Pale wox I, and in vapours hid my face.
Art thou, too, near such doom ? vague fear there is
For I have seen my sons most unlike Gods.
Divine ye were created, and divine
In sad demeanour, solemn, undisturb'd,
Unruffled, like high Gods, ye lived and ruled·
Now I behold in you fear, hope, and wrath;
Actions of rage and passion; even as
I see them, on the mortal world beneath,
In men who die. — This is the grief, O Son !
Sad sign of ruin, sudden dismay, and fall !
Yet do thou strive ; as thou art capable,
As thou canst move about, an evident God,
And canst oppose to each malignant hour
Ethereal presence : — I am but a voice;
My life is but the life of winds and tides, —
No more than winds and tides can I avail: —
But thou canst. — Be thou therefore in the van
Of circumstance ; yea, seize the arrow's barb
Before the tense string murmur. — To the earth
For there thou wilt find Saturn, and his woes.
Meantime I will keep watch on thy bright sun,
And of thy seasons be a careful nurse."—
Ere half this region-whisper had come down
Hyperion arose, and on the stars
Lifted his curvèd lids, and kept them wide
Until it ceased ; and still he kept them wide :
And still they were the same bright, patient stars.
Then with a slow incline of his broad breast,
           diver in the pearly seas,
                 stoop'd over the airy shore,
                     all noiseless into the deep night.

BOOK II.

JUST at the self-same beat of Time's wide wings
Hyperion slid into the rustled air,
And Saturn gain'd with Thea that sad place
Where Cybele and the bruised Titans mourn'd.
It was a den where no insulting light
Could glimmer on their tears; where their own
  groans
They felt, but heard not, for the solid roar
Of thunderous waterfalls and torrents hoarse,
Pouring a constant bulk, uncertain where.
Crag jutting forth to crag, and rocks that seem'd
Ever as if just rising from a sleep,
Forehead to forehead held their monstrous horns;
And thus in thousand hugest phantasies
Made a fit roofing to this nest of woe.
Instead of thrones, hard flint they sat upon,
Couches of rugged stone, and slaty ridge
Stubborn'd with iron.   All were not assembled:
Some chain'd in torture, and some wandering.
Cœus, and Gyges, and Briareus,
Typhon, and Dolor, and Porphyrion,
With many more, the brawniest in assault,
Were pent in regions of laborious breath;
Dungeon'd in opaque element to keep
Their clenched teeth still clench'd, and all their
  limbs
Locked up like veins of metal, cramped and
  screwed;
Without a motion, save of their big hearts
Heaving in pain, and horribly convulsed
With sanguine, feverous, boiling gurge of pulse.
Mnemosyne was straying in the world,
Far from her moon had Phœbe wanderèd;
And many else were free to roam abroad,
But for the main, here found they covert **drear.**

Scarce images of life, one here, one there,
Lay vast and edgeways; like a dismal cirque
Of Druid stones, upon a forlorn moor,
When the chill rain begins at shut of eve,
In dull November, and their chancel vault,
The heaven itself, is blinded throughout night.
Each one kept shroud, nor to his neighbour gave
Or word, or look, or action of despair.
Creüs was one; his ponderous iron mace
Lay by him, and a shatter'd rib of rock
Told of his rage, ere he thus sank and pined.
Iapetus another; in his grasp,
A serpent's plashy neck; its barbed tongue
Squeezed from the gorge, and all its uncurl'd
        length
Dead; and because the creature could not spit
Its poison in the eyes of conquering Jove.
Next Cottus: prone he lay, chin uppermost,
As though in pain for still upon the flint
He ground severe his skull, with open mouth
And eyes at horrid working Nearest him
Asia, born of most enormous Caf,
Who cost her mother Tellus keener pangs,
Though feminine, than any of her sons:
More thought than woe was in her dusky face
For she was prophesying of her glory;
And in her wide imagination stood
Palm-shaded temples, and high rival fanes,
By Oxus or in Ganges' sacred isles.
Even as Hope upon her anchor leans,
So leant she, not so fair, upon a tusk
Shed from the broadest of her elephants.
Above her, on a crag's uneasy shelve,
Upon his elbow raised, all prostrate else,
Shadow'd Enceladus; once tame and mild
As grazing ox unworried in the meads;
Now tiger-passion'd, lion-thoughted, wroth,
He meditated, plotted, and even now

Was hurling mountains in that second war,
Not long delay'd, that scared the younger Gods
To hide themselves in forms of beast and bird.
Not far hence Atlas; and beside him prone
Phorcus, the sire of Gorgons.   Neighbour'd close
Oceanus, and Tethys, in whose lap
Sobb'd Clymene among her tangled hair
In midst of all lay Themis, at the feet
Of Ops the queen all clouded round from sight;
No shape distinguishable, more than when
Thick night confounds the pine-tops with the
        clouds :
And many else whose names may not be told.
For when the muse's wings are air-ward spread,
Who shall delay her flight?   And she must chant
Of Saturn, and his guide, who now had climbed
With damp and slippery footing from a depth
More horrid still.   Above a sombre cliff
Their heads appear'd, and up their stature grew
Till on the level height their steps found ease :
Then Thea spread abroad her trembling arms
Upon the precincts of this nest of pain,
And sidelong fix'd her eye on Saturn's face :
There saw she direst strife; the supreme God
At war with all the frailty of grief,
Of rage, of fear, anxiety, revenge,
Remorse, spleen, hope, but most of all despair.
Against these plagues he strove in vain : for Fate
Had pour'd a mortal oil upon his head,
A disanointing poison . so that Thea,
Affrighted, kept her still, and let him pass
First onwards in, among the fallen tribe.

    As with us mortal men, the laden heart
Is persecuted more, and fever'd more,
When it is nighing to the mournful house
Where other hearts are sick of the same bruise:
So Saturn, as he walk'd into the midst,

Felt faint, and would have sunk among the rest,
But that he met Enceladus's eye,
Whose mightiness, and awe of him, at once
Came like an inspiration ; and he shouted,
" Titans, behold your God !" at which some
     groan'd ;
Some started on their feet ; some also shouted ;
Some wept, some wail'd — all bow'd with reverence
And Ops, uplifting her black folded veil,
Show'd her pale cheeks, and all her forehead wan,
Her eyebrows thin and jet, and hollow eyes.
There is a roaring in the bleak-grown pines
When Winter lifts his voice ; there is a noise
Among immortals when a God gives sign,
With hushing finger, how he means to load
His tongue with the full weight of utterless thought,
With thunder, and with music, and with pomp :
Such noise is like the roar of bleak-grown pines ;
Which, when it ceases in this mountain'd world,
No other sound succeeds ; but ceasing here,
Among these fallen, Saturn's voice therefrom
Grew up like organ, that begins anew
Its strain, when other harmonies, stopt short,
Leave the dinn'd air vibrating silverly.
Thus grew it up : — " Not in my own sad breast,
Which is its own great judge and searcher out,
Can I find reason why ye should be thus :
Not in the legends of the first of days,
Studied from that old spirit-leaved book
Which starry Uranus with finger bright
Saved from the shores of darkness, when the waves
Low-ebb'd still hid it up in shallow gloom ;
And the which book ye know I ever kept
For my firm-based footstool. — Ah, infirm !
Not there, nor in sign, symbol, or portent
Of element, earth, water, air, and fire, —
At war, at peace, or inter-quarrelling
One against one, or two, or three, or all,

Each several one against the other three,
As fire with air loud warring when rain-floods
Drown both, and press them both against earth's
    face,
Where, finding sulphur, a quadruple wrath
Unhinges the poor world;— not in that strife,
Wherefrom I take strange lore, and read it deep,
Can I find reason why ye should be thus:
No, nowhere can unriddle, though I search,
And pore on Nature's universal scroll
Even to swooning, why ye, Divinities,
The first-born of all shaped and palpable Gods,
Should cower beneath what, in comparison,
Is untremendous might. Yet ye are here,
O'erwhelm'd, and spurn'd, and batter'd, ye are
    here !
O Titans, shall I say 'Arise !' — Ye groan:
Shall 1 say 'Crouch !'— Ye groan. What can I
    then ?
O Heaven wide ! O unseen parent dear !
What can I ? Tell me, all ye brethren Gods,
How we can war, how engine our great wrath !
O speak your counsel now, for Saturn's ear
Is all a-hunger'd. Thou, Oceanus,
Ponderest high and deep; and in thy face
I see, astonied, that severe content
Which comes of thought and musing: give us
    help !"

    So ended Saturn ; and the God of the Sea,
Sophist and sage, from no Athenian grove,
But cogitation in his watery shades,
Arose, with locks not oozy, and began,
In murmurs, which his first endeavouring tongue
Caught infant-like from the far-foamed sands.
"O ye, whom wrath consumes ! who, passion-stung,
Writhe at defeat, and nurse your agonies !
Shut up your senses, stifle up your ears,

My voice is not a bellows unto ire.
Yet listen, ye who will, whilst l bring proof
How ye, perforce, must be content to stoop :
And in the proof much comfort will I give,
If ye will take that comfort in its truth.
We fall by course of Nature's law, not force
Of thunder, or of Jove.   Great Saturn, thou
Hast sifted well the atom-universe ;
But for this reason, that thou art the King,
And only blind from sheer supremacy,
One avenue was shaded from thine eyes,
Through which I wander'd to eternal truth
And first, as thou wast not the first of powers,
So art thou not the last ; it cannot be
Thou art not the beginning nor the end
From chaos and parental darkness came
Light, the first fruits of that intestine broil,
That sullen ferment, which for wondrous ends
Was ripening in itself.   The ripe hour came,
And with it light, and light engendering
Upon its own producer, forthwith touch'd
The whole enormous matter into life.
Upon that very hour, our parentage,
The Heavens and the Earth, were manifest :
Then thou first-born, and we the giant-race,
Found ourselves ruling new and beauteous realms
Now comes the pain of truth, to whom 'tis pain ;
O folly ! for to bear all naked truths,
And to envisage circumstance, all calm,
That is the top of sovereignty.   Mark well !
As Heaven and Earth are fairer, fairer far
Than Chaos and blank Darkness, though once
           chiefs ;
And as we show beyond that Heaven and **Earth**
In form and shape compact and beautiful,
In will, in action free, companionship,
And thousand other signs of purer life ;
So on our heels a fresh perfection treads,

A power more strong in beauty, born of us
And fated to excel us, as we pass
In glory that old Darkness · nor are we
Thereby more conquered than by us the rule
Of shapeless Chaos. Say, doth the dull soil
Quarrel with the proud forests it hath fed,
And feedeth still, more comely than itself?
Can it deny the chiefdom of green groves?
Or shall the tree be envious of the dove
Because it cooeth, and hath snowy wings
To wander wherewithal and find its joys?
We are such forest-trees, and our fair boughs
Have bred forth, not pale solitary doves,
But eagles golden-feather'd, who do tower
Above us in their beauty, and must reign
In right thereof; for 'tis the eternal law
That first in beauty should be first in might:
Yea, by that law, another race may drive
Our conquerors to mourn as we do now.
Have ye beheld the young God of the Seas,
My dispossessor? Have ye seen his face?
Have ye beheld his chariot, foam'd along
By noble winged creatures he hath made?
I saw him on the calmed waters scud,
With such a glow of beauty in his eyes,
That it enforced me to bid sad farewell
To all my empire; farewell sad I took,
And hither came, to see how dolorous fate
Had wrought upon ye; and how I might best
Give consolation in this woe extreme.
Receive the truth, and let it be your balm"

Whether through pozed conviction, or disdain.
They guarded silence, when Oceanus
Left murmuring, what deepest thought can tell?
But so it was, none answer'd for a space,
Save one whom none regarded, Clymene ·
And yet she answer'd not, only complain'd,

With hectic lips, and eyes up-looking mild,
Thus wording timidly among the fierce :
" O Father ! I am here the simplest voice,
And all my knowledge is that joy is gone,
And this thing woe crept in among our hearts,
There to remain for ever, as I fear ·
I would not bode of evil, if I thought
So weak a creature could turn off the help
Which by just right should come of mighty Gods ,
Yet let me tell my sorrow, let me tell
Of what I heard, and how it made me weep,
And know that we had parted from all hope.
I stood upon a shore, a pleasant shore,
Where a sweet clime was breathed from a land
Of fragrance, quietness, and trees, and flowers
Full of calm joy it was, as I of grief ;
Too full of joy and soft delicious warmth ;
So that I felt a movement in my heart
To chide, and to reproach that solitude
With songs of misery, music of our woes ;
And sat me down, and took a mouthed shell
And murmur'd into it, and made melody —
O melody no more ! for while I sang,
And with poor skill let pass into the breeze
The dull shell's echo, from a bowery strand
Just opposite, an island of the sea,
There came enchantment with the shifting wind
That did both drown and keep alive my ears.
I threw my shell away upon the sand,
And a wave fill'd it, as my sense was fill'd
With that new blissful golden melody.
A living death was in each gush of sounds,
Each family of rapturous hurried notes,
That fell, one after one, yet all at once,
Like pearl beads dropping sudden from their string
And then another, then another strain,
Each like a dove leaving its olive perch,
With music wing'd instead of silent plumes,

To hover round my head, and make me sick
Of joy and grief at once.   Grief overcame,
And I was stopping up my frantic ears,
When, past all hindrance of my trembling hands,
A voice came sweeter, sweeter than all tune,
And still it cried, ' Apollo ! young Apollo !
The morning-bright Apollo ! young Apollo !'
I fled, it follow'd me, and cried, ' Apollo !'
O Father, and O Brethren ! had ye felt
Those pains of mine ! O Saturn, hadst thou felt,
Ye would not call this too indulged tongue
Presumptuous, in thus venturing to be heard !"

So far her voice flow'd on, like timorous brook
That, lingering along a pebbled coast,
Doth fear to meet the sea : but sea it met,
And shudder'd ; for the overwhelming voice
Of huge Enceladus swallow'd it in wrath :
The ponderous syllables, like sullen waves
In the half-glutted hollows of reef-rocks,
Came booming thus, while still upon his arm
He lean'd ; not rising, from supreme contempt.
" Or shall we listen to the over-wise,
Or to the over-foolish giant, Gods ?
Not thunderbolt on thunderbolt, till all
That rebel Jove's whole armoury were spent,
Not world on world upon these shoulders piled,
Could agonize me more than baby-words
In midst of this dethronement horrible.
Speak ! roar ! shout ! yell ! ye sleepy Titans all.
Do ye forget the blows, the buffets vile ?
Are ye not smitten by a youngling arm ?
Dost thou forget, sham Monarch of the Waves,
Thy scalding in the seas ?   What ! have I roused
Your spleens with so few simple words as these ?
O joy ! for now I see ye are not lost :
O joy ! for now I see a thousand eyes
Wide glaring for revenge." — As this he said,

He lifted up his stature vast, and stood,
Still without intermission speaking thus:
" Now ye are flames, I'll tell you how to burn,
And purge the ether of our enemies;
How to feed fierce the crooked stings of fire,
And singe away the swollen clouds of Jove,
Stifling that puny essence in its tent.
O let him feel the evil he hath done;
For though I scorn Oceanus's lore,
Much pain have I for more than loss of realms.
The days of peace and slumberous calm are fled;
Those days, all innocent of scathing war,
When all the fair Existences of heaven
Came open-eyed to guess what we would speak:—
That was before our brows were taught to frown,
Before our lips knew else but solemn sounds;
That was before we knew the winged thing,
Victory, might be lost, or might be won.
And be ye mindful that Hyperion,
Our brightest brother, still is undisgraced —
Hyperion, lo! his radiance is here!"

All eyes were on Enceladus's face,
And they beheld, while still Hyperion's name
Flew from his lips up to the vaulted rocks,
A pallid gleam across his features stern:
Not savage, for he saw full many a God
Wroth as himself.   He look'd upon them all,
And in each face he saw a gleam of light,
But splendider in Saturn's, whose hoar locks
Shone like the bubbling foam about a keel
When the prow sweeps into a midnight cove.
In pale and silver silence they remain'd,
Till suddenly a splendour, like the morn,
Pervaded all the beetling gloomy steeps,
All the sad spaces of oblivion,
And every gulf, and every chasm old,
And every height, and every sullen depth,

Voiceless, or hoarse with loud tormented streams.
And all the everlasting cataracts,
And all the headlong torrents far and near,
Mantled before in darkness and huge shade,
Now saw the light and made it terrible.
It was Hyperion: — a granite peak
His bright feet touch'd, and there he staid to view
The misery his brilliance had betray'd
To the most hateful seeing of itself
Golden his hair of short Numidian curl,
Regal his shape majestic, a vast shade
In midst of his own brightness, like the bulk
Of Memnon's image at the set of sun
To one who travels from the dusking East:
Sighs, too, as mournful as that Memnon's harp,
He utter'd, while his hands, contemplative,
He press'd together, and in silence stood
Despondence seized again the fallen Gods
At sight of the dejected King of Day,
And many hid their faces from the light:
But fierce Enceladus sent forth his eyes
Among the brotherhood; and, at their glare,
Uprose Iapetus, and Creüs too,
And Phorcus, sea-born, and together strode
To where he tower'd on his eminence.
There those four shouted forth old Saturn's name;
Hyperion from the peak loud answer'd "Saturn!"
Saturn sat near the Mother of the Gods,
In whose face was no joy, though all the Gods
Gave from their hollow throats the name of
  "Saturn!"

BOOK III.

THUS in alternate uproar and sad peace,
Amazed were those Titans utterly.
O leave them, Muse! O leave them to their woe
For thou art weak to sing such tumults dire:
A solitary sorrow best befits
Thy lips, and antheming a lonely grief
Leave them, O Muse! for thou anon wilt find
Many a fallen old Divinity
Wandering in vain about bewilder'd shores.
Meantime touch piously the Delphic harp,
And not a wind of heaven but will breathe
In aid soft warble from the Dorian flute;
For lo! 'tis for the Father of all verse.
Flush every thing that hath a vermeil hue,
Let the rose glow intense and warm the air,
And let the clouds of even and of morn
Float in voluptuous fleeces o'er the hills;
Let the red wine within the goblet boil,
Cold as a bubbling well; let faint-lipp'd shells,
On sands or in great deeps, vermilion turn
Through all their labyrinths; and let the maid
Blush keenly, as with some warm kiss surprised.
Chief isle of the embowered Cyclades,
Rejoice, O Delos, with thine olives green,
And poplars, and lawn-shading palms, and beech,
In which the Zephyr breathes the loudest song,
And hazels thick, dark-stemm'd beneath the shade
Apollo is once more the golden theme!
Where was he, when the Giant of the Sun
Stood bright, amid the sorrow of his peers?
Together had he left his mother fair
And his twin-sister sleeping in their bower,
And in the morning twilight wander'd forth
Beside the osiers of a rivulet,
Full ankle-deep in lilies of the vale.

The nightingale had ceased, and a few stars
Were lingering in the heavens, while the thrush
Began calm-throated.   Throughout all the isle
There was no covert, no retired cave
Unhaunted by the murmurous noise of waves,
Though scarcely heard in many a green recess.
He listen'd, and he wept, and his bright tears
Went trickling down the golden bow he held.
Thus with half-shut suffused eyes he stood,
While from beneath some cumbrous boughs hard (
With solemn step an awful Goddess came,
And there was purport in her looks for him,
Which he with eager guess began to read
Perplex'd, the while melodiously he said ·
" How camest thou over the unfooted sea ?
Or hath that antique mien and robed form
Moved in these vales invisible till now ?
Sure I have heard those vestments sweeping o'er
The fallen leaves, when I have sat alone
In cool mid-forest.   Surely I have traced
The rustle of those ample skirts about
These grassy solitudes, and seen the flowers
Lift up their heads, and still the whisper pass'd.
Goddess ! I have beheld those eyes before,
And their eternal calm, and all that face,
Or I have dream'd." — " Yes, " said the supreme
        shape,
'' Thou hast dream'd of me ; and awaking up
Didst find a lyre all golden by thy side,
·Whose strings touch'd by thy fingers, all the vast
Unwearied ear of the whole universe
Listen'd in pain and pleasure at the birth
Of such new tuneful wonder.   Is't not strange
That thou shouldst weep, so gifted ? Tell me, youth,
What sorrow thou canst feel ; for I am sad
When thou dost shed a tear : explain thy grief
To one who in this lonely isle hath been
The watcher of thy sleep and hours of life,
15

From the young day when first thy infant hand
Pluck'd witless the weak flowers, till thine arm
Could bend that bow heroic to all times.
Show thy heart's secret to an ancient Power
Who hath forsaken old and sacred thrones
For prophecies of thee, and for the sake
Of loveliness new-born." — Apollo then,
With sudden scrutiny and gloomless eyes,
Thus answer'd, while his white melodious throat
Throbb'd with the syllables : —"Mnemosyne !
Thy name is on my tongue, I know not how ;
Why should I tell thee what thou so well seest ?
Why should I strive to show what from thy lips
Would come no mystery ?   For me, dark, dark,
And painful vile oblivion seals my eyes :
I strive to search wherefore I am so sad,
Until a melancholy numbs my limbs ;
And then upon the grass I sit, and moan,
Like one who once had wings. — O why should I
Feel cursed and thwarted, when the liegeless air
Yields to my step aspirant ? why should I
Spurn the green turf as hateful to my feet ?
Goddess benign ! point forth some unknown thing
Are there not other regions than this isle ?
What are the stars ?   There is the sun, the sun !
And the most patient brilliance of the moon !
And stars by thousands !   Point me out the way
To any one particular beauteous star,
And I will flit into it with my lyre,
And make its silvery splendour pant with bliss.
I have heard the cloudy thunder : Where is power
Whose hand, whose essence, what divinity
Makes this alarum in the elements,
While I here idle listen on the shores
In fearless yet in aching ignorance ?
O tell me, lonely Goddess ! by thy harp,
That waileth every morn and eventide,
Tell me why thus I rave, about these groves !

Mute thou remainest — Mute? yet I can read
A wondrous lesson in thy silent face :
Krowledge enormous makes a God of me.
Names, deeds, grey legends, dire events, rebellions,
Majesties, sovran voices, agonies,
Creations and destroyings, all at once
Pour into the wide hollows of my brain,
And deify me, as if some blithe wine
Or bright elixir peerless I had drunk,
And so become immortal." — Thus the God,
While his enkindled eyes, with level glance
Beneath his white soft temples, steadfast kept
Trembling with light upon Mnemosyne.
Soon wild commotions shook him, and made flush
All the immortal fairness of his limbs :
Most like the struggle at the gate of death ;
Or like still to one who should take leave
Of pale immortal death, and with a pang
As hot as death's is chill, with fierce convulse
Die into life : so young Apollo anguish'd ;
His very hair, his golden tresses famed
Kept undulation round his eager neck.
During the pain Mnemosyne upheld
Her arms as one who prophesied. — At length
Apollo shriek'd ; — and lo ! from all his limbs
Celestial   .   .   .   .   .   .

                    .   .

MISCELLANEOUS POEMS.

———◦———

What more felicity can fall to creature
Than to enjoy delight with liberty ?
           Fate of the Butterfly. — SPENSER

DEDICATION.

———◆———

TO LEIGH HUNT, ESQ.

GLORY and loveliness have pass'd away ;
  For if we wander out in early morn,
  No wreathed incense do we see upborne
Into the east to meet the smiling day :
No crowds of nymphs soft-voiced and young and gay
  In woven baskets bringing ears of corn,
  Roses, and pinks, and violets, to adorn
The shrine of Flora in her early May.
But there are left delights as high as these,
  And I shall ever bless my destiny,
That in a time when under pleasant trees
  Pan is no longer sought, I feel a free,
A leafy luxury, seeing I could please
  With these poor offerings, a man like thee

MISCELLANEOUS POEMS.

Places of nestling green for poets made. — *Story of Rimini*

I STOOD tiptoe upon a little hill,
The air was cooling, and so very still,
That the sweet buds which with a modest pride
Pull droopingly, in slanting curve aside,
Their scanty-leaved, and finely-tapering stems,
Had not yet lost the starry diadems
Caught from the early sobbing of the morn.
The clouds were pure and white as flocks new-
shorn,
And fresh from the clear brook; sweetly they slept
On the blue fields of heaven, and then there crept
A little noiseless noise among the leaves,
Born of the very sigh that silence heaves;
For not the faintest motion could be seen
Of all the shades that slanted o'er the green.
There was wide wandering for the greediest eye,
To peer about upon variety;
Far round the horizon's crystal air to skim,
And trace the dwindled edgings of its brim;
To picture out the quaint and curious bending
Of a fresh woodland alley never-ending:
Or by the bowery clefts, and leafy shelves,
Guess where the jaunty streams refresh themselves.
I gazed awhile, and felt as light, and free
As though the fanning wings of Mercury
Had play'd upon my heels: I was light-hearted,
And many pleasures to my vision started;
So I straightway began to pluck a posy
Of luxuries bright, milky, soft and rosy.

A bush of May-flowers with the bees about **them**;
Ah, sure no tasteful nook could be without **them**!
And let a lush laburnum oversweep them,
And let long grass grow round the roots, to keep
      them
Moist, cool, and green; and shade the violets,
That they may bind the moss in leafy nets.

A filbert-hedge with wild-briar overtwined,
And clumps of woodbine taking the soft wind
Upon their summer thrones; there too should be
The frequent-chequer of a youngling tree,
That with a score of light green brethren shoots
From the quaint mossiness of aged roots:
Round which is heard a spring-head of clear waters,
Babbling so wildly of its lovely daughters,
The spreading blue-bells: it may haply mourn
That such fair clusters should be rudely torn
From their fresh beds, and scatter'd thoughtlessly
By infant hands, left on the path to die.

Open afresh your round of starry folds,
Ye ardent marigolds!
Dry up the moisture from your golden lids,
For great Apollo bids
That in these days your praises should be sung
On many harps, which he has lately strung;
And when again your dewiness he kisses,
Tell him, I have you in my world of blisses:
So haply when I rove in some far vale,
His mighty voice may come upon the gale.

Here are sweet peas, on tiptoe for a flight:
With wings of gentle flush o'er delicate white,
And taper fingers catching at all things,
To bind them all about with tiny rings.
Linger awhile upon some bending planks
That lean against a streamlet's rushy banks,

And watch intently Nature's gentle doings,
They will be found softer than ring-doves' cooings
How silent comes the water round that bend!
Not the minutest whisper does it send
To the o'erhanging sallows: blades of grass
S'owly accross the chequer'd shadows pass.
Why you might read two sonnets, ere they reach
To where the hurrying freshnesses aye preach
A natural sermon o'er their pebbly beds;
Where swarms of minnows show their little heads.
Staying their wavy bodies 'gainst the streams,
To taste the luxury of sunny beams
Temper'd with coolness.   How they ever wrestle
With their own sweet delight, and ever nestle
Their silver bellies on the pebbly sand!
If you but scantily hold out the hand,
That very instant not one will remain
But turn your eye, and they are there again.
The ripples seem right glad to reach those cresses,
And cool themselves among the emerald tresses;
The while they cool themselves, they freshness give,
And moisture, that the bowery green may live:
So keeping up an interchange of favours,
Like good men in the truth of their behaviours.
Sometimes goldfinches one by one will drop
From low-hung branches: little space they stop;
But sip, and twitter, and their feathers sleek;
Then off at once, as in a wanton freak:
Or perhaps, to show their black and golden wings,
Pausing upon their yellow flutterings
Were I in such a place, I sure should pray
That nought less sweet might call my thoughts
     away,
Than the soft rustle of a maiden's gown
Fanning away the dandelion's down;
Than the light music of her nimble toes
Patting against the sorrel as she goes.
How she would start, and blush, thus to be caught

Playing in all her innocence of thought!
O let me lead her gently o'er the brook,
Watch her half-smiling lips and downward look
O let me for one moment touch her wrist;
Let me one moment to her breathing list;
And as she leaves me, may she often turn
Her fair eyes looking through her locks auburne
What next? a tuft of evening primroses,
O'er which the mind may hover till it dozes;
O'er which it well might take a pleasant sleep,
But that 'tis ever startled by the leap
Of buds into ripe flowers, or by the flitting
Of divers moths, that aye their rest are quitting
Or by the moon lifting her silver rim
Above a cloud, and with a gradual swim
Coming into the blue with all her light.
O Maker of sweet poets! dear delight
Of this fair world and all its gentle livers;
Spangler of clouds, halo of crystal rivers,
Mingler with leaves, and dew and tumbling stream
Closer of lovely eyes to lovely dreams,
Lover of loneliness, and wandering,
Of upcast eye, and tender pondering!
Thee must I praise above all other glories
That smile us on to tell delightful stories.
For what has made the sage or poet write
But the fair paradise of Nature's light?
In the calm grandeur of a sober line,
We see the waving of the mountain pine;
And when a tale is beautifully staid,
We feel the safety of a hawthorn glade:
When it is moving on luxurious wings,
The soul is lost in pleasant smotherings:
Fair dewy roses brush against our faces,
And flowering laurels spring from diamond vases
O'erhead we see the jasmine and sweet-briar,
And bloomy grapes laughing from green attire
While at our feet, the voice of crystal bubbles

Charms us at once away from all our troubles:
So that we feel uplifted from the world,
Walking upon the white clouds wreath'd and curl'd.
So felt he, who first told how Psyche went
On the smooth wind to realms of wonderment;
What Psyche felt, and Love, when their full lips
First touch'd; what amorous and fondling nips
They gave each other's cheeks; with all their sighs,
And how they kist each other's tremulous eyes:
The silver lamp,— the ravishment — the wonder —
The darkness —loneliness — the fearful thunder;
Their woes gone by, and both to heaven up flown,
To bow for gratitude before Jove's throne.
So did he feel, who pull'd the boughs aside,
That we might look into a forest wide,
To catch a glimpse of Fauns, and Dryades
Coming with softest rustle through the trees;
And garlands woven of flowers wild, and sweet,
Upheld on ivory wrists, or sporting feet:
Telling us how fair trembling Syrinx fled
Arcadian Pan, with such a fearful dread.
Poor Nymph, — poor Pan, — how did he weep to
        find
Nought but a lovely sighing of the wind
Along the reedy stream! a half-heard strain,
Full of sweet desolation — balmy pain.

What first inspired a bard of old to sing
Narcissus pining o'er the untainted spring?
In some delicious ramble, he had found
A little space, with boughs all woven round;
And in the midst of all, a clearer pool
Than e'er reflected in its pleasant cool
The blue sky, here and there serenely peeping,
Through tendril wreaths fantastically creeping.
And on the bank a lonely flower he spied,
A meek and forlorn flower, with nought of pride,
Drooping its beauty o'er the watery clearness,

To woo its own sad image into nearness:
Deaf to light Zephyrus it would not move;
But still would seem to droop, to pine, to love.
So while the poet stood in this sweet spot,
Some fainter gleamings o'er his fancy shot·
Nor was it long ere he had told the tale
Of young Narcissus, and sad Echo's bale.

Where had he been, from whose warm head
        outflew
That sweetest of all songs, that ever new,
That aye refreshing, pure deliciousness,
Coming ever to bless
The wanderer by moonlight? to him bringing
Shapes from the invisible world, unearthly singing
From out the middle air, from flowery nests,
And from the pillowy silkiness that rests
Full in the speculation of the stars.
Ah! surely he had burst our mortal bars;
Into some wondrous region he had gone,
To search for thee, divine Endymion!

He was a Poet, sure a lover too,
Who stood on Latmus' top, what time there blew
Soft breezes from the myrtle vale below;
And brought, in faintness solemn, sweet, and slow,
A hymn from Dian's temple; while upswelling,
The incense went to her own starry dwelling.
But though her face was clear as infants' eyes,
Though she stood smiling o'er the sacrifice,
The poet wept at her so piteous fate,
Wept that such beauty should be desolate:
So in fine wrath some golden sounds he won,
And gave meek Cynthia her Endymion

Queen of the wide air; thou most lovely queen
Of all the brightness that mine eyes have seen!
As thou exceedest all things in thy shine,

So every tale does this sweet tale of thine.
O for three words of honey, that 1 might
Tell but one wonder of thy bridal night '

    Where distant ships do seem to show their keels
Phœbus awhile delay'd his mighty wheels,
And turn'd to smile upon thy bashful eyes,
Ere he his unseen pomp would solemnize.
The evening weather was so bright, and clear,
That men of health were of unusual cheer;
Stepping like Homer at the trumpet's call,
Or young Apollo on the pedestal:
And lovely women were as fair and warm,
As Venus looking sideways in alarm.
The breezes were ethereal, and pure.
And crept through half-closed lattices to cure
The languid sick: it cool'd their fever'd sleep,
And soothed them into slumbers full and deep.
Soon they awoke clear-eyed: nor burn'd with
        thirsting,
Nor with hot fingers, nor with temples bursting:
And springing up, they met the wondering sight
Of their dear friends, nigh foolish with delight;
Who feel their arms, and breasts, and kiss, and stare
And on their placid foreheads part the hair.
Young men and maidens at each other gazed,
With hands held back, and motionless, amazed
To see the brightness in each other's eyes;
And so they stood, fill'd with a sweet surprise,
Until their tongues were loosed in poesy.
Therefore no lover did of anguish die:
But the soft numbers, in that moment spoken,
Made silken ties, that never may be broken.
Cynthia! I cannot tell the greater blisses
That follow'd thine, and thy dear shepherd's kisses
Was there a poet born? — But now no more —
My wandering spirit must no farther soar

SPECIMEN OF AN INDUCTION TO A POEM.

L O! I must tell a tale of chivalry;
 For large white plumes are dancing in mine
  eye
Not like the formal crest of latter days
But bending in a thousand graceful ways,
So graceful, that it seems no mortal hand,
Or e'en the touch of Archimago's wand,
Could charm them into such an attitude.
We must think rather, that in playful mood,
Some mountain breeze had turn'd its chief delight
To show this wonder of its gentle might.
Lo! I must tell a tale of chivalry;
For while I muse, the lance points slantingly
Athwart the morning air; some lady sweet,
Who cannot feel for cold her tender feet,
From the worn top of some old battlement
Hails it with tears, her stout defender sent;
And from her own pure self no joy dissembling,
Wraps round her ample robe with happy trem-
 bling.
Sometimes when the good knight his rest could
 take,
It is reflected, clearly, in a lake,
With the young ashen boughs, 'gainst which it rests
And th' half-seen mossiness of linnets' nests.
Ah! shall I ever tell its cruelty,
When the fire flashes from a warrior's eye,
And his tremendous hand is grasping it,
And his dark brow for very wrath is knit?
Or when his spirit, with more calm intent
Leaps to the honours of a tournament,

And makes the gazers round about the ring
Stare at the grandeur of the balancing?
No, no! this is far off — then how shall I
Revive the dying tones of minstrelsy,
Which linger yet about long gothic arches,
In dark green ivy, and among wild larches?
How sing the splendour of the revelries,
When butts of wine are drank off to the lees?
And that bright lance, against the fretted wall,
Beneath the shade of stately banneral,
Is slung with shining cuirass, sword, and shield?
Where ye may see a spur in bloody field,
Light-footed damsels move with gentle paces
Round the wide hall, and show their happy faces:
Or stand in courtly talk by fives and sevens:
Like those fair stars that twinkle in the heavens.
Yet must I tell a tale of chivalry·
Or wherefore comes that knight so proudly by?
Wherefore more proudly does the gentle knight
Rein in the swelling of his ample might?
Spenser! thy brows are arched, open, kind,
And come like a clear sun-rise to my mind;
And always does my heart with pleasure dance,
When I think on thy noble countenance:
Where never yet was aught more earthly seen
Than the pure freshness of thy laurels green.
Therefore, great bard, I not so fearfully
Call on thy gentle spirit to hover nigh
My daring steps: or if thy tender care,
Thus startled unaware,
Be jealous that the foot of other wight
Should madly follow that bright path of light
Traced by thy loved Libertas; he will speak,
And tell thee that my prayer is very meek;
That I will follow with due reverence,
And start with awe at mine own strange pretence
Him thou wilt hear; so I will rest in hope
To see wide plains, fair trees, and lawny slope;

The morn, the eve, the light, the shade, the
     flowers;
Clear streams, smooth lakes, and overlooking
    towers.

———◆———

CALIDORE.

A FRAGMENT.

YOUNG Calidore is paddling o'er the lake;
  His healthful spirit eager and awake
    To feel the beauty of a silent eve,
Which seem'd full loth this happy world to leave
The light dwelt o'er the scene so lingeringly.
He bares his forehead to the cool blue sky,
And smiles at the far clearness all around,
Until his heart is well nigh overwound,
And turns for calmness to the pleasant green
Of easy slopes, and shadowy trees that lean
So elegantly o'er the waters' brim
And show their blossoms trim.
Scarce can his clear and nimble eyesight follow
The freaks and dartings of the black-wing'd swal
    low,
Delighting much, to see it half at rest,
Dip so refreshingly its wings and breast
'Gainst the smooth surface, and to mark anon,
The widening circles into nothing gone.

  And now the sharp keel of his little boat
Comes up with ripple, and with easy float
And glides into a bed of water-lilies:
Broad-leaved are they, and their white canopies
Are upward turn'd to catch the heavens' dew.
Near to a little island's point they grew;
Whence Calidore might have the goodliest view

Heard melodies are sweet, but those unheard
   Are sweeter; therefore, ye soft pipes, play on;
Not to the sensual ear, but, more endear'd
   Pipe to the spirit ditties of no tone:
Fair youth, beneath the trees, thou canst not leave
   Thy song, nor ever can those trees be bare;
     Bold Lover, never, never, canst thou kiss,
Though winning near the goal — yet, do not grieve
     She cannot fade, though thou hast not thy bliss,
For ever wilt thou love, and she be fair!

Ah, happy, happy boughs! that cannot shed
   Your leaves, nor ever bid the Spring adieu;
And, happy melodist, unwearied,
   For ever piping songs for ever new;
More happy love! more happy, happy love!
   For ever warm, and still to be enjoy'd,
     For ever panting and for ever young;
All breathing human passion far above,
   That leaves a heart high sorrowful and cloy'd,
     A burning forehead, and a parching tongue.

Who are these coming to the sacrifice?
   To that green altar, O mysterious priest,
Lead'st thou that heifer lowing at the skies,
   And all her silken flanks with garlands drest?
What little town by river or sea-shore,
   Or mountain-built with peaceful citadel,
     Is emptied of its folk, this pious morn?
And, little town, thy streets for evermore
   Will silent be; and not a soul to tell
     Why thou art desolate, can e'er return.

O Attic shape! Fair attitude! with brede
   Of marble men and maidens overwrought,
With forest branches and the trodden weed;
   Thou, silent form! dost tease us out of thought
As doth eternity: Cold Pastoral!

17

When old age shall this generation waste,
   Thou shalt remain, in midst of other woe
Than ours, a friend to man, to whom thou say'st,
" Beauty is truth, truth beauty," — that is all
   Ye know on earth, and all ye need to know

———◆———

ODE TO PSYCHE.

O GODDESS! hear these tuneless numbers
            wrung
   By sweet enforcement and remembrance dear,
And pardon that thy secrets should be sung,
   Even into thine own soft-conched ear :
Surely I dreamt to-day, or did I see
   The winged Psyche with awaken'd eyes ?
I wander'd in a forest thoughtlessly,
   And, on the sudden, fainting with surprise,
Saw two fair creatures, couched side by side
   In deepest grass, beneath the whispering roof
   Of leaves and trembled blossoms, where there ran
         A brooklet, scarce espied :
'Mid hush'd, cool-rooted flowers fragrant-eyed,
   Blue, silver-white, and budded Tyrian.
They lay calm-breathing on the bedded grass;
   Their arms embraced, and their pinions too;
   Their lips touch'd not, but had not bade adieu,
As if disjoined by soft-harded slumber,
And ready still past kisses to outnumber
   At tender eye-dawn of aurorean love :
        The winged boy I knew ;
   But who wast thou, O happy, happy dove ?
        His Psyche true !
O latest-born and loveliest vision far
   Of all Olympus' faded hierarchy !

Fairer than Phœbe's sapphire-region'd star,
  Or Vesper, amorous glow-worm of the sky;
Fairer than these, though temple thou hast none,
    Nor altar heap'd with flowers;
Nor Virgin-choir to make delicious moan
    Upon the midnight hours;
No voice, no lute, no pipe, no incense sweet
  From chain-swung censer teeming;
No shrine, no grove, no oracle, no heat
  Of pale-mouth'd prophet dreaming.
O brightest! though too late for antique vows,
  Too, too late for the fond believing lyre,
When holy were the haunted forest boughs,
  Holy the air, the water, and the fire;
Yet even in these days so far retired
  From happy pieties, thy lucent fans,
  Fluttering among the faint Olympians,
I see, and sing, by my own eyes inspired.
  So let me be thy choir, and make a moan
    Upon the midnight hours!
Thy voice, thy lute, thy pipe, thy incense sweet
  From swinged censer teeming:
Thy shrine, thy grove, thy oracle, thy heat
  Of pale-mouth'd prophet dreaming.

Yes, I will be thy priest, and build a fane
  In some untrodden region of my mind,
Where branched thoughts, new-grown with pleasant
    pain,
  Instead of pines shall murmur in the wind:
Far, far around shall those dark-cluster'd trees
  Fledge the wild-ridged mountains steep by steep
And there by zephyrs, streams, and birds, and bees,
  The moss-lain Dryads shall be lull'd to sleep;
And in the midst of this wide quietness
A rosy sanctuary will I dress
With the wreathed trellis of a working brain,
  With buds, and bells, and stars without a name,

With all the gardener Fancy e'er could feign,
  Who breeding flowers, will never breed the same
And there shall be for thee all soft delight
  That shadowy thought can win,
A bright torch, and a casement ope at night,
  To let the warm Love in !

——◆——

FANCY.

EVER let the Fancy roam,
  Pleasure never is at home :
    At a touch sweet Pleasure melteth,
Like to bubbles when rain pelteth ;
Then let winged Fancy wander
Through the thought still spread beyond her
Open wide the mind's cage-door,
She'll dart forth, and cloudward soar.
O sweet Fancy ! let her loose ;
Summer's joys are spoilt by use,
And the enjoying of the Spring
Fades as does its blossoming :
Autumn's red-lipp'd fruitage too,
Blushing through the mist and dew,
Cloys with tasting : What do then ?
Sit thee by the ingle, when
The sear fagot blazes bright,
Spirit of a winter's night ;
When the soundless earth is muffled,
And the caked snow is shuffled
From the ploughboy's heavy shoon ;
When the Night doth meet the Noon
In a dark conspiracy
To banish Even from her sky.
Sit thee there, and send abroad,
With a mind self-overawed,
Fancy, high-commission'd : — send her

She has vassals to attend her:
She will bring, in spite of frost,
Beauties that the earth hath lost;
She will bring thee, all together,
All delights of summer weather;
All the buds and bells of May,
From dewy sward or thorny spray;
All the heaped Autumn's wealth,
With a still, mysterious stealth:
She will mix these pleasures up
Like three fit wines in a cup,
And thou shalt quaff it: — thou shalt hear
Distant harvest-carols clear;
Rustle of the reaped corn;
Sweet birds antheming the morn:
And, in the same moment — hark!
'Tis the early April lark,
Or the rooks, with busy caw,
Foraging for sticks and straw.
Thou shalt, at one glance, behold
The daisy and the marigold;
White-plumed lilies, and the first
Hedge-grown primrose that hath burst
Shaded hyacinth, alway
Sapphire queen of the mid-May;
And every leaf, and every flower
Pearled with the self-same shower.
Thou shalt see the field-mouse peep
Meagre from its celled sleep;
And the snake all winter-thin
Cast on sunny bank its skin;
Freckled nest eggs thou shalt see
Hatching in the hawthorn-tree,
When the hen-bird's wing doth rest
Quiet on her mossy nest;
Then the hurry and alarm
When the bee-hive casts its swarm;
Acorns ripe down-pattering
While the autumn breezes sing.

OL, sweet Fancy! let her loose
Every thing is spoilt by use;
Where's the check that doth not fade,
Too much gazed at? Where's the **maid**
Whose lip mature is ever new?
Where's the eye, however blue,
Doth not weary? Where's the face
One would meet in every place?
Where's the voice, however soft,
One would hear so very oft?
At a touch sweet Pleasure melteth
Like to bubbles when rain pelteth.
Let, then, winged Fancy find
Thee a mistress to thy mind:
Dulcet-eyed as Ceres' daughter
Ere the God of Torment taught her
How to frown and how to chide;
With a waist and with a side
White as Hebe's, when her zone
Slipt its golden clasp, and down
Fell her kirtle to her feet,
While she held the goblet sweet,
And Jove grew languid. — Break the **mesh**
Of the Fancy's silken leash;
Quickly break her prison-string,
And such joys as these she'll bring. —
Let the winged Fancy roam,
Pleasure never is at home.

———◆———

ODE.

BARDS of Passion and of Mirth,
Ye have left your souls on earth!
Have ye souls in heaven too,
Double-lived in regions new?
Yes, and those of heaven commune
With the spheres of sun and moon;

With the noise of fountains wondrous,
And the parle of voices thund'rous;
With the whisper of heaven's trees
And one another, in soft ease
Seated on Elysian lawns
Browsed by none but Dian's fawns;
Underneath large blue-bells tented,
Where the daisies are rose-scented,
And the rose herself has got
Perfume which on earth is not;
Where the nightingale doth sing
Not a senseless, tranced thing,
But divine melodious truth;
Philosophic numbers smooth;
Tales and golden histories
Of heaven and its mysteries.

Thus ye live on high, and then
On the earth ye live again;
And the souls ye left behind you
Teach us, here, the way to find you,
Where your other souls are joying,
Never slumber'd, never cloying.
Here, your earth-born souls still speak
To mortals, of their little week;
Of their sorrows and delights;
Of their passions and their spites;
Of their glory and their shame;
What doth strengthen and what maim.
Thus ye teach us, every day,
Wisdom, though fled far away.

Bards of Passion and of Mirth,
Ye have left your souls on earth!
Ye have souls in heaven too,
Double-lived in regions new!

TO AUTUMN.

SEASON of mists and mellow fruitfulness!
    Close bosom-friend of the maturing sun;
    Conspiring with him how to load and bless
    With fruit the vines that round the thatch-eaves
            run;
To bend with apples the moss'd cottage-trees,
    And fill all fruit with ripeness to the core;
        To swell the gourd, and plump the hazel shells
    With a sweet kernel; to set budding more,
And still more, later flowers for the bees,
Until they think warm days will never cease,
        For Summer has o'er-brimm'd their clammy
            cells.

Who hath not seen thee oft amid thy store?
    Sometimes whoever seeks abroad may find
Thee sitting careless on a granary floor,
    Thy hair soft-lifted by the winnowing wind;
Or on a half-reap'd furrow sound asleep,
    Drowsed with the fume of poppies, while thy
            hook
        Spares the next swath and all its twined
            flowers;
And sometime like a gleaner thou dost keep
    Steady thy laden head across a brook;
    Or by a cider-press, with patient look,
        Thou watchest the last oozings, hours by hours

Where are the songs of Spring? Ay, where are
            they?
    Think not of them, thou hast thy music too,
While barred clouds bloom the soft-dying day,

And touch the stubble-plains with rosy hue;
Then in a wailful choir the small gnats mourn
Among the river sallows, borne aloft
Or sinking as the light wind lives or dies;
And full-grown lambs loud bleat from hilly bourn;
Hedge-crickets sing; and now with treble soft
The redbreast whistles from a garden-croft,
And gathering swallows twitter in the skies.

ODE ON MELANCHOLY.

NO, no! go not to Lethe, neither twist
Wolf's-bane, tight-rooted, for its poisonous
wine;
Nor suffer thy pale forehead to be kiss'd
By nightshade, ruby grape of Proserpine;
Make not your rosary of yew-berries,
Nor let the beetle, nor the death-moth be
Your mournful Psyche, nor the downy owl
A partner in your sorrow's mysteries;
For shade to shade will come too drowsily,
And drown the wakeful anguish of the soul.

But when the melancholy fit shall fall
Sudden from heaven like a weeping cloud,
That fosters the droop-headed flowers all,
And hides the green hill in an April shroud;
Then glut thy sorrow on a morning rose,
Or on the rainbow of the salt sand-wave,
Or on the wealth of globed peonies;
Or if thy mistress some rich anger shows,
Emprison her soft hand, and let her rave,
And feed deep, deep upon her peerless eyes.

She dwells with Beauty — Beauty that must die;
And Joy, whose hand is ever at his lips

Bidding adieu ; and aching Pleasure nigh,
   Turning to poison while the bee-mouth sips :
Ay, in the very temple of Delight
   Veil'd Melancholy has her sovran shrine,
      Though seen of none save him whose strenuous
         tongue
Can burst Joy's grape against his palate fine
His soul shall taste the sadness of her might,
      And be among her cloudy trophies hung.

———◆———

LINES ON THE MERMAID TAVERN

SOULS of poets dead and gone,
  What Elysium have ye known,
    Happy field or mossy cavern,
Choicer than the Mermaid Tavern ?
Have ye tippled drink more fine
Than mine host's Canary wine ?
Or are fruits of Paradise
Sweeter than those dainty pies
Of venison ?   O generous food !
Drest as though bold Robin Hood
Would, with his maid Marian,
Sup and bowse from horn and can.

    I have heard that on a day
Mine host's sign-board flew away,
Nobody knew whither, till
An astrologer's old quill
To a sheepskin gave the story, —
Said he saw you in your glory,
Underneath a new old-sign
Sipping beverage divine,
And pledging with contented smack
The Mermaid in the Zodiac.

Souls of poets dead and gone,
What Elysium have ye known,
Happy field or mossy cavern,
Choicer than the Mermaid Tavern?

———•———

ROBIN HOOD.

TO A FRIEND.

NO! those days are gone away,
And their hours are old and gray
And their minutes buried all
Under the down-trodden pall
Of the leaves of many years:
Many times have Winter's shears,
Frozen North, and chilling East,
Sounded tempests to the feast
Of the forest's whispering fleeces,
Since men knew nor rent nor lease:

No, the bugle sounds no more,
And the twanging bow no more;
Silent is the ivory shrill
Past the heath and up the hill;
There is no mid-forest laugh,
Where lone Echo gives the half
To some wight, amazed to hear
Jesting, deep in forest drear.

On the fairest time of June
You may go, with sun or moon,
Or the seven stars to light you,
Or the polar ray to right you;
But you never may behold
Little John, or Robin bold,
Never one, of all the clan,
Thrumming on an empty can

Some old hunting ditty, while
He doth his green way beguile
To fair hostess Merriment,
Down beside the pasture Trent;
For he left the merry tale,
Messenger for spicy ale.

Gone, the merry morris din;
Gone, the song of Gamelyn;
Gone, the tough-belted outlaw
Idling in the " greené shawe; "
All are gone away and past!
And if Robin should be cast
Sudden from his tufted grave,
And if Marian should have
Once again her forest days,
She would weep, and he would craze:
He would swear, for all his oaks,
Fall'n beneath the dock-yard strokes,
Have rotted on the briny seas,
She would weep that her wild bees
Sang not to her — strange! that honey
Can't be got without hard money!

So it is; yet let us sing
Honour to the old bow-string!
Honour to the bugle horn!
Honour to the woods unshorn!
Honour to the Lincoln green!
Honour to the archer keen!
Honour to tight Little John,
And the horse he rode upon!
Honour to bold Robin Hood,
Sleeping in the underwood!
Honour to Maid Marian,
And to all the Sherwood clan!
Though their days have hurried by,
Let us two a burden try.

SLEEP AND POETRY.

As I lay in my bed slepe full unmete
Was unto me, but why that I ne might
Rest I ne wist, for there n' as erthly wight
(As I suppose) had more of hertis ese
Than I, for I n' ad sicknesse nor disese. —Chaucer.

WHAT is more gentle than a wind in summer?
 What is more soothing than the pretty hum-
   mer
That stays one moment in an open flower,
And buzzes cheerily from bower to bower?
What is more tranquil than a musk-rose blowing
In a green island, far from all men's knowing?
More healthful than the leafiness of dales?
More secret than a nest of nightingales?
More serene than Cordelia's countenance?
More full of visions than a high romance?
What, but thee, Sleep? Soft closer of our eyes!
Low murmurer of tender lullabies!
Light hoverer around our happy pillows!
Wreather of poppy buds, and weeping willows!
Silent entangler of a beauty's tresses!
Most happy listener! when the morning blesses
Thee for enlivening all the cheerful eyes
That glance so brightly at the new sun-rise.

But what is higher beyond thought than thee?
Fresher than berries of a mountain-tree?
More strange, more beautiful, more smooth, more
   regal,
Than wings of swans, than doves, than dim-seen
   eagle?
What is it? And to what shall I compare it?
It has a glory, and nought else can share it:

The thought thereof is awful, sweet, and **holy**,
Chasing away all worldliness and folly:
Coming sometimes like fearful claps of thunder;
Or the low rumblings earth's regions **under**;
And sometimes like a gentle whispering
Of all the secrets of some wondrous thing
That breathes about us in the vacant air;
So that we look around with prying stare,
Perhaps to see shapes of light, aerial limning;
And catch soft floatings from a faint-heard **hymn**
     ing;
To see the laurel-wreath, on high suspended,
That is to crown our name when life is ended.
Sometimes it gives a glory to the voice,
And from the heart up-springs, rejoice! rejoice!
Sounds which will reach the Framer of all **things**,
And die away in ardent mutterings.

No one who once the glorious sun has seen,
And all the clouds, and felt his bosom clean
For his great Maker's presence, but must **know**
What 'tis I mean, and feel his being glow:
Therefore no insult will I give his spirit,
By telling what he sees from native **merit.**

O Poesy! for thee I hold my pen,
That am not yet a glorious denizen
Of thy wide heaven — should I rather kneel
Upon some mountain-top until I feel
A glowing splendour round about me hung,
And echo back the voice of thine own tongue?
O Poesy! for thee I grasp my pen,
That am not yet a glorious denizen
Of thy wide heaven; yet, to my ardent **prayer,**
Yield from thy sanctuary some clear **air,**
Smooth'd for intoxication by the breath
Of flowering bays, that I may die a **death**
Of luxury, and my young spirit follow

The morning sunbeams to the great Apollo,
Like a fresh sacrifice; or, if I can bear
The o'erwhelming sweets, 'twill bring me to the fair
Visions of all places: a bowery nook
Will be elysium — an eternal book
Whence I may copy many a lovely saying
About the leaves, and flowers — about the playing
Of nymphs in woods, and fountains; and the shade
Keeping a silence round a sleeping maid;
And many a verse from so strange influence
That we must ever wonder how, and whence
It came.   Also imaginings will hover
Round my fire-side, and haply there discover
Vistas of solemn beauty, where I'd wander
In happy silence, like the clear Meander
Through its lone vales; and where I found a spot
Of awfuller shade, or an enchanted grot,
Or a green hill o'erspread with chequer'd dress
Of flowers, and fearful from its loveliness,
Write on my tablets all that was permitted,
All that was for our human senses fitted.
Then the events of this wide world I'd seize
Like a strong giant, and my spirit tease
'Till at its shoulders it should proudly see
Wings to find out an immortality.

Stop and consider! life is but a day;
A fragile dewdrop on its perilous way
From a tree's summit; a poor Indian's sleep
While his boat hastens to the monstrous steep
Of Montmorenci.   Why so sad a moan?
Life is the rose's hope while yet unblown;
The reading of an ever-changing tale;
The light uplifting of a maiden's veil;
A pigeon tumbling in clear summer air;
A laughing school-boy, without grief or care,
Riding the springy branches of an elm.

O for ten years, that I may overwhelm
Myself in poesy! so I may do the deed
That my own soul has to itself decreed.
Then I will pass the countries that I see
In long perspective, and continually
Taste their pure fountains.   First the realm I'll pass
Of Flora, and Old Pan: sleep in the grass,
Feed upon apples red, and strawberries,
And choose each pleasure that my fancy sees,
Catch the white-handed nymphs in shady places,
To woo sweet kisses from averted faces —
Play with their fingers, touch their shoulders white
Into a pretty shrinking with a bite
As hard as lips can make it : till agreed,
A lovely tale of human life we'll read.
And one will teach a tame dove how it best
May fan the cool air gently o'er my rest :
Another, bending o'er her nimble tread,
Will set a green robe floating round her head,
And still will dance with ever-varied ease,
Smiling upon the flowers and the trees :
Another will entice me on, and on,
Through almond blossoms and rich cinnamon ;
Till in the bosom of a leafy world
We rest in silence, like two gems upcurl'd
In the recesses of a pearly shell.

And can I ever bid these joys farewell ?
Yes, I must pass them for a nobler life,
Where I may find the agonies, the strife
Of human hearts : for lo ! I see afar,
O'er-sailing the blue cragginess, a car
And steeds with streamy manes — the charioteer
Looks out upon the winds with glorious fear :
And now the numerous tramplings quiver lightly
Along a huge cloud's ridge ; and now with sprightly
Wheel downward come they into fresher skies,
Tipt round with silver from the sun's bright eyes.

Still downward with capacious whirl they glide;
And now I see them on a green hill side
In breezy rest among the nodding stalks
The charioteer with wondrous gesture talks
To the trees and mountains; and there soon **appear**
Shapes of delight, of mystery, and fear,
Passing along before a dusky space
Made by some mighty oaks · as they would **chase**
Some ever-fleeting music, on they sweep.
Lo! how they murmur, laugh, and smile, and **weep**
Some with upholden hand and mouth severe;
Some with their faces muffled to the ear
Between their arms; some clear in youthful **bloom,**
Go glad and smilingly athwart the gloom;
Some looking back, and some with upward **gaze;**
Yes, thousands in a thousand different ways
Flit onward — now a lovely wreath of girls
Dancing their sleek hair into tangled curls;
And now broad wings   Most awfully intent
The driver of those steeds is forward bent,
And seems to listen: O that I might know
All that he writes with such a hurrying glow!

The visions all are fled — the car is fled
Into the light of heaven, and in their stead
A sense of real things comes doubly strong,
And, like a muddy stream, would bear along
My soul to nothingness: but I will strive
Against all doubtings, and will keep alive
The thought of that same chariot, and the **strange**
Journey it went.

              Is there so small a range
In the present strength of manhood, that **the high**
Imagination cannot freely fly
As she was wont of old? prepare her steeds,
Paw up against the light, and do strange **deeds**
Upon the clouds? Has she not shown us **all?**
    18

From the clear space of ether, to the small
Breath of new buds unfolding ? From the meaning
Of Jove's large eyebrow, to the tender greening
Of April meadows ? here her altar shone,
E'en in this isle ; and who could paragon
The fervid choir that lifted up a noise
Of harmony, to where it aye will poise
Its mighty self of convoluting sound,
Huge as a planet, and like that roll round,
Eternally around a dizzy void ?
Ay, in those days the Muses were nigh cloy'd
With honours ; nor had any other care
Than to sing out and soothe their wavy hair.

   Could all this be forgotten ?   Yes, a schism
Nurtured by foppery and barbarism,
Made great Apollo blush for this his land.
Men were thought wise who could not understand
His glories : with a puling infant's force
They sway'd about upon a rocking-horse,
And thought it Pegasus.   Ah, dismal-soul'd !
The winds of heaven blew, the ocean roll'd
Its gathering waves — ye felt it not.   The blue
Bared its eternal bosom. and the dew
Of summer night collected still to make
The morning precious : Beauty was awake !
Why were ye not awake ?   But ye were dead
To things ye knew not of, — were closely wed
To musty laws lined out with wretched rule
And compass vile · so that ye taught a school
Of dolts to smooth, inlay, and clip, and fit,
Till, like the certain wands of Jacob's wit,
Their verses tallied.   Easy was the task :
A thousand handicraftsmen wore the mask
Of Poesy.   Ill-fated, impious race !
That blasphemed the bright Lyrist to his face,
And did not know it, — no, they went about,
Holding a poor, decrepit standard out,

Mark'd with most flimsy mottoes, and in large
The name of one Boileau !

                   O ye whose charge
It is to hover round our pleasant hills !
Whose congregated majesty so fills
My boundly reverence, that I cannot trace
Your hallow'd names, in this unholy place,
So near those common folk : did not their shames
Affright you ?   Did our old lamenting Thames
Delight you ?   Did ye never cluster round
Delicious Avon, with a mournful sound,
And weep ?   Or did ye wholly bid adieu
To regions where no more the laurel grew ?
Or did ye stay to give a welcoming
To some lone spirits who could proudly sing
Their youth away, and die ?   'Twas even so :
But let me think away those times of woe ·
Now 'tis a fairer season ; ye have breathed
Rich benedictions o'er us ; ye have wreathed
Fresh garlands : for sweet music has been heard
In many places ; some has been upstirr'd
From out its crystal dwelling in a lake,
By a swan's ebon bill ; from a thick brake,
Nested and quiet in a valley mild,
Bubbles a pipe ; fine sounds are floating wild
About the earth : happy are ye and glad.
These things are, doubtless . yet in truth we've ha'
Strange thunders from the potency of song ;
Mingled indeed with what is sweet and strong,
From majesty : but in clear truth the themes
Are ugly cubs, the Poet's Polyphemes
Disturbing the grand sea.   A drainless shower
Of light is poesy ; 'tis the supreme of power ;
'Tis might half slumbering on its own right arm.
The very archings of her eyelids charm
A thousand willing agents to obey,
And still she governs with the mildest sway :

But strength alone though of the Muses born
Is like a fallen angel : trees uptorn,
Darkness, and worms, and shrouds, and sepulchres
Delight it ; for it feeds upon the burrs
And thorns of life ; forgetting the great end
Of poesy, that it should be a friend
To soothe the cares, and lift the thoughts of man.

Yet I rejoice : a myrtle fairer than
E'er grew in Paphos, from the bitter weeds
Lifts its sweet heap into the air, and feeds
A silent space with ever-sprouting green.
All tenderest birds there find a pleasant screen,
Creep through the shade with jaunty fluttering,
Nibble the little cupped flowers and sing.
Then let us clear away the choking thorns
From round its gentle stem ; let the young fawns
Yeaned in after-times, when we are flown,
Find a fresh sward beneath it, overgrown
With simple flowers : let there nothing be
More boisterous than a lover's bended knee ,
Nought more ungentle than the placid look
Of one who leans upon a closed book ;
Nought more untranquil than the grassy slopes
Between two hills.   All hail, delightful hopes !
As she was wont, th' imagination
Into most lovely labyrinths will be gone,
And they shall be accounted poet kings
Who simply tell the most heart-easing things.
O may these joys be ripe before I die !

Will not some say that I presumptuously
Have spoken ? that from hastening disgrace
'Twere better far to hide my foolish face ?
That whining boyhood should with reverence bow
Ere the dread thunderbolt could reach me ? How
If I do hide myself, it sure shall be
In the very fane, the light of Poesy :

If I do fall, at least I will be laid
Beneath the silence of a poplar shade ;
And over me the grass shall be smooth shaven ,
And there shall be a kind memorial graven.
But off, Despondence ! miserable bane !
They should not know thee, who athirst to gain
A noble end, are thirsty every hour.
What though I am not wealthy in the dower
Of spanning wisdom ; though I do not know
The shiftings of the mighty winds that blow
Hither and thither all the changing thoughts
Of man: though no great ministering **reason**
     sorts
Out the dark mysteries of human souls
To clear conceiving : yet there ever rolls
A vast idea before me, and I glean
Therefrom my liberty : thence too I've seen
The end and aim of Poesy. 'Tis clear
As anything most true ; as that the year
Is made of the four seasons — manifest
As a large cross, some old cathedral's crest,
Lifted to the white clouds. Therefore should **I**
Be but the essence of deformity,
A coward, did my very eyelids wink
At speaking out what I have dared to think.
Ah ! rather let me like a madman run
Over some precipice ; let the hot sun
Melt my Dedalian wings, and drive me down
Convulsed and headlong ? Stay ! an **inward**
     frown
Of conscience bids me be more calm awhile.
An ocean dim, sprinkled with many an isle,
Spreads awfully before me. How much toil
How many days ! what desperate turmoil !
Ere I can have explored its widenesses.
Ah, what a task ! upon my bended **knees,**
I could unsay those — no, impossible !
Impossible !

For sweet relief I'll dwell
On humbler thoughts, and let this strange assay
Begun in gentleness die so away.
E'en now all tumult from my bosom fades :
I turn full-hearted to the friendly aids
That smooth the path of honour; brotherhood,
And friendliness, the nurse of mutual good.
The hearty grasp that sends a pleasant sonnet
Into the brain ere one can think upon it :
The silence when some rhymes are coming out;
And when they're come, the very pleasant rout:
The message certain to be done to-morrow.
'Tis perhaps as well that it should be to borrow
Some precious book from out its snug retreat,
To cluster round it when we next shall meet.
Scarce can I scribble on; for lovely airs
Are fluttering round the room like doves in pair:
Many delights of that glad day recalling,
When first my senses caught their tender falling
And with these airs come forms of elegance
Stooping their shoulders o'er a horse's prance,
Careless, and grand — fingers soft and round
Parting luxuriant curls ; and the swift bound
Of Bacchus from his chariot, when his eye
Made Ariadne's cheek look blushingly.
Thus I remember all the pleasant flow
Of words at opening a portfolio.

Things such as these are ever harbingers
To trains of peaceful images : the stirs
Of a swan's neck unseen among the rushes.
A linnet starting all about the bushes :
A butterfly, with golden wings broad-parted,
Nestling a rose, convulsed as though it smarted
With over-pleasure — many, many more,
Might I indulge at large in all my store
Of luxuries · yet I must not forget
Sleep, quiet with his poppy coronet:

For what there may be worthy in these rhymes
I partly owe to him . and thus, the chimes
Of friendly voices had just given place
To as sweet a silence, when I 'gan retrace
The pleasant day, upon a couch at ease.
It was a poet's house who keeps the keys
Of pleasure's temple — round about were hung
The glorious features of the bards who sung
In other ages — cold and sacred busts
Smiled at each other.   Happy he who trusts
To clear Futurity his darling fame !
Then there were fauns and satyrs taking aim
At swelling apples with a frisky heap
And reaching fingers, 'mid a luscious heap
Of vine-leaves.   Then there rose to view a fane
Of liney marble, and thereto a train
Of nymphs approaching fairly o'er the sward :
One, loveliest, holding her white hand toward
The dazzling sun-rise : two sisters sweet
Bending their graceful figures till they meet
Over the trippings of a little child :
And some are hearing, eagerly, the wild
Thrilling liquidity of dewy piping.
See, in another picture, nymphs are wiping
Cherishingly Diana's timorous limbs ;
A fold of lawny mantle dabbling swims
At the bath's edge, and keeps a gentle motion
With the subsiding crystal : as when ocean
Heaves calmly its broad swelling smoothness o'er
Its rocky marge, and balances once more
The patient weeds ; that now unshent by foam
Feel all about their undulating home
Sappho's meek head was there half smiling down
At nothing ; just as though the earnest frown
Of over-thinking had that moment gone
From off her brow, and left her all alone

   Great Alfred's too, with anxious, pitying eyes,
As if he always listen'd to the sighs

Of the goaded world; and Kosciusko's, worn
By horrid suffrance — mightily forlorn.

Petrarch, outstepping from the shady green,
Starts at the sight of Laura; nor can wean
His eyes from her sweet face. Most happy **they!**
For over them was seen a free display
Of outspread wings, and from between them **shone**
The face of Poesy: from off her throne
She overlook'd things that I scarce could tell,
The very sense of where I was might well
Keep sleep aloof: but more than that there **came**
Thought after thought to nourish up the **flame**
Within my breast; so that the morning **light**
Surprised me even from a sleepless night;
And up I rose refresh'd, and glad, and **gay,**
Resolving to begin that very day
These lines; and howsoever they be **done,**
I leave them as a father does his son.

STANZAS.

IN a drear-nighted December,
  Too happy, happy tree,
    Thy branches ne'er **remember**
Their green felicity:
The north cannot undo them,
With a sleety whistle through **them;**
Nor frozen thawings glue them
From budding at the prime.

In a drear-nighted December,
Too happy, happy brook,
Thy bubblings ne'er **remember**
Apollo's summer look;
But with a sweet **forgetting,**

They stay their crystal fretting,
Never, never petting
About the frozen time.

Ah ! would 'twere so with many
A gentle girl and boy !
But were there ever any
Writhed not at passed joy ?
To know the change and feel it,
When there is none to heal it,
Nor numbed sense to steal it,
Was never said in rhyme.

EPISTLES.

Among the rest a shepherd (though but young
Yet hartned to his pipe) with all the skill
His few yeeres could, began to fill his quill.
Britannia's Pastorals. — BROWNE

EPISTLES.

——◆——

TO GEORGE FELTON MATHEW.

SWEET are the pleasures that to verse belong,
  And doubly sweet a brotherhood in song;
    Nor can remembrance, Mathew! bring to view
A fate more pleasing, a delight more true
Than that in which the brother poets joy'd,
Who, with combined powers, their wit employ'd
To raise a trophy to the drama's muses.
The thought of this great partnership diffuses
Over the genius-loving heart, a feeling
Of all that's high, and great, and good, and healing
Too partial friend! fain would I follow thee
Past each horizon of fine poesy;
Fain would I echo back each pleasant note
As o'er Sicilian seas, clear anthems float
'Mong the light skimming gondolas far parted,
Just when the sun his farewell beam has darted
But 'tis impossible, far different cares
Beckon me sternly from soft " Lydian airs,"
And hold my faculties so long in thrall,
That I am oft in doubt whether at all
I shall again see Phœbus in the morning:
Or flush'd Aurora in the roseate dawning!
Or a white Naiad in a rippling stream;
Or a wrapt seraph in a moonlight beam;
Or again witness what with thee I've seen,
The dew by fairy feet swept from the green,
After a night of some quaint jubilee
Which every elf and fay had come to see

When bright processions took their airy **march**
Beneath the curved moon's triumphal arch.

But might I now each passing moment give
To the coy Muse, with me she would not live
In this dark city, nor would condescend
'Mid contradictions her delights to lend.
Should e'er the fine-eyed maid to me be kind,
Ah! surely it must be whene'er I find
Some flowery spot, sequester'd, wild, romantic,
That often must have seen a poet frantic,
Where oaks, that erst the Druid knew, are growing,
And flowers, the glory of one day, are blowing;
Where the dark-leaved laburnum's drooping clusters
Reflect athwart the stream their yellow lustres,
And intertwined the cassia's arms unite,
With its own drooping buds, but very white.
Where on one side are covert branches hung,
'Mong which the nightingales have always sung
In leafy quiet; where to pry, aloof
Atween the pillars of the sylvan roof,
Would be to find where violet beds were nestling,
And where the bee with cowslip bells was wrestling
There must be too a ruin dark and gloomy,
To say " Joy not too much in all that's bloomy."

Yet this is vain — O Mathew! lend thy aid
To find a place where I may greet the maid —
Where we may soft humanity put on,
And sit, and rhyme, and think on Chatterton;
And that warm-hearted Shakspeare sent to meet
        him
Four laurell'd spirits, heavenward to entreat him
With reverence would we speak of all the sages
Who have left streaks of light athwart their ages.
And thou shouldst moralize on Milton's blindness,
And mourn the fearful dearth of human kindness
To those who strove with the bright golden wing

Of genius, to flap away each sting
Thrown by the pitiless world.   We next could te
Of those who in the cause of freedom fell;
Of our own Alfred, of Helvetian Tell;
Of him whose name to every heart 's a solace,
High-minded and unbending William Wallace.
While to the rugged north our musing turns,
We well might drop a tear for him and Burns.
Felton! without incitements such as these,
How vain for me the niggard Muse to tease!
For thee, she will thy every dwelling grace,
And make " a sunshine in a shady place · "
For thou wast once a flow'ret blooming wild,
Close to the source, bright, pure, and undefiled,
Whence gush the streams of song · in happy hour
Came chaste Diana from her shady bower,
Just as the sun was from the east uprising;
And, as for him some gift she was devising,
Beheld thee, pluck'd thee, cast thee in the strean
To meet her glorious brother's greeting beam.
I marvel much that thou hast never told
How, from a flower, into a fish of gold
Apollo changed thee: how thou next didst seem
A black-eyed swan upon the widening stream;
And when thou first didst in that mirror trace
The placid features of a human face;
That thou hast never told thy travels strange,
And all the wonders of the mazy range
O'er pebbly crystal, and o'er golden sands:
Kissing thy daily food from Naiads' pearly hands

November, 1815

———◆———

TO MY BROTHER GEORGE.

FULL many a dreary hour have I past,
My brain bewilder'd, and my mind o'ercast
With heaviness; in seasons when I've thought

No sphery strains by me could e'er be caught
From the blue dome, though I to dimness gaze
On the far depth where sheeted lightning plays ;
Or, on the wavy grass outstretch'd supinely,
Pry 'mong the stars, to strive to think divinely :
That I should never hear Apollo's song,
Though feathery clouds were floating all along
The purple west, and, two bright streaks between,
The golden lyre itself were dimly seen :
That the still murmur of the honey-bee
Would never teach a rural song to me :
That the bright glance from beauty's eyelids slanting
Would never make a lay of mine enchanting,
Or warm my breast with ardour to unfold
Some tale of love and arms in time of old.

But there are times, when those that love the bay
Fly from all sorrowing far, far away ;
A sudden glow comes on them, nought they see
In water, earth, or air, but poesy.
It has been said, dear George, and true I hold it,
(For knightly Spenser to Libertas told it,)
That when a Poet is in such a trance,
In air he sees white coursers paw and prance,
Bestridden of gay knights, in gay apparel,
Who at each other tilt in playful quarrel ;
And what we, ignorantly, sheet-lightning call,
Is the swift opening of their wide portal,
When the bright warder blows his trumpet clear,
Whose tones reach nought on earth but poet's ear
When these enchanted portals open wide,
And through the light the horsemen swiftly glide,
The Poet's eye can reach those golden halls,
And view the glory of their festivals :
Their ladies fair, that in the distance seem
Fit for the silvering of a seraph's dream ;
Their rich brimm'd goblets, that incessant run,
Like the bright spots that move about the sun ;

And when upheld, the wine from each bright **jar**
Pours with the lustre of a falling star.
Yet further off are dimly seen their bowers,
Of which no mortal eye can reach the flowers;
And 'tis right just, for well Apollo knows
'Twould make the Poet quarrel with the rose.
All that's reveal'd from that far seat of blisses,
Is, the clear fountains' interchanging kisses,
As gracefully descending, light and thin,
Like silver streaks across a dolphin's fin,
When he upswimmeth from the coral caves,
And sports with half his tail above the **waves**.

These wonders strange he sees, and many **more**,
Whose head is pregnant with poetic lore:
Should he upon an evening ramble fare
With forehead to the soothing breezes bare,
Would he nought see but the dark, silent blue,
With all its diamonds trembling through **and**
    through?
Or the coy moon, when in the waviness
Of whitest clouds she does her beauty dress,
And staidly paces higher up, and higher,
Like a sweet nun in holiday attire?
Ah, yes! much more would start into his sight —
The revelries and mysteries of night:
And should I ever see them, I will tell you
Such tales as needs must with amazement spell **you**.

These are the living pleasures of the bard:
But richer far posterity's award.
What does he murmur with his latest breath,
While his proud eye looks through the film **of**
    death?
" What though I leave this dull and earthly **mould**
Yet shall my spirit lofty converse hold
With after times. — The patriot shall **feel**
My stern alarum, and unsheath his steel;
19

Or in the senate thunder out my numbers,
To startle princes from their easy slumbers.
The sage will mingle with each moral theme
My happy thoughts sententious : he will teem
With lofty periods when my verses fire him,
And then I'll stoop from heaven to inspire him
Lays have I left of such a dear delight
That maids will sing them on their bridal-night.
Gay villagers, upon a morn of May,
When they have tired their gentle limbs with pla
And form'd a snowy circle on the grass,
And placed in midst of all that lovely lass
Who chosen is their queen, — with her fine head
Crowned with flowers purple, white, and red :
For there the lily and the musk-rose sighing,
Are emblems true of hapless lovers dying :
Between her breasts, that never yet felt trouble,
A bunch of violets full blown, and double,
Serenely sleep : — she from a casket takes
A little book, — and then a joy awakes
About each youthful heart, — with stifled cries,
And rubbing of white hands, and sparkling eyes
For she's to read a tale of hopes and fears ;
One that I foster'd in my youthful years :
The pearls, that on each glistening circlet sleep,
Gush ever and anon with silent creep,
Lured by the innocent dimples.   To sweet rest
Shall the dear babe, upon its mother's breast,
Be lull'd with songs of mine.   Fair world adieu !
Thy dales and hills are fading from my view ·
Swiftly I mount, upon wide-spreading pinions,
Far from the narrow bounds of thy dominions.
Full joy I feel, while thus I cleave the air,
That my soft verse will charm thy daughters fair,
And warm thy sons !"   Ah, my dear friend and
        brother,
Could I, at once, my mad ambition smother,
For tasting joys like these, sure I should be

Happier, and dearer to society.
At times, 'tis true, I've felt relief from pain
When some bright thought has darted through my
     brain :
Through all that day I've felt a greater pleasure
Than if I had brought to light a hidden treasure.
As to my sonnets, though none else should heed
     them,
I feel delighted, still, that you should read them.
Of late, too, I have had much calm enjoyment,
Stretch'd on the grass at my best loved employ
     ment
Of scribbling lines for you. These things I thought
While, in my face, the freshest breeze I caught.
E'en now I am pillow'd on a bed of flowers
That crowns a lofty cliff, which proudly towers
Above the ocean waves. The stalks and blades
Chequer my tablet with their quivering shades.
On one side is a field of drooping oats,
Through which the poppies show their scarlet coats,
So pert and useless, that they bring to mind
The scarlet coats that pester human-kind.
And on the other side, outspread, is seen
Ocean's blue mantle, streak'd with purple and
     green;
Now 'tis I see a canvas'd ship, and now
Mark the bright silver curling round her prow.
I see the lark down-dropping to his nest,
And the broad-wing'd sea-gull never at rest;
For when no more he spreads his feathers free,
His breast is dancing on the restless sea.
Now I direct my eyes into the west,
Which at this moment is in sun-beams drest.
Why westward turn ? 'Twas but to say adieu!
'Twas but to kiss my hand, dear George, to you

August, 1816

TO CHARLES COWDEN CLARKE

OFT have you seen a swan superbly frowning,
  And with proud breast his own white shadow
        crowning;
He slants his neck beneath the waters bright
So silently, it seems a beam of light
Come from the galaxy . anon he sports, —
With outspread wings the Naiad Zephyr courts,
Or ruffles all the surface of the lake
In striving from its crystal face to take
Some diamond water-drops, and them to treasure
In milky nest, and sip them off at leisure.
But not a moment can he there ensure them,
Nor to such downy rest can he allure them;
For down they rush as though they would be free
And drop like hours into eternity.
Just like that bird am I in loss of time,
Whene'er I venture on the stream of rhyme;
With shatter'd boat, oar snapt, and canvas rent,
I slowly sail, scarce knowing my intent;
Still scooping up the water with my fingers,
In which a trembling diamond never lingers.

  By this, friend Charles, you may full plainly see
Why I have never penn'd a line to thee:
Because my thoughts were never free and clear,
And little fit to please a classic ear;
Because my wine was of too poor a savour
For one whose palate gladdens in the flavour
Of sparkling Helicon: — small good it were
To take him to a desert rude and bare,
Who had on Baiæ's shore reclined at ease,
While Tasso's page was floating in a breeze
That gave soft music from Armida's bowers,
Mingled with fragrance from her rarest flowers:

Small good to one who had by Mulla's stream
Fondled the maidens with the breasts of cream;
Who had beheld Belphœbe in a brook,
And lovely Una in a leafy nook,
And Archimago leaning o'er his book:
Who had of all that's sweet tasted, and seen,
From silvery ripple, up to beauty's queen;
From the sequester'd haunts of gay Titania,
To the blue dwelling of divine Urania:
One, who of late had ta'en sweet forest walks
With him who elegantly chats and talks —
The wrong'd Libertas — who has told you stories
Of laurel chaplets, and Apollo's glories;
Of troops chivalrous prancing through a city,
And tearful ladies, made for love and pity:
With many else which I have never known.
Thus have I thought; and days on days have flown
Slowly, or rapidly — unwilling still
For you to try my dull, unlearned quill.
Nor should I now, but that I've known you long,
That you first taught me all the sweets of song:
The grand, the sweet, the terse, the free, the fine,
What swell'd with pathos, and what right divine.
Spenserian vowels that elope with ease,
And float along like birds o'er summer seas.
Miltonian storms, and more, Miltonian tenderness:
Michael in arms, and more, meek Eve's fair slen-
      derness.
Who read for me the sonnet swelling loudly
Up to its climax, and then dying proudly?
Who found for me the grandeur of the ode,
Growing, like Atlas, stronger from its load?
Who let me taste that more than cordial dram,
The sharp, the rapier-pointed epigram?
Show'd me that epic was of all the king,
Round, vast, and spanning all, like Saturn's ring?
You too upheld the veil from Clio's beauty,
And pointed out the patriot's stern duty;

The might of Alfred, and the shaft of **Tell**;
The hand of Brutus, that so grandly fell
Upon a tyrant's head.   Ah! had I never seen,
Or known your kindness, what might I have been
What my enjoyments in my youthful years,
Bereft of all that now my life endears?
And can I e'er these benefits forget?
And can I e'er repay the friendly debt?
No, doubly no; — yet should these rhyming
          please,
I shall roll on the grass with twofold ease,
For I have long time been my fancy feeding
With hopes that you would one day think the
          reading
Of my rough verses not an hour misspent;
Should it e'er be so, what a rich content!
Some weeks have pass'd since last I saw the spires
In lucent Thames reflected: — warm desires
To see the sun o'er-peep the eastern dimness,
And morning-shadows streaking into slimness
Across the lawny fields, and pebbly water;
To mark the time as they grow broad and shorter
To feel the air that plays about the hills,
And sips its freshness from the little rills;
To see high, golden corn wave in the light
When Cynthia smiles upon a summer's night,
And peers among the cloudlets, jet and white,
As though she were reclining in a bed
Of bean-blossoms, in heaven freshly shed.
No sooner had I stepp'd into these pleasures,
Than I began to think of rhymes and measures
The air that floated by me seem'd to say
" Write! thou wilt never have a better day."
And so I did.   When many lines I'd written,
Though with their grace I was not oversmitten,
Yet, as my hand was warm, I thought I'd better
Trust to my feelings, and write you a letter.
Such an attempt required an inspiration

Of a peculiar sort, — a consummation ; —
Which, had I felt, these scribblings might have
    been
Verses from which the soul would never ween ;
But many days have past since last my heart
Was warm'd luxuriously by divine Mozart ;
By Arne delighted, or by Handel madden'd ;
Or by the song of Erin pierced and sadden'd :
What time you were before the music sitting,
And the rich notes to each sensation fitting.
Since I have walk'd with you through shady lanes
That freshly terminate in open plains,
And revell'd in a chat that ceased not,
When, at night-fall, among your books we got :
No, nor when supper came, nor after that, —
Nor when reluctantly I took my hat ;
No, nor till cordially you shook my hand
Mid-way between our homes : — your accents
    bland
Still sounded in my ears, when I no more
Could hear your footsteps touch the gravelly floor.
Sometimes I lost them, and then found again ;
You changed the foot-path for the grassy plain.
In those still moments I have wish'd you joys
That well you know to honour : — " Life's very toys
With him," said I, " will take a pleasant charm ;
It cannot be that aught will work him harm."
These thoughts now come o'er me with all their
    might : —
Again I shake your hand, — friend Charles, good
    night.

September, 1816

SONNETS.

SONNETS.

I.

TO A FRIEND WHO SENT ME SOME ROSES.

AS late I rambled in the happy fields,
    What time the skylark shakes the tremulous
       dew
  From his lush clover covert ; — when anew
Adventurous knights take up their dinted shields ;
I saw the sweetest flower wild nature yields,
    A fresh-blown musk-rose ; 'twas the first that
       threw
    Its sweets upon the summer : graceful it grew
As is the wand that queen Titania wields.
And, as I feasted on its fragrancy,
    I thought the garden-rose it far excell'd ;
But when, O Wells ! thy roses came to me,
    My sense with their deliciousness was spell'd
Soft voices had they, that with tender plea
    Whisper'd of peace, and truth, and friendliness
       unquell'd.

II.

TO MY BROTHER GEORGE.

MANY the wonders I this day have seen :
The sun, when first he kist away the tears
That fill'd the eyes of Morn ; — the laurell'd
peers
Who from the feathery gold of evening lean ; —
The Ocean with its vastness, its blue green,
Its ships, its rocks, its caves, its hopes, its fears, —
Its voice mysterious, which whoso hears
Must think on what will be, and what has been.
E'en now, dear George, while this for you I write,
Cynthia is from her silken curtains peeping
So scantly, that it seems her bridal night,
And she her half-discover'd revels keeping.
But what, without the social thought of thee,
Would be the wonders of the sky and sea ?

III.

TO ——.

HAD I a man's fair form, then might my sighs
Be echoed swiftly through that ivory shell
Thine ear, and find thy gentle heart ; so well
Would passion arm me for the enterprise :
But ah ! I am no knight whose foeman dies ;
No cuirass glistens on my bosom's swell ;
I am no happy shepherd of the dell
Whose lips have trembled with a maiden's eyes.
Yet must I doat upon thee, — call thee sweet.
Sweeter by far than Hybla's honey'd roses
When steep'd in dew rich to intoxication.
Ah ! I will taste that dew. for me 'tis meet,
And when the moon her pallid face discloses,
I'll gather some by spells. and incantation.

IV.

O SOLITUDE! if I must with thee dwell,
Let it not be among the jumbled heap
Of murky buildings : climb with me the
    steep, —
Nature's observatory — whence the dell.
In flowery slopes, its river's crystal swell,
  May seem a span ; let me thy vigils keep
  'Mongst boughs pavilion'd, where the deer's
    swift leap
Startles the wild bee from the foxglove bell.
  But though I'll gladly trace these scenes with
    thee,
Yet the sweet converse of an innocent mind,
Whose words are images of thoughts refined,
  Is my soul's pleasure ; and it sure must be
Almost the highest bliss of human-kind,
  When to thy haunts two kindred spirits flee.

v.

HOW many bards gild the lapses of time !
  A few of them have ever been the food
  Of my delighted fancy, — I could brood
Over their beauties, earthly, or sublime ·
And often, when I sit me down to rhyme,
  These will in throngs before my mind intrude :
  But no confusion, no disturbance rude
Do they occasion ; 'tis a pleasing chime.
  So the unnumber'd sounds that evening store ;
The songs of birds — the whispering of the leaves —
The voice of waters — the great bell that heaves
  With solemn sound, — and thousand others
    more,
That distance of recognizance bereaves,
  Make pleasing music, and not wild uproar.

VL.

TO G. A. W.

NYMPH of the downward smile and sidelong
        glance!
    In what diviner moments of the day
  Art thou most lovely? when gone far astray
Into the labyrinths of sweet utterance?
Or when serenely wandering in a trance
    Of sober thought?   Or when starting away,
    With careless robe to meet the morning ray,
Thou sparest the flowers in thy mazy dance?
Haply 'tis when thy ruby lips part sweetly,
    And so remain, because thou listenest:
But thou to please wert nurtured so completely
    That I can never tell what mood is best,
I shall as soon pronounce which Grace more neatly
    Trips it before Apollo than the rest.

VII.

WRITTEN ON THE DAY THAT MR. LEIGH HUNT
LEFT PRISON.

WHAT though, for showing truth to flatter'd
        state,
    Kind Hunt was shut in prison, yet has he,
  In his immortal spirit, been as free
As the sky-searching lark, and as elate.
Minion of grandeur! think you he did wait?
    Think you he nought but prison-walls did see,
    Till, so unwilling, thou unturn'dst the key?
Ah, no! far happier, nobler was his fate!
In Spenser's halls he stray'd, and bowers fair,
    Culling enchanted flowers; and he flew
With daring Milton through the fields of air:
    To regions of his own his genius true
Took happy flights.   Who shall his fame impair
    When thou art dead, and all thy wretched crew?

VIII.

TO MY BROTHER.

SMALL, busy flames play through the fresh-laid
    coals,
  And their faint cracklings o'er our silence creep
  Like whispers of the household gods that keep
A gentle empire o'er fraternal souls.
And while, for rhymes, I search around the poles,
  Your eyes are fix'd, as in poetic sleep,
  Upon the lore so voluble and deep,
That aye at fall of night our care condoles.
This is your birth-day, Tom, and I rejoice
  That thus it passes smoothly, quietly :
Many such eves of gently whispering noise
  May we together pass, and calmly try
What are this world's true joys, — ere the great
    Voice
  From its fair face shall bid our spirits fly.

IX.

ADDRESSED TO HAYDON

HIGH-MINDEDNESS, a jealousy for good,
  A loving-kindness for the great man's fame,
  Dwells here and there with people of no name,
In noisome alley, and in pathless wood :
And where we think the truth least understood,
  Oft may be found a " singleness of aim,"
  That ought to frighten into hooded shame
A money-mongering, pitiable brood.
How glorious this affection for the cause
  Of steadfast genius, toiling gallantly !
What when a stout unbending champion awes
  Envy, and malice to their native sty ?
Unnumber'd souls breathe out a still applause,
  Proud to behold him in his country's eye.

X.

ADDRESSED TO THE SAME.

GREAT spirits now on earth are sojourning:
  He of the cloud, the cataract. the lake,
    Who on Helvellyn's summit, wide awake,
Catches his freshness from Archangel's wing:
He of the rose, the violet, the spring,
    The social smile, the chain for Freedom's sake
    And lo! whose steadfastness would never take
A meaner sound than Raphael's whispering.
And other spirits there are standing apart
    Upon the forehead of the age to come;
These, these will give the world another heart,
    And other pulses.   Hear ye not the hum
Of mighty workings? ——
Listen awhile, ye nations, and be dumb.

XI

ON FIRST LOOKING INTO CHAPMAN'S HOMER.

MUCH have I travell'd in the realms of gold,
  And many goodly states and kingdoms seen
    Round many western islands have I been
Which bards in fealty to Apollo hold.
Oft of one wide expanse had I been told
    That deep-brow'd Homer ruled as his demesne
    Yet did I never breathe its pure serene
Till I heard Chapman speak out loud and bold:
Then felt I like some watcher of the skies
    When a new planet swims into his ken,
Or like stout Cortez when with eagle eyes
    He stared at the Pacific — and all his men
Look'd at each other with a wild surmise —
    Silent, upon a peak in Darien.

XII.

ON LEAVING SOME FRIENDS AT AN EARLY HOUR.

GIVE me a golden pen, and let me lean
  On heap'd-up flowers, in regions clear, and far
    Bring me a tablet whiter than a star,
Or hand of hymning angel, when 'tis seen
The silver strings of heavenly harp atween:
  And let there glide by many a pearly car,
    Pink robes, and wavy hair, and diamond jar,
And half-discover'd wings, and glances keen.
The while let music wander round my ears,
And as it reaches each delicious ending,
  Let me write down a line of glorious tone,
And full of many wonders of the spheres:
For what a height my spirit is contending!
  'Tis not content so soon to be alone.

XIII.

KEEN fitful gusts are whispering here and there
  Among the bushes, half leafless and dry;
    The stars look very cold about the sky,
And I have many miles on foot to fare,
Yet feel I little of the cool bleak air,
  Or of the dead leaves rustling drearily,
    Or of those silver lamps that burn on high,
Or of the distance from home's pleasant lair.
For I am brimful of the friendliness
  That in a little cottage I have found;
Of fair-hair'd Milton's eloquent distress,
  And all his love for gentle Lycid' drown'd
Of lovely Laura in her light green dress,
  And faithful Petrarch gloriously crown'd.

XIV.

TO one who has been long in city pent,
   'Tis very sweet to look into the fair
   And open face of heaven, — to breathe a prayer
Full in the smile of the blue firmament.
Who is more happy, when, with heart's content,
   Fatigued he sinks into some pleasant lair
   Of wavy grass, and reads a debonair
And gentle tale of love and languishment?
Returning home at evening, with an ear
   Catching the notes of Philomel, — an eye
Watching the sailing cloudlet's bright career,
   He mourns that day so soon has glided by:
E'en like the passage of an angel's tear
   That falls through the clear ether silently.

XV.

ON THE GRASSHOPPER AND CRICKET.

THE poetry of earth is never dead:
   When all the birds are faint with the hot sun,
   And hide in cooling trees, a voice will run
From hedge to hedge about the new-mown mead·
That is the grasshopper's — he takes the lead
   In summer luxury, — he has never done
   With his delights, for when tired out with fun,
He rests at ease beneath some pleasant weed.
The poetry of earth is ceasing never:
   On a lone winter evening, when the frost
Has wrought a silence, from the stove there shrills
The Cricket's song, in warmth increasing ever,
   And seems to one in drowsiness half lost,
The Grasshopper's among some grassy hills.

XVI.

TO KOSCIUSKO.

GOOD Kosciusko! thy great name alone
  Is a full harvest whence to reap high feeling;
    It comes upon us like the glorious pealing
Of the wide spheres — an everlasting tone.
And now it tells me, that in worlds unknown,
    The names of heroes, burst from clouds concealing,
    Are changed to harmonies, for ever stealing
Through cloudless blue, and round each silver
        throne.
It tells me too, that on a happy day,
    When some good spirit walks upon the earth,
Thy name with Alfred's. and the great of yore,
    Gently commingling, gives tremendous birth
To a loud hymn, that sounds far, far away
To where the great God lives for evermore

XVII.

HAPPY is England! I could be content
  To see no other verdure than its own;
    To feel no other breezes than are blown
Through its tall woods with high romances blent
Yet do I sometimes feel a languishment
    For skies Italian, and an inward groan
    To sit upon an Alp as on a throne,
And half forget what world or worldling meant.
Happy is England, sweet her artless daughters;
    Enough their simple loveliness for me,
Enough their whitest arms in silence clinging:
    Yet do I often warmly burn to see
Beauties of deeper glance, and hear their singing,
And float with them about the summer waters.

XVIII.

THE HUMAN SEASONS.

FOUR Seasons fil' the measure of the year;
  There are four seasons in the mind of man:
  He has his lusty Spring, when fancy clear
  Takes in all beauty with an easy span :
He has his Summer, when luxuriously
  Spring's honey'd cud of youthful thought he loves
To ruminate, and by such dreaming high
  Is nearest unto heaven : quiet coves
His soul has in its Autumn, when his wings
  He furleth close ; contented so to look
On mists in idleness — to let fair things
  Pass by unheeded as a threshold brook.
He has his Winter too of pale misfeature,
Or else he would forego his mortal nature.

XIX.

ON A PICTURE OF LEANDER.

COME hither, all sweet maidens soberly,
  Down-looking aye, and with a chasten'd light,
  Hid in the fringes of your eyelids white,
And meekly let your fair hands joined be,
As if so gentle that ye could not see,
  Untouch'd, a victim of your beauty bright,
  Sinking away to his young spirit's night,
Sinking bewilder'd 'mid the dreary sea :
'Tis young Leander toiling to his death ;
  Nigh swooning, he doth purse his weary lips
For Hero's cheek, and smiles against her smile.
  O horrid dream ! see how his body dips
Dead-heavy ; arms and shoulders gleam awhile :
He's gone ; up bubbles all his amorous breath !

XX.

TO AILSA ROCK.

HEARKEN, thou craggy ocean pyramid!
  Give answer from thy voice, the sea-fowl's
    screams!
  When were thy shoulders mantled in huge
    streams!
When, from the sun, was thy broad forehead hid?
How long is't since the mighty power bid
  Thee heave to airy sleep from fathom dreams?
  Sleep in the lap of thunder or sun-beams,
Or when gray clouds are thy cold cover-lid?
Thou answer'st not, for thou art dead asleep!
  Thy life is but two dead eternities —
The last in air, the former in the deep;
  First with the whales, last with the eagle-skies —
Drown'd wast thou till an earthquake made thee
    steep,
  Another cannot wake thy giant size.

XXI.

ON SEEING THE ELGIN MARBLES.

MY spirit is too weak, mortality
  Weighs heavily on me like unwilling sleep,
  And each imagined pinnacle and steep
Of godlike hardship tells me I must die
Like a sick eagle looking at the sky.
  Yet 'tis a gentle luxury to weep,
  That I have not the cloudy winds to keep
Fresh for the opening of the morning's eye.
Such dim-conceived glories of the brain,
  Bring round the heart an indescribable feud:
So do these wonders a most dizzy pain,
  That mingles Grecian grandeur with the rude
Wasting of old Time — with a billowy main
  A sun, a shadow of a magnitude.

XXII.

TO HAYDON.

(WITH THE PRECEDING SONNET.)

HAYDON! forgive me that I cannot speak
  Definitively of these mighty things;
    Forgive me, that I have not eagle's wings,
That what I want I know not where to seek.
And think that I would not be over-meek,
  In rolling out upfollowed thunderings,
    Even to the steep of Heliconian springs,
Were I of ample strength for such a freak.
Think, too, that all these numbers should be thine
  Whose else? In this who touch thy vesture'
      hem?
For, when men stared at what was most divine
  With brainless idiotism and o'erwise phlegm,
Thou hadst beheld the full Hesperian shine
  Of their star in the east, and gone to worship
      them!

XXIII.

WRITTEN IN THE COTTAGE WHERE BURNS WAS BORN.

THIS mortal body of a thousand days
  Now fills, O Burns, a space in thine own room,
    Where thou didst dream alone on budded bays
Happy and thoughtless of thy day of doom!
My pulse is warm with thine old Barley-bree,
  My head is light with pledging a great soul,
My eyes are wandering, and I cannot see,
  Fancy is dead and drunken at its goal;
Yet can I stamp my foot upon thy floor,
  Yet can I ope thy window-sash to find
The meadow thou hast tramped o'er and o'er —
  Yet can I think of thee till thought is blind, —
Yet can I gulp a bumper to thy name, —
O smile among the shades, for this is fame!

XXIV.

TO THE NILE

SON of the old moon-mountains African!
Stream of the Pyramid and Crocodile!
We call thee fruitful, and that very while
A desert fills our seeing's inward span:
Nurse of swart nations since the world began,
Art thou so fruitful? or dost thou beguile
Those men to honour thee, who, worn with toil,
Rest them a space 'twixt Cairo and Decan?
O may dark fancies err! They surely do;
'Tis ignorance that makes a barren waste
Of all beyond itself. Thou dost bedew
Green rushes like our rivers, and dost taste
The pleasant sun-rise. Green isles hast thou too,
And to the sea as happily dost haste.

XXV.

ON SITTING DOWN TO READ "KING LEAR" ONCE AGAIN

O GOLDEN-TONGUED Romance with serene
lute!
Fair plumed Syren! Queen! if far away!
Leave melodizing on this wintry day,
Shut up thine olden volume, and be mute.
Adieu! for once again the fierce dispute,
Betwixt hell torment and impassioned clay
Must I burn through; once more assay
The bitter sweet of this Shakspearian fruit.
Chief Poet! and ye clouds of Albion,
Begetters of our deep eternal theme,
When I am through the old oak forest gone,
Let me not wander in a barren dream,
But when I am consumed with the Fire,
Give me new Phœnix-wings to fly at my desire.

XXVI.

READ me a lesson, Muse, and speak it loud
  Upon the top of Nevis, blind in mist !
  I look into the chasms, and a shroud
Vaporous doth hide them, — just so much I wist
Mankind do know of hell ; I look o'erhead,
  And there is sullen mist, — even so much
Mankind can tell of heaven ; mist is spread
  Before the earth, beneath me, — even such,
Even so vague is man's sight of himself !
  Here are the craggy stones beneath my feet, —
Thus much I know that, a poor witless elf,
  I tread on them, — that all my eye doth meet
Is mist and crag, not only on this height,
But in the world of thought and mental might !

POSTHUMOUS POEMS.

———◆———

FINGAL'S CAVE.

NOT Aladdin magian
Ever such a work began;
Not the wizard of the Dee
Ever such a dream could see;
Not St. John, in Patmos' isle,
In the passion of his toil,
When he saw the churches seven,
Golden aisled, built up in heaven,
Gazed at such a rugged wonder!—
As I stood its roofing under,
Lo! I saw one sleeping there,
On the marble cold and bare;
While the surges washed his feet,
And his garments white did beat,
Drenched about the sombre rocks;
On his neck his well-grown locks,
Lifted dry above the main,
Were upon the curl again.
"What is this? and what art thou?"
Whispered I, and touch'd his brow;
"What art thou? and what is this?"
Whispered I, and strove to kiss
The spirit's hand, to wake his eyes;
Up he started in a trice:
"I am Lycidas," said he,
"Fam'd in fun'ral minstrelsy!
This was architectur'd thus
By the great Oceanus!—
Here his mighty waters play
Hollow organs all the day;

Here, by turns, his dolphins all,
Finny palmers, great and small,
Come to pay devotion due, —
Each a mouth of pearls must strew :
Many a mortal of these days
Dares to pass our sacred ways ;
Dares to touch, audaciously,
This cathedral of the sea !
I have been the pontiff-priest,
Where the waters never rest,
Where a fledgy sea-bird choir
Soars for ever !   Holy fire
I have hid from mortal man ;
Proteus is my Sacristan !
But the dulled eye of mortal
Hath passed beyond the rocky portal ;
So for ever will I leave
Such a taint, and soon unweave
All the magic of the place."
So saying, with a Spirit's glance
He dived !

TO ——.

WHAT can I do to drive away
     Remembrance from my eyes ? for they have
          seen,
Aye, an hour ago, my brilliant Queen '
Touch has a memory.   O say, love, say,
What can I do to kill it and be free
In my old liberty ?
When every fair one that I saw was fair,
Enough to catch me in but half a snare,
Not keep me there :
When, howe'er poor or particolour'd things,
My muse had wings,

And ever ready was to take her course
Whither I bent her force,
Unintellectual, yet divine to me ; —
Divine, I say ! — What sea-bird o'er the sea
Is a philosopher the while he goes
Winging along where the great water throes ?

How shall I do
To get anew
Those moulted feathers, and so mount once more
Above, above
The reach of fluttering Love,
And make him cower lowly while I soar ?
Shall I gulp wine ?   No, that is vulgarism,
A heresy and schism,
Foisted into the canon law of love ; —
No, — wine is only sweet to happy men ;
More dismal cares
Seize on me unawares, —
Where shall I learn to get my peace again ?
To banish thoughts of that most hateful land,
Dungeoner of my friends, that wicked strand
Where they were wreck'd and live a wrecked life
That monstrous region, whose dull rivers pour,
Ever from their sordid urns unto the shore,
Unown'd of any weedy-haired gods ;
Whose winds, all zephyrless, hold scourging rods,
Iced in the great lakes, to afflict mankind ;
Whose rank-grown forests, frosted, black, and
      blind,
Would fright a Dryad ; whose harsh herbaged
      meads
Make lean and lank the starv'd ox while he feeds ;
There bad flowers have no scent, birds no sweet
      song,
And great unerring Nature once seems wrong.

O, for some sunny spell
To dissipate the shadows of this hell !

Say they are gone, — with the new dawning light
Steps forth my lady bright !
O, let me once more rest
My soul upon that dazzling breast !
Let once again these aching arms be placed,
The tender gaolers of thy waist !
And let me feel that warm breath here and there
To spread a rapture in my very hair, —
O, the sweetness of the pain !
Give me those lips again !
Enough ! Enough ! it is enough for me
To dream of thee !

———◆———

HYMN TO APOLLO.

GOD of the golden bow,
   And of the golden lyre,
  And of the golden hair,
 And of the golden fire,
    Charioteer
   Of the patient year,
Where — where slept thine ire,
When like a blank idiot I put on thy wreath,
   Thy laurel, thy glory,
   The light of thy story,
Or was I a worm — too low crawling, for death ?
   O Delphic Apollo !

The Thunderer grasp'd and grasp'd,
  The Thunderer frown'd and frown'd ;
The eagle's feathery mane
  For wrath became stiffen'd — the sound
   Of breeding thunder
   Went drowsily under,
Muttering to be unbound.
O why didst thou pity, and for a worm
  Why touch thy soft lute

Till the thunder was mute,
Why was not I crush'd — such a pitiful germ ?
O Delphic Apollo !

The Pleiades were up,
    Watching the silent air ;
The seeds and roots in the Earth
    Were swelling for summer fare ;
        The Ocean, its neighbour,
        Was at its old labour,
When, who — who did dare
To tie, like a madman, thy plant round his brow,
        And grin and look proudly,
        And blaspheme so loudly,
And live for that honour, to stoop to thee now ?
    O Delphic Apollo !

———◆———

LINES.

UNFELT, unheard, unseen,
    I've left my little queen,
        Her languid arms in silver slumber ly-
            ing :
    Ah ! through their nestling touch,
    Who — who could tell how much
There is for madness — cruel, or complying ?

    Those faery lids how sleek !
    Those lips how moist ! — they speak,
In ripest quiet, shadows of sweet sounds :
    Into my fancy's ear
    Melting a burden dear,
How "Love doth know no fulness, and no bounds."

    True ! — tender monitors !
    I bend unto your laws :

This sweetest day for dalliance was born !
       So, without more ado,
       I'll feel my heaven anew,
For all the blushing of the hasty morn.

       1817.

———◆———

SONG.

I.

HUSH, hush ! tread softly ! hush, hush, **my dear**
       All the house is asleep, but we know very well
       That the jealous, the jealous old bald-pate **may**
           hear,
   Tho you've padded his night-cap — O sweet
           Isabel !
   Tho' your feet are more light than a Faery's
           feet,
   Who dances on bubbles where brooklets meet,—
Hush, hush ! soft tiptoe ! hush, hush, my dear !
For less than a nothing the jealous can hear.

II.

No leaf doth tremble, no ripple is there
   On the river, — all's still, and the night's sleepy eye
Closes up, and forgets all its Lethean care,
   Charm'd to death by the drone of the humming
           May-fly ;
   And the moon, whether prudish or complaisant
   Has fled to her bower, well knowing I want
No light in the dusk, no torch in the gloom,
But my Isabel's eyes, and her lips pulp'd with bloom

III.

Lift the latch ! ah gently ! ah tenderly — sweet !
   We are dead if that latchet gives one little clink

Well done — now those lips, and a flowery seat —
  The old man may sleep, and the planets may
      wink;
    The shut rose shall dream of our loves and
      awake
    Full-blown, and such warmth for the morning
      take,
The stock-dove shall hatch his soft twin-eggs and coo,
While I kiss to the melody, aching all through!

    1818.

FAERY SONG.

SHED no tear! O shed no tear!
  The flower will bloom another year.
    Weep no more! O weep no more!
Young buds sleep in the root's white core.
Dry your eyes! O dry your eyes!
For I was taught in Paradise
To ease my breast of melodies —
        Shed no tear.

Overhead! look overhead!
'Mong the blossoms white and red —
Look up, look up. I flutter now
On this fresh pomegranate bough.
See me! 'tis this silvery bill
Ever cures the good man's ill.
Shed no tear! O shed no tear!
The flower will bloom another year.
Adieu, Adieu — I fly, adieu,
I vanish in the heaven's blue —
        Adieu, Adieu!

LA BELLE DAME SANS MERCI.

A BALLAD.

I.

O WHAT can ail thee, knight-at-arms,
  Alone and palely loitering?
The sedge has wither'd from the lake,
And no birds sing.

II.

O what can ail thee, knight-at-arms!
  So haggard and so woe-begone?
The squirrel's granary is full,
  And the harvest's done.

III.

I see a lily on thy brow
  With anguish moist and fever dew,
And on thy cheeks a fading rose
  Fast withereth too.

IV.

I met a lady in the meads,
  Full beautiful — a faery's child,
Her hair was long, her foot was light,
  And her eyes were wild.

V.

I made a garland for her head,
  And bracelets too, and fragrant zone;
She look'd at me as she did love,
  And made sweet moan.

VI.

I set her on my pacing steed
   And nothing else saw all d† long,
For sidelong would she bend, a ’ ng
   A faery song.

VII.

She found me roots of relish   eet,
   And honey wild, and manna dew,
And sure in language strange she said —
   " I love thee true."

VIII.

She took me to her elfin grot,
   And there she wept, and sigh'd full sore,
And there I shut her wild wild eyes
   With kisses four.

IX.

And there she lulled me asleep,
   And there I dream'd — Ah ! woe betide
The latest dream I ever dream'd
   On the cold hill's side.

X.

I saw pale kings and princes too,
   Pale warriors, death-pale were they all ;
They cried — " La Belle Dame sans Merci
   Hath thee in thrall ! "

XI.

I saw their starved lips in the gloam,
   With horrid warning gaped wide,

And I awoke and found me here,
  On the cold hill's side.

XII.

And this is why I sojourn here,
  Alone and palely loitering,
Though the sedge is wither'd from the lake,
  And no birds sing.

    1819

———◆———

THE EVE OF ST. MARK.

(UNFINISHED.)

UPON a Sabbath-day it fell;
  Twice holy was the Sabbath-bell,
  That call'd the folk to evening prayer
The city streets were clean and fair
From wholesome drench of April rains,
And, on the western window-panes,
The chilly sunset faintly told
Of unmatured green, valleys cold,
Of the green thorny bloomless hedge,
Of rivers new with spring-tide sedge,
Of primroses by shelter'd rills,
And daisies on the aguish hills.

Twice holy was the Sabbath-bell:
The silent streets were crowded well
With staid and pious companies,
Warm from their fireside orat'ries;
And moving, with demurest air,
To even-song, and vesper prayer.
Each arched porch, and entry low,
Was fill'd with patient folk and slow,

With whispers push, and shuffling feet,
While play'd the organ loud and sweet.

The bells had ceased, the prayers begun,
And Bertha had not yet half done
A curious volume, patch'd and torn,
That all day long. from earliest morn,
Had taken captive her two eyes,
Among its golden broideries;
Perplex'd her with a thousand things, —
The stars of Heaven, and angels' wings,
Martyrs in a fiery blaze,
Azure saints and silver rays,
Moses' breastplate, and the seven
Candlesticks John saw in Heaven,
The winged Lion of Saint Mark,
And the Covenantal Ark,
With its many mysteries,
Cherubim and golden mice

Bertha was a maiden fair,
Dwelling in th' old Minster-square;
From her fireside she could see,
Sidelong. its rich antiquity,
Far as the Bishop's garden-wall;
Where sycamores and elm-trees tall,
Full-leaved, the forest had outstript,
By no sharp north-wind ever nipt,
So shelter'd by the mighty pile,
Bertha arose, and read awhile,
With forehead 'gainst the window-pane.
Again she tried, and then again,
Until the dusk eve left her dark
Upon the legend of St. Mark.
From plaited lawn-frill, fine and thin,
She lifted up her soft warm chin,
With aching neck and swimming eyes
And dazed with saintly imag'ries.

All was gloom, and silent all,
Save now and then the still foot-fall
Of one returning homewards late,
Past the echoing minster-gate.
The clamorous daws, that all the day
Above tree-tops and towers play,
Pair by pair had gone to rest,
Each in its ancient belfry-nest,
Where asleep they fall betimes,
To music and the drowsy chimes.

All was silent, all was gloom,
Abroad and in the homely room :
Down she sat, poor cheated soul !
And struck a lamp from the dismal coal;
Leaned forward, with bright drooping hair
And slant book, full against the glare.
Her shadow, in uneasy guise,
Hover'd about, a giant size,
On ceiling-beam and old oak chair,
The parrot's cage, and panel square;
And the warm angled winter-screen,
On which were many monsters seen,
Call'd doves of Siam. Lima mice,
And legless birds of Paradise,
Macaw, and tender Av'davat,
And silken-furr'd Angora cat.
Untired she read, her shadow still
Glower'd about, as it would fill
The room with wildest forms and shades,
As though some ghostly queer. of spades
Had come to mock behind her back,
And dance, and ruffle her garments black.
Untired she read the legend page,
Of holy Mark, from youth to age,
On land, on sea, in pagan chains.
Rejoicing for his many pains.
Sometimes the learned eremite,

With golden star, or dagger bright,
Referr'd to pious poesies
Written in smallest crow-quill size
Beneath the text; and thus the rhyme
Was parcell'd out from time to time:
—— "Als writith he of swevenis,
Men han beforne they wake in bliss,
Whanne that hir friendes thinke him **bound**
In crimped shroude farre under grounde;
And how a litling child mote be
A saint er its nativitie,
Gif that the modre (God **her blesse!**)
Kepen in solitarinesse,
And kissen devoute the holy croce,
Of Goddes love, and Sathan's force, —
He writith; and thinges many **mo**
Of swiche thinges I may not **shew.**
Bot I must tellen verilie
Somdel of Saintè Cicilie,
And chieflie what he auctorethe
Of Saintè Markis life and dethe:"

At length her constant eyelids **come**
Upon the fervent martyrdom;
Then lastly to his holy shrine,
Exalt amid the tapers' shine
At Venice, —

1819

——◆——

TO FANNY.

PHYSICIAN Nature! let my spirit blood!
    O ease my heart of verse and let me **rest;**
    Throw me upon thy Tripod, till the flood
Of stifling numbers ebbs from my full breast.
A theme! a theme! Great Nature! give **a theme**

Let me begin my dream.
I come — I see thee, as thou standest there;
Beckon me not into the wintry air.

Ah! dearest love, sweet home of all my fears,
And hopes, and joys, and panting miseries, —
To-night, if I may guess, thy beauty wears
    A smile of such delight,
    As brilliant and as bright,
As when with ravished, aching, vassal eyes,
    Lost in soft amaze,
    I gaze, I gaze!

Who now, with greedy looks, eats up my feast?
What stare outfaces now my silver moon!
Ah! keep that hand unravished at the least;
    Let, let the amorous burn —
    But, pr'ythee, do not turn
The current of your heart from me so soon.
    O! save, in charity,
    The quickest pulse for me.

Save it for me, sweet love! though music breathe
Voluptuous visions into the warm air,
Though swimming through the dance's dangerou
      wreath;
    Be like an April day,
    Smiling and cold and gay,
A temperate lily, temperate as fair;
    Then, Heaven! there will be
    A warmer June for me.

Why, this — you'll say, my Fanny! is not true:
Put your soft hand upon your snowy side,
Where the heart beats: confess — 'tis nothing
    new —
    Must not a woman be
    A feather on the sea,

Sway'd to and fro by every wind and tide ?
　　Of as uncertain speed
　　As blow-ball from the mead ?

I know it — and to know it is despair
To one who loves you as I love, sweet Fanny !
Whose heart goes flutt'ring for you every where,
　　Nor, when away you roam,
　　Dare keep its wretched home,
Love, love alone, his pains severe and many ·
　　Then, loveliest ! keep me free,
　　From torturing jealousy.

Ah ! if you prize my subdued soul above
The poor, the fading, brief, pride of an hour;
Let none profane my Holy See of love,
　　Or with a rude hand break
　　The sacramental cake :
Let none else touch the just new-budded flower:
　　If not — may my eyes close,
　　Love ! on their lost repose.

SONNETS.

—◆—

I.

OH! how I love, on a fair summer's eve,
  When streams of light pour down the golden
      west,
  And on the balmy zephyrs tranquil rest
The silver clouds, — far, far away to leave
All meaner thoughts, and take a sweet reprieve
  From little cares ; to find, with easy quest,
  A fragrant wild, with Nature's beauty drest,
And there into delight my soul deceive.
There warm my breast with patriotic lore,
  Musing on Milton's fate — on Sydney's bier —
  Till their stern forms before my mind arise :
Perhaps on wing of Poesy upsoar,
  Full often dropping a delicious tear,
  When some melodious sorrow spells mine eyes.
    1816.

II.

TO A YOUNG LADY WHO SENT ME A LAUREL CROWN.

FRESH morning gusts have blown away all fear
    From my glad bosom — now from gloominess
    I mount forever — not an atom less
Than the proud laurel shall content my bier.
No! by the eternal stars! or why sit here
    In the Sun's eye, and 'gainst my temples press
    Apollo's very leaves, woven to bless
By thy white fingers and thy spirit clear.
Lo! who dares say, "Do this?" Who dares call
    down
    My will from its high purpose? Who say,
    " Stand,"
Or " Go?" This mighty moment I would frown
    On abject Cæsars — not the stoutest band
Of mailed heroes should tear off my crown.
    Yet would I kneel and kiss thy gentle hand!

III.

AFTER dark vapors have oppress'd our plains
    For a long dreary season, comes a day
    Born of the gentle south, and clears away
From the sick heavens all unseemly stains.
The anxious month, relieved from its pains,
    Takes as a long-lost right the feel of May,
    The eyelids with the passing coolness play,
Like rose-leaves with the drip of summer rains.
And calmest thoughts come round us — as, of leaves
    Budding, — fruit ripening in stillness, — autumn
    suns
Smiling at eve upon the quiet sheaves, —
Sweet Sappho's cheek, — a sleeping infant's
    breath, —
    The gradual sand that through an hour-glass
    runs, —
A woodland rivulet, — a Poet's death.

Jan. 1817

IV.

**WRITTEN ON THE BLANK SPACE OF A LEAF
AT THE END OF CHAUCER'S TALE OF "THE
FLOWRE AND THE LEFE."**

THIS pleasant tale is like a little copse :
    The honeyed lines so freshly interlace,
    To keep the reader in so sweet a place,
So that he here and there full-hearted stops ;
And oftentimes he feels the dewy drops
    Come cool and suddenly against his face,
    And, by the wandering melody, may trace
Which way the tender-legged linnet hops.
Oh ! what a power has white simplicity !
    What mighty power has this gentle story !
    I, that do ever feel athirst for glory,
Could at this moment be content to lie
    Meekly upon the grass, as those whose sobbings
    Were heard of none beside the mournful robins.

    Feb. 1817

V.

ON THE SEA.

IT keeps eternal whisperings around
    Desolate shores, and with its mighty swell
    Gluts twice ten thousand caverns, till the spell
Of Hecate leaves them their old shadowy sound.
Often 'tis in such gentle temper found,
    That scarcely will the very smallest shell
    Be moved for days from where it sometime fell,
When last the winds of heaven were unbound.
O ye ! who have your eyeballs vexed and tired,
    Feast them upon the wideness of the Sea ;
O ye ! whose ears are dinn'd with uproar rude,
    Or fed too much with cloying melody, —
Sit ye near some old cavern's mouth, and brood
Until ye start, as if the sea-nymphs quired !

VI.

ON LEIGH HUNT'S POEM, THE "STORY OF RIMINI."

WHO loves to peer up at the morning sun,
  With half-shut eyes and comfortable cheek,
    Let him, with this sweet tale, full often seek
For meadows where the little rivers run;
Who loves to linger with that brightest one
  Of Heaven — Hesperus — let him lowly speak
    These numbers to the night, and starlight meek,
Or moon, if that her hunting be begun.
He who knows these delights, and too is prone
  To moralize upon a smile or tear,
Will find at once a region of his own,
  A bower for his spirit, and will steer
To alleys, where the fir-tree drops its cone,
  Where robins hop, and fallen leaves are sear.

1817

VII.

WHEN I have fears that I may cease to be
  Before my pen has glean'd my teeming
        brain,
Before high-piled books, in charact'ry,
  Hold like rich garners the full-ripen'd grain;
When I behold, upon the night's starr'd face,
  Huge cloudy symbols of a high romance,
And think that I may never live to trace
  Their shadows, with the magic hand of chance;
And when I feel, fair creature of an hour!
  That I shall never look upon thee more,
Never have relish in the faery power
  Of unreflecting love! — then on the shore
Of the wide world I stand alone, and think
Till Love and Fame to nothingness do sink.

1817

VIII.

TO HOMER.

STANDING aloof in giant ignorance,
 Of thee I hear and of the Cyclades,
  As one who sits ashore and longs perchance
 To visit dolphin-coral in deep seas.
So thou wast blind ! — but then the veil was rent,
 For Jove uncurtain'd Heaven to let thee live,
And Neptune made for thee a spermy tent,
 And Pan made sing for thee his forest-hive ;
Aye, on the shores of darkness there is light,
 And precipices show untrodden green ;
There is a budding morrow in midnight ;
 There is a triple sight in blindness keen :
Such seeing hadst thou, as it once befell
To Dian, Queen of Earth, and Heaven, and Hell

 1818

IX.

ANSWER TO A SONNET ENDING THUS : —

"Dark eyes are dearer far
Than those that made the hyacinthine bell."
   By J. H REYNOLDS

BLUE ! 'Tis the life of heaven, — the domain
 Of Cynthia, — the wide palace of the sun, —
  The tent of Hesperus, and all his train, —
 The bosomer of clouds, gold, gray, and dun.
Blue ! 'Tis the life of waters — ocean
 And all its vassal streams : pools numberless
May range, and foam, and fret, but never can
 Subside, if not to dark-blue nativeness.
Blue ! Gentle cousin of the forest-green,
 Married to green in all the sweetest flowers —
Forget-me-not, — the blue-bell, — and, that queen
 Of secrecy, the violet : what strange powers
Hast thou, as a mere shadow ! But how great,
When in an Eye thou art alive with fate !

 Feb. 1818.

X.

TO J. H. REYNOLDS.

O THAT a week could be an age, and we
    Felt parting and warm meeting every week ,
    Then one poor year a thousand years would be,
  The flush of welcome ever on the cheek :
So could we live long life in little space,
    So time itself would be annihilate,
So a day's journey in oblivious haze
    To serve our joys would lengthen and dilate.
O to arrive each Monday morn from Ind !
    To land each Tuesday from the rich Levant !
In little time a host of joys to bind,
    And keep our souls in one eternal pant !
This morn, my friend, and yester-evening taught
Me how to harbor such a happy thought.

XI.

TO ———.*

TIME'S sea hath been five years at its low ebb,
    Long hours have to and fro let creep the sand,
    Since I was tangled in thy beauty's web,
  And snared by the ungloving of thine hand.
And yet I never look on midnight sky,
    But I behold thine eyes' well-memoried light·
I cannot look upon the rose's dye,
    But to thy cheek my soul doth take its flight:
I cannot look on any budding flower,
    But my fond ear, in fancy at thy lips,
And hearkening for a love-sound, doth devour
    Its sweets in the wrong sense :— Thou dost
        eclipse
Every delight with sweet remembering,
And grief unto my darling joys dost bring.

* A lady whom he saw for some moments at Vauxhall.

XII.

TO SLEEP.

O SOFT embalmer of the still midnight !
   Shutting, with careful fingers and benign,
   Our gloom-pleased eyes, embower'd from the
      light,
   Enshaded in forgetfulness divine ;
O soothest Sleep ! if so it please thee, close,
   In midst of this thine hymn, my willing eyes,
Or wait the amen, ere thy poppy throws
   Around my bed its lulling charities ;
   Then save me, or the passed day will shine
Upon my pillow, breeding many woes ;
   Save me from curious conscience. that still lords
Its strength, for darkness burrowing like a mole ;
   Turn the key deftly in the oiled wards,
And seal the hushed casket of my soul.

   1819.

XIII.

ON FAME.

FAME, like a wayward girl, will still be coy
   To those who woo her with too slavish knees,
   But makes surrender to some thoughtless boy
   And dotes the more upon a heart at ease.
She is a Gipsey, — will not speak to those
   Who have not learnt to be content without her ;
A Jilt, whose ear was never whisper'd close,
   Who thinks they scandal her who talk about
      her ;
A very Gipsey is she, Nilus-born,
   Sister-in-law to jealous Potiphar,
Ye lovesick Bards ! repay her scorn for scorn ;
   Ye Artists lovelorn ! madmen that ye are
Make your best bow to her and bid adieu,
Then, if she likes it, she will follow you.

XIV.

ON FAME.

"You cannot eat your cake and have it too."— *Proverb*

HOW fever'd is the man, who cannot look
   Upon his mortal days with temperate blood,
   Who vexes all the leaves of his life's book,
And robs his fair name of its maidenhood:
It is as if the rose should pluck herself,
   Or the ripe plum finger its misty bloom;
As if a Naiad, like a meddling elf,
   Should darken her pure grot with muddy gloom,
But the rose leaves herself upon the brier,
   For winds to kiss and grateful bees to feed,
And the ripe plum still wears its dim attire,
   The undisturbed lake has crystal space:
   Why then should man, teasing the world for
      grace,
Spoil his salvation for a fierce miscreed?

   1819.

XV

WHY did I laugh to-night? No voice will tell;
   No God, no Demon of severe response,
      Deigns to reply from Heaven or from Hell
Then to my human heart I turn at once. —
Heart! Thou and I are here sad and alone;
   I say, why did I laugh? O mortal pain!
O Darkness! Darkness! ever must I moan,
   To question Heaven and Hell and Heart in vain
Why did I laugh? I know this Being's lease,
   My fancy to its utmost blisses spreads;
Yet would I on this very midnight cease,
   And the world's gaudy ensigns see in shreds;
Verse, Fame, and Beauty are intense indeed,
But Death intenser — Death is Life's high meed.

XVI.

ON A DREAM.

AS Hermes once took to his feathers light,
  When lulled Argus, baffled, swoon'd and
    slept,
So on a Delphic reed, my idle spright,
  So play'd, so charm'd, so conquer'd, so bereft
The dragon-world of all its hundred eyes,
  And seeing it asleep, so fled away,
Not to pure Ida with its snow-cold skies,
  Nor unto Tempe, where Jove grieved a day,
But to that second circle of sad Hell,
  Where in the gust, the whirlwind, and the flaw
Of rain and hailstones, lovers need not tell
  Their sorrows: — pale were the sweet lips I saw,
Pale were the lips I kiss'd, and fair the form
I floated with, about that melancholy storm.

    1819.

XVII.

IF by dull rhymes our English must be chain'd,
  And, like Andromeda, the Sonnet sweet
    Fetter'd, in spite of pained loveliness,
Let us find out, if we must be constrain'd,
  Sandals more interwoven and complete
    To fit the naked foot of poesy ;
Let us inspect the lyre, and weigh the stress
Of every chord, and see what may be gain'd
  By ear industrious, and attention meet ;
Misers of sound and syllable, no less
  Than Midas of his coinage, let us be
  Jealous of dead leaves in the bay-wreath crown
So, if we may not let the Muse be free,
  She will be bound with garlands of her own.

    1819.

XVIII.

THE day is gone, and all its sweets are gone !
  Sweet voice, sweet lips, soft hand, and softer
    breast,
Warm breath, light whisper, tender semitone,
  Bright eyes, accomplish'd shape, and lang'rous
    waist !
Faded the flower and all its budded charms,
  Faded the sight of beauty from my eyes,
Faded the shape of beauty from my arms,
  Faded the voice, warmth, whiteness, paradise !
Vanish'd unseasonably at shut of eve,
  When the dusk holiday — or holinight —
Of fragrant-curtain'd love begins to weave
  The woof of darkness thick, for hid delight :
But, as I've read love's missal through to-day,
He'll let me sleep, seeing I fast and pray.

  1819

XIX.

I CRY your mercy — pity — love — ay, love !
  Merciful love that tantalizes not,
    One-thoughted, never-wandering, guileless love,
  Unmask'd, and being seen — without a blot !
O ! let me have thee whole, — all — all — be mine !
  That shape, that fairness, that sweet minor zest
Of love, your kiss, — those hands, those eyes divine,
  That warm, white, lucent, million-pleasured
    breast, —
Yourself — your soul — in pity give me all,
  Withhold no atom's atom, or I die,
Or living on perhaps, your wretched thrall,
  Forget, in the mist of idle misery,
Life's purposes — the palate of my mind
Losing its gust, and my ambition blind !

  1819.

XX.

KEATS'S LAST SONNET.

BRIGHT star, would I were steadfast as ~~thou~~
    art !
    Not in lone splendor hung aloft the night,
And watching, with eternal lids apart,
    Like Nature's patient sleepless Eremite,
The moving waters at their priestlike task
    Of pure ablution round earth's human shores,
Or gazing on the new soft fallen mask
    Of snow upon the mountains and the moors —
No — yet still steadfast, still unchangeable,
    Pillow'd upon my fair love's ripening breast,
To feel forever its soft fall and swell,
    Awake forever in a sweet unrest,
Still, still to hear her tender-taken breath,
And so live ever — or else swoon to death.

    Another reading : —
        Half-passionless, and so swoon on to death

THE END.

CPSIA information can be obtained at www.ICGtesting.com
Printed in the USA
LVOW110427121212

311267LV00006B/120/P